Jules William Press JWP

This Book

Old Norse – Old Icelandic: Concise Introduction is a modern "primer" for learning to read the Icelandic sagas in their original language. This straightforward, easy-to-use primer requires no previous language knowledge. It is designed for self-learning, in-class use, and distance learning. Starting with the first page, students read Old Norse passages from Icelandic sagas as well as episodes from Scandinavian myth and medieval sources. The language and thought of the Viking Age come alive in these critical, Old Norse reading segments. For a free Answer Key to the exercises, visit our website: www.oldnorse.org.

About the Authors

JESSE BYOCK is distinguished professor of Old Norse and Medieval Scandinavian at UCLA. He earned his Ph.D. from Harvard University and specializes in the Viking World: its language, sagas, history, and archaeology. He is professor at the UCLA Cotsen Institute of Archaeology. In Iceland, he directs the Mosfell Archaeological Project (MAP) and teaches at the University of Iceland (Háskóli Íslands) in the Department of History and the programs of Medieval Icelandic and Viking Studies.

RANDALL GORDON is a specialist in historical linguistics of Celtic and Germanic Languages, with concentrations on the development and grammar of Old Norse and Old Irish. He received his Ph.D. in Indo-European Studies from UCLA.

www.juleswilliampress.com & www.oldnorse.org

Jules William Press publishes a range of books about the Viking Age. Its series of Old Norse primers, grammars, texts, studies, and audio pronunciation albums answer the needs of the modern student, instructor, and self-learner. The books and materials are purposely affordable. JWP also publishes a series of novels and eBooks as well as archaeological reports about the Viking period.

Old Norse – Old Icelandic
Concise Introduction
to the Language of the Sagas

by
Jesse Byock and Randall Gordon

A Volume in the Viking Language Old Norse Series

www.juleswilliampress.com
www.oldnorse.org

Jules William Press

www.juleswilliampress.com

www.oldnorse.org

Old Norse – Old Icelandic: Concise Introduction to the Language of the Sagas in the *Viking Language Old Norse Series*

Paperback ISBN: 978-1-953947-09-3

eBook ISBN: 978-0-9881764-3-0

Cover design by Basil Arnould Price

Printed in Cambria font

Keywords: Old Norse, Old Icelandic, Icelandic saga, how to learn Old Norse, Icelandic, Norse, Viking, Scandinavian languages, Germanic languages, Germanic, textbook, Old Norse primer, grammar, language, saga, Altnordisch

About This
Old Norse – Old Icelandic "Primer"

This new book answers the need for a concise primer for learning Old Icelandic. It requires no previous foreign language knowledge, and in a straightforward, incremental way, it teaches how to read Icelandic sagas and Old Norse texts in the original. The lessons supply all necessary information (grammar, vocabulary, and exercises) and are designed for in-class teaching, self-instruction, and distance learning. It is a resource for today's students and instructors.

Free Answer Key on www.oldnorse.org

For a free downloadable Answer Key to the exercises this Old Norse – Old Icelandic primer, visit our webpage: www.oldnorse.org.

Arrangement of the Book

Old Norse – Old Icelandic is divided into 17 short lessons. Each lesson opens with a passage in Old Icelandic drawn from sagas or mythological sources. Lessons focus on the grammar and vocabulary necessary to master the reading(s). In this way, original texts determine the instruction, and students master grammatical elements as they are needed. To speed the learning, each lesson contains a short vocabulary of new words and phrases, as well as practice exercises, reinforcing the grammatical explanations. Reading passages are drawn from the following Old Icelandic texts.

Egils saga Skalla-Grímssonar (*Egil's Saga*)
Fóstbrœðra saga (*Saga of the Foster-Brothers*)
Gísla saga Súrssonar (*Saga of Gisli Sursson*)
Gunnlaugs saga ormstungu (*Gunnlaug's Saga Serpent-Tongue*)
Hávarðar saga (*Havard's Saga*)
Heimskringla (*History of the Kings of Norway*)
Hrafnkels saga Freysgoða (*Saga of Hrafnkel the Priest of Frey*)
Landnámabók (*Sturlubók*) (*The Book of Settlements*)
Magnúss saga Erlingssonar (*Saga of Magnus Erlingsson*)
Njáls saga (*Njal's Saga*)
Óláfs saga Tryggvasonar (*Saga of Olaf Tryggvason*)
Ragnars saga loðbrókar (*Ragnar´s Saga Lodbrok*)
Snorra Edda (*Snorri's Edda* [*The Prose Edda*])
Vápnfirðinga saga (*Saga of the Families of Weapon's Fjord*)
Ynglinga saga (*Saga of the Ynglings*)
Þorsteins þáttr stangarhǫggs (*The Tale of Thorstein Staff-Struck*)

Appendices

The rear of the book contains several helpful appendices:

- a Pronunciation Guide to Old Icelandic (with a discussion of Modern Icelandic pronunciation),
- an extensive Reference Grammar of Old Norse – Old Icelandic,
- a full Vocabulary of all Words and Phrases in the volume.

Additional Resources

This introductory primer, *Old Norse – Old Icelandic: Concise Introduction to the Language of the Sagas*, is complemented by an **eBook** version and a series of additional texts.

Supplementary Exercises for Old Norse – Old Icelandic. This stand-alone volume of additional exercises augments the exercises found in the lessons of the *Old Norse – Old Icelandic: Concise Introduction to the Language of the Sagas*. The volume of *Supplementary Exercises* also includes a series of original Old Norse readings. Some are drawn from the *Saga of Ragnar Lodbrok* and recount Ragnar's attack on England and his death in the snake pit. Others are mythological tales from *The Prose Edda*, which tell of a strange journey of the gods and events involving the treasure and magical ring taken from the dragon by Sigurd the Volsung. *Supplementary Exercises* features a complete vocabulary with all words and phrases found in the exercises and readings. It is a workbook useful for anyone learning Old Norse. For a free downloadable Answer Key to the *Supplementary Exercises for Old Norse – Old Icelandic*, visit our webpage: www.oldnorse.org.

The Saga of the Families of Weapon's Fjord (***Vápnfirðinga saga***) is a classic Icelandic prose tale of blood feud in Viking Age Iceland. Issues of vengeance, honor, and survival dominate as two rival chieftain families struggle for power in Iceland's East Fjords. This saga edition offers a new translation and includes the original Old Norse text presented in a way that teaches how to read a complete saga in both English and Old Icelandic. The edition contains extensive notes, maps, vocabulary, and cultural explanations. The student has everything necessary to master a saga of feud, violence, and the claims of honor.

The Tale of Thorstein Staff-Struck (***Þorsteins þáttr stangar-hǫggs***). This short and not-so-sweet Icelandic *þáttr* ('tale', in this instance a short saga) weighs the role of violence, while exploring insult and the duty of vengeance. *Þorsteins þáttr* captures the essence of the Icelandic sagas, but with an unusual twist. This edition offers a new English translation along with the original Old Norse text, extensive vocabulary, detailed notes, and grammar explanations. Here is a compact volume that teaches how to read sagas and to evaluate how these medieval narratives are constructed.

Books Co-authored by Jesse Byock & Randall Gordon

Old Norse – Old Icelandic: Concise Introduction to the Language of the sagas. Jules William Press (JWP)

Supplementary Exercises for Old Norse – Old Icelandic. JWP

The Tale of Thorstein Staff-Struck (Þorsteins saga stangarhöggs). JWP

Saga of the Families of Weapon's Fjord (Vápnfirðinga saga). JWP

Books by Jesse Byock

Viking Age Iceland. Penguin Books

   L'Islande des Vikings. Flammarion, Editions Aubier (France)

   La Stirpe di Odino: La Civiltà Vichinga in Islanda. Oscar Mondadori (Italy)

   Исландия эпохи викингов. Corpus Books (Russia)

Feud in the Icelandic Saga. University of California Press (UC Press)

   サガ ノ シャカイカイシ チューセイアイスランド ノ シュウコッカ. Tokai University Press (Japan)

Medieval Iceland: Society, Sagas, and Power. UC Press

   Island i sagatiden: Samfund, magt og fejde. C.A. Reitzel (Denmark)

   アイスランド サカ Tokai University Press (Japan)

Viking Archaeology in Iceland: Mosfell Archaeological Project. Editors Davide Zori and Jesse Byock. Brepols Publisher, Cursor Mundi

Grettir's Saga. Oxford University Press

The Prose Edda: Norse Mythology. Penguin Books

The Saga of the Volsungs: The Norse Epic of Sigurd the Dragon Slayer. Penguin Books

The Saga of King Hrolf Kraki. Penguin Books

The Viking Language Old Norse Series (JWP)

Viking Language 1: Learn Old Norse, Runes, and Icelandic Sagas (2nd Edition)

Viking Language 2: The Old Norse Reader

   Viking Language 1 Audio Lessons 1-8: Pronounce Old Norse

   Viking Language 1 Audio Lessons 9-15: Pronounce Old Norse

Altnordisch 1: Die Sprache der Wikinger, Runen, und isländischen Sagas (*Altnordisch 1*, *Viking Language 2*, and the pronunciation MP3 downloads, Hörbeispiele zur Aussprache, available on Amazon.de)

Table of Contents
for *Old Norse – Old Icelandic:*
Concise Introduction to the Language of the Sagas

The Old Icelandic Alphabet, Spelling, and Vowels viii

Abbreviations ix

LESSON 1 1
Ór *Gunnlaugs sǫgu ormstungu* (**1. kap.**) (From the *Saga of Gunnlaug Serpent-Tongue*, Chap. 1) 1
1.1. Stems and Endings. 1
1.2. Cases of Old Icelandic. 1
1.3. No Indefinite Article. 3
1.4. Strong Nouns and Adjectives: Masculine Nominative Singular. 3
1.5. Strong Nouns: Masculine Genitive Singular. 3
1.6. Strong Adjectives: Genitive Singular Masculine. 4
Ór *Fóstbrœðra sǫgu* (**2. kap.**) (From the *Saga of the Foster-Brothers*, Chap. 2) 4
1.7. Agreement of Adjectives with Nouns; Noun Apposition. 4
1.8. Review Paradigms: Nom. and Gen. Sing. of Strong Masc. Nouns and Adjectives. 5
1.9. Prepositions: A First Look. 6

LESSON 2 9
Ór *Hrafnkels sǫgu Freysgoða* (**2. kap.**) (From the *Saga of Hrafnkel the Priest of Frey*, Chap. 2) 9
2.1. Special Stem Rules. 9
2.2. Other Uses of the Genitive. 10
2.3. Strong Nouns: Masculine Accusative and Dative Singular. 11
2.4. Strong Adjectives: Accusative and Dative Singular Masculine. 11
2.5. Review Paradigms: Endings of Masc. Sing. Strong Nouns and Adjectives (See 1.8). 11
2.6. The Noun *maðr*. 11

LESSON 3 14
Ór *Egils sǫgu Skalla-Grímssonar* (**50. kap.**) (From the *Saga of Egil Skalla-Grimsson*, Chap. 50) 14
3.1. Definite Article: Singular Masculine. 14
3.2. Weak Adjectives: Singular Masculine. 14
3.3. Weak Nouns: Masculine Singular. 14
3.4. The Noun *sonr* (*-son*). 15
3.5. Disyllabic Adjectives and Nouns. 15
3.6. Personal Pronouns: First and Second Persons. 15
3.7. Preview of the Verb: The Infinitive. 15
3.8. Infinitive Marker *at*. 16
3.9. Additional Reading. 16

Ór *Þorsteins þætti stangarhǫggs* (1. kap.) (From the *Tale of Thorstein Staff-Struck*, Chap. 1) 16

LESSON 4 .... **19**
Ór *Egils sǫgu Skalla-Grímssonar* (36. kap.) (From the *Saga of Egil Skalla-Grimsson*, Chap. 36) 19
4.1. Strong Nouns: Neuter Singular 19
4.2. Review Paradigms: Masc. and Neut. Sing. Strong Noun Endings (See 2.5). 19
4.3. Definite Article: Singular Neuter. 20
4.4. Review Paradigms: Masc. and Neut. Sing. Forms of the Article (See 3.1, 4.3) 20
4.5. Strong and Weak Adjectives: Singular Neuter 20
Ór *Magnúss sǫgu Erlingssonar* (16. kap.) (From the *Saga of Magnus Erlingsson*, Chap. 16) 20
4.6. Review Paradigms: Sing. Masc. and Neut. of Strong and Weak Adjectives (See 2.5, 3.2, 4.5). 20
4.7. Weak Nouns: Neuter Singular 21
4.8. Suffixed Definite Article 21
4.9. More on the Accusative and Dative Cases. 21

LESSON 5 .... **25**
Ór *Snorra Eddu, Gylfaginning* (6. kap.) (From *Snorri's Edda* [*The Prose Edda*], *The Beguiling of Gylfi*, Chap. 6) 25
5.1. Personal Pronouns: 3rd Person 25
5.2. Verbs: Weak and Strong Verbs. 26
5.3. Weak Verbs: Formation of the Past Tense. 26
5.4. Weak Verbs: Variation in the Dental Suffix 27
5.5. Weak Verbs: 3rd Person Past-Tense Endings. 28
5.6. Weak Verbs: Vowel Alternation in Short Roots with *j*-Suffix 28

LESSON 6 .... **32**
Ór *Ragnars sǫgu loðbrókar* (3. kap.) (From the *Saga of Ragnar Lodbrok*, Chap. 3) 32
6.1. Strong Verbs: Formation of the Past Tense. 32
6.2. Verbs: 3rd Person Past-Tense Endings. 33
6.3. Review Paradigms: 3rd Person Past-Tense Endings of the Verb. 33
6.4. Strong Verbs: Singular and Plural Past-Tense Stems (See 6.1). 33
6.5. The Verbs *vera* and *hafa* 34
6.6. Additional Reading. 34
Ór *Vápnfirðinga sǫgu* (1. kap.) (From the *Saga of the Families of Weapon's Fjord*, Chap. 1) 34
6.7. Additional Adjectives 35

LESSON 7 .... **43**
Ór *Snorra Eddu, Gylfaginning* (22. kap.) (From *Snorri's Edda* [*The Prose Edda*], *The Beguiling of Gylfi*, Chap. 22) 43
7.1. Strong Nouns: Neuter Nouns with Stem-Final -*i*. 43
7.2. Nouns and Adjectives: Genitive Plural. 43

7.3. Definite Article: Genitive Plural..44
Ór *Egils sǫgu Skalla-Grímssonar* (20. kap.) (From the *Saga of Egil Skalla-Grimsson*, Chap. 20)..44
7.4. Strong Adjectives: Nominative/Accusative Singular Neuter Stem Rules (See 4.5)..44
7.5. Superlative Adjective Formation..44
7.6. Adverb Formation..44
7.7. Verbs: 3rd Person Singular Present-Tense Endings..45
7.8. Verbs: Assimilation of the 3rd Person Singular Present-Tense Ending -*r*..45
7.9. Verbs: 3rd Person Plural Present-Tense Endings..46
7.10. Review Paradigms: 3rd Person Endings (Past and Pres.) of Weak and Strong Verbs (See 6.3)..46

LESSON 8..**52**
Ór *Gunnlaugs sǫgu ormstungu* (9. kap.) (From the *Saga of Gunnlaug Serpent-Tongue*, Chap. 9)..52
8.1. Definite Article: Singular Feminine..52
(1) Ór *Landnámabók (Sturlubók)* (112. kap.) (From the *Book of Settlements* [*Sturla's Book*], Chap. 112)..52
(2) Ór *Egils sǫgu Skalla-Grímssonar* (55. kap.) (From the *Saga of Egill Skalla-Grimsson*, Chap. 55)..53
8.2. Definite Article: Complete Declension (See 4.4, 7.2, 8.1)..53
8.3. Pronouns: Apposition..53
8.4. Verbs: 1st and 2nd Person Past-Tense Endings..54
8.5. Verbs: Moods and the Subjunctive..54
8.6. Verbs: 3rd Person Singular Subjunctive Endings..55
8.7. Participles: A First Look..55
8.8. Participles: Past Participles in Compound Tenses..56

LESSON 9..**61**
Ór *Egils sǫgu Skalla-Grímssonar* (32. kap.) (From the *Saga of Egil Skalla-Grimsson*, Chap. 32)..61
9.1. Weak Nouns and Adjectives: Feminine Singular..62
9.2. Review Paradigms: Complete Weak Noun and Adj. Endings in the Sing. (See 4.7, 9.1)..62
9.3. Strong Nouns: Feminine Singular..62
Ór *Gísla sǫgu Súrssonar* (5. kap.) (From the *Saga of Gisli Sursson*, Chap. 5)..62
9.4. Review Paradigms: Complete Strong Noun Endings in the Singular (See 4.2, 9.3)..63
9.5. Kinship Terms in -*ir*: Singular Declension..63
9.6. Strong Adjectives: Singular Feminine..64
(1) Ór *Hávarðar sǫgu* (1. kap.) (From the *Saga of Havard*, Chap. 1).. 64
(2) Ór *Snorra Eddu* (10. kap.) (From *Snorri's Edda* [*The Prose Edda*], Chap. 10)..64
9.7. Review Paradigms: Complete Strong Adj. Endings in the Sing. (See 4.6, 9.6)..64

9.8. Verbs: 1st and 2nd Person Present-Tense Endings. 65
9.9. Review Paradigms: Pres. and Past-Tense Endings of Verbs
    (See 7.9, 8.4, 9.8). 65

Suggested Readings: *Viking Language 2* 72

LESSON 10 75
Ór *Óláfs sǫgu Tryggvasonar* **(108. kap.)** (From the *Saga of Olaf*
    Tryggvason, Chap. 108).. 75
10.1. Verbs: The Imperative. 75
10.2. Stem Variation in -*j*- and -*v*-. 76
10.3. Verbs: Past Participle Formation. 77
10.4. Verbs: Function of Reflexive Verbs. 78
10.5. Reflexive Verbs: Formation of the 3rd Person. 79

LESSON 11 85
Ór *Fóstbrœðra sǫgu* **(23. kap.)** (From the *Saga of the Foster-*
    Brothers, Chap. 23).. 85
11.1. Strong Verbs: Present-Stem Vowel Alternation. 85
11.2. Umlaut: An Explanation. 86
11.3. Weak Feminine Nouns: *a~ǫ* Alternation in the Singular. 88
11.4. Strong Feminine Nouns: *a~ǫ* Alternation in the Singular. 88
11.5. Strong Masculine Nouns: *a~ǫ~e* Alternation in the Singular. 89
11.6. Strong Feminine Noun *hǫnd*: *a~ǫ~e* Alternation in the
    Singular. 90
11.7. Strong Adjectives: *a~ǫ* Alternation in the Singular. 90

LESSON 12 95
(1) Ór *Ragnars sǫgu loðbrókar* **(7. kap. 'Frá Ragnarssonum')**
    (From the *Saga of Ragnar Lodbrok*, Chap. 7 'About the Sons of
    Ragnar').. 95
(2) Ór *Heimskringlu* **(1. kap.)** (From *Heimskringla* or the *History of*
    the Kings of Norway, Chap. 1) 95
12.1. Demonstrative Pronouns: *sá* 'that, that one'and *þessi* (*sjá*) 'this,
    this one'. 96
12.2. Relative Particles *er* and *sem*. 96
12.3. Strong Nouns: Plural of All Genders. 97
12.4. Weak Nouns: Plural of All Genders. 98
12.5. Review Paradigms: Noun Endings, Sing. and Pl. 99

LESSON 13 104
(1) Ór *Egils sǫgu Skalla-Grímssonar* **(25. kap.)** (From the *Saga of*
    Egil Skalla-Grimsson, Chap. 25) 104
(2) Ór *Egils sǫgu Skalla-Grímssonar* **(25. kap.)** (From the *Saga of*
    Egil Skalla-Grimsson, Chap. 25) 104
(3) Ór *Egils sǫgu Skalla-Grímssonar* **(57. kap.)** (From the *Saga of*
    Egil Skalla-Grimsson, Chap. 57) 104
(4) Ór *Egils sǫgu Skalla-Grímssonar* **(66. kap.)** (From the *Saga of*
    Egil Skalla-Grimsson, Chap. 66) 105
13.1. Strong Adjectives: Plural. 105

13.2. Review Paradigms: Complete Endings of Strong Adjectives (See 9.7, 13.1). 106

13.3. The Adjective *annarr* '(an)other, second'. 106

13.4. Weak Adjectives: Plural. 107

(1) Ór *Egils sǫgu Skalla-Grímssonar* **(25. kap.)** (From the *Saga of Egil Skalla-Grimsson*, Chap. 25) 107

(2) Ór *Ynglinga sǫgu* **(29. kap.)** (From the *Saga of the Ynglings*, Chap. 29) 107

(3) Ór *Egils sǫgu Skalla-Grímssonar* **(36. Kap.)** (From the *Saga of Egil Skalla-Grimsson*, Chap. 36) 107

(4) Ór *Egils sǫgu Skalla-Grímssonar* **(77. kap.)** (From the *Saga of Egil Skalla-Grimsson*, Chap. 77) 107

13.5. *u*-Umlaut: *a~u* Alternation. 108

13.6. Review Paradigms: Complete Endings of Weak Adjectives and Nouns (See 9.2, 12.4, 13.4). 108

13.7. Adjectives: Examples of Complete Declensions. 109

LESSON 14 .... **115**

Ór *Ynglinga sǫgu* **(3. Kap. 'Frá brœðrum Óðins')** (From the *Saga of the Ynglings*, Chap. 3 'About Odin's Brothers') 115

14.1. Numerals 115

14.2. Verbs: Weak Verbs with Vowel Alternation. 116

14.3. Reflexive Possessive Adjective 116

Ór *Egils sǫgu Skalla-Grímssonar* **(59. Kap.)** (From the *Saga of Egil Skalla-Grimsson*, Chap. 59) 118

14.4. Declension of *sonr* in the Singular and Plural 118

14.5. Suffixed article: Plural 118

14.6. Review Paradigms: Suffixed Art. in the Sing. and Pl. 119

14.7. Suffixed Article: Contraction with Monosyllabic Strong Nouns Ending in a Vowel. 119

Ór *Njáls sǫgu* **(146. Kap.)** (From *Njal's Saga*, Chap. 146) 120

14.8. Kinship Terms in the Plural 120

LESSON 15 .... **124**

Ór *Egils sǫgu Skalla-Grímssonar* **(81. kap.)** (From the *Saga of Egil Skalla-Grimsson*, Chap. 81) 124

15.1. Preterite-Present Verbs: Present Tense. 125

15.2. *Munu* 'will, shall, be likely' vs. *muna* 'remember'. 126

15.3. Preterite-Present Verbs: Past Tense. 127

15.4. Verbs: More on *vera*. 128

15.5. Verbs: Present Subjunctive (See Also 8.5, 8.6). 128

15.6. Verbs: Impersonal Constructions Expressing Opinion or Belief. 128

LESSON 16 .... **133**

Ór *Njáls sǫgu* **(58. kap.)** (From *Njal's Saga*, Chap. 58) 133

16.1. Verbs: Past Subjunctive. 134

16.2. The Verb *vera*: Present and Past Subjunctive 135

16.3. Personal Pronouns: 1st and 2nd Person Dual. 135

16.4. Adjectives: Possessive Adjectives. 136

16.5. The Indefinite Pronoun *hvárrtveggja.* 137

LESSON 17 ....**143**
Ór *Snorra Eddu* (15., 17. kap.) (From *Snorri's Edda*, Chaps. 15, 17) 143
17.1. Adjectives: Declension of Comparative Adjectives........................... 144
17.2. Adjectives: Formation of Comparatives. 145
17.3. Adjectives and Adverbs: Irregular Comparatives and
Superlatives... 145
17.4. Verbs: Present Participles... 146
17.5. Verbs: Preterite Infinitive. 146
Ór *Þorsteins þætti stangarhǫggs* (3. Kap.) (From the *Tale of
Thorstein Staff-Struck*, Chap. 3) 147
17.6. Nouns: Plural of Strong Nouns with *a~ǫ~e* alternation. 147

Appendices **153**

**Appendix 1 Pronunciation Guide to Old Icelandic (With a
Discussion of Modern Icelandic Pronunciation)** **154**

Appendix 2 Reference Grammar of Old Norse – Old Icelandic...159

Appendix 3 Vocabulary of Words and Phrases **172**

DEDICATION

This book is dedicated to Kenneth Chapman, whose ideas, examples, and approach to teaching Old Icelandic were the inspiration for this work. Ken was a brilliant linguist, a wonderful friend, and a generous teacher who thoroughly enjoyed sharing his great knowledge and helping students and colleagues. Ken passed away as we were beginning the project, and we greatly miss him.

ACKNOWLEDGEMENTS

We thank Basil A. Price, Chad Laidlow, Kevin Elliott, Ágúst Guðmundsson, Cassandra Ruiz, Jack Hartley, Gunnar Karlsson, Meg Morrow, Helgi Þorláksson, and Ilya Sverdlov. In one way or another, they assisted us with the completion of this book. Ilya's and Basil's suggestions and assistance with the grammar and exercises were especially insightful. We also thank our editor Ashley M. Byock, who was instrumental in publishing this book.

Norwegian Wood Carving,
thought to be Odin, the one-
eyed god.

The Old Icelandic Alphabet, Spelling, and Vowels

a, á, b, d, ð, e, é, f, g, h, i, í, j, k, l, m, n, o, ó,
p, r, s, t, u, ú, v, x, y, ý, z, þ, æ, œ, ǫ(ö), ø

The Latin alphabet adopted by the Icelanders in the 11th century was probably modeled on Anglo-Saxon writing brought to the northern lands by English missionaries and clerics during the Viking Age. From this source, Icelanders may have learned the use of ink and parchment. By the 12th century, Icelandic writers were utilizing the newly acquired Latin alphabet and writing vernacular texts in considerable numbers. However, they did not follow a standardized spelling.

The variety of spellings in the manuscripts greatly complicated the task of making Old Icelandic/Old Norse vocabularies and dictionaries when the sagas and Old Norse were rediscovered by European and British scholars in the late 1700s. Scholars in the early 1800s addressed this issue by adopting a normalized Old Icelandic spelling and alphabetic order. The reading passages and vocabularies in this current book follow the normalized spelling as found in the standard Icelandic *Íslenzk fornrit* saga editions. This spelling convention, which is found in most of today's saga editions and dictionaries, maintains the medieval distinction between the vowels *æ* and *œ*, and *ǫ* and *ø*.

In the Old Norse/Icelandic alphabet, long vowels are distinguished from short vowels by an acute accent (for ex., long *é* and short *e*). The long vowels *æ*, *œ*, and *ø* are listed at the end of the Icelandic alphabet, as is *ǫ* (the medieval form of umlauted *a*, which becomes modern *ö*). The letters *c*, *q*, and *w* are occasionally found in manuscripts, but these foreign letters have not been adopted into the standardized alphabet.

Abbreviations

acc.	accusative	MI.	Modern Icelandic
adj.	adjective	num.	numeral
adv.	adverb	obj.	object
art.	article	OI	Old Icelandic
comp.	comparative	ON	Old Norse
conj.	Conjunction	ord.	ordinal
Dan.	Danish	part.	participle
dat.	dative	pers.	personal
def.	definite	pl.	plural
dem.	demonstrative	poet.	poetical usage
dir. obj.	direct object	poss.	possessive
f.ex.	for example	ppart.	past participle
fem., f.	feminine	pref.	prefix
gen.	genitive	prep.	preposition
i.e.	that is	pres.	present
impers.	impersonal	pret.	preterite
ind. obj.	indirect object	pron.	pronoun
indecl.	indeclinable	refl.	reflexive
indef.	indefinite	rel.	relative
indic.	indicative	R.S.	reading selection
inf.	infinitive	sing., sg.	singular
int.	interrogative	subj.	subject
intrans.	intransitive	subjunct.	subjunctive
lit.	literally	superl.	superlative
masc., m.	masculine	Swed.	Swedish
NB	Nota Bene	trans.	transitive
neut., n.	neuter	var.	variant
nom.	nominative	vb.	verb
Norw.	Norwegian	w.	with

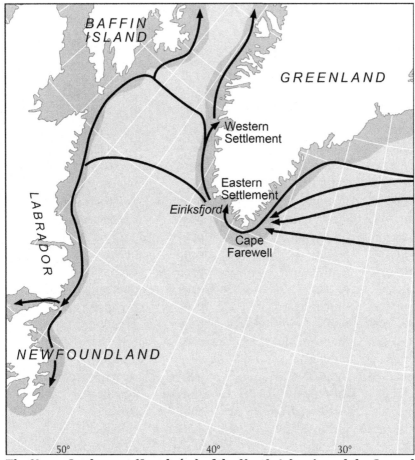

The Norse Settlement (*Landnám*) of the North Atlantic and the Spread of Old Norse Across the Atlantic. The islands of Shetland, Orkney, and the Faroes were known to Norse seamen by the 8th century. Iceland was discovered and first settled in the 9th century during the Viking Age (ca. 780–1100 CE). Most settlers, who were called *landnámsmenn*, a term that includes women, came from Norway, but some arrived from other regions of mainland Scandinavia, as well as from the Viking colonies in Ireland, Scotland, Shetland, Orkney and the Hebrides. The settlers were mostly Old Norse speakers, but there were also Celts among them, especially women.

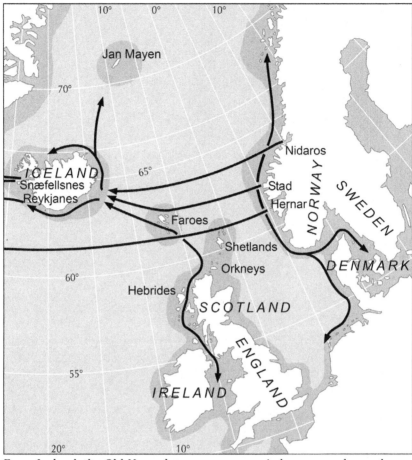

From Iceland, the Old Norse language was carried over seas by explorers and settlers to Greenland and Vínland (North America). The map shows the major sailing routes across the North Atlantic, connecting the large geographical region where Old Norse was spoken. Old Icelandic, the language of the sagas, is the dialect that developed in Iceland from the variants of Old Norse brought to the island by the Viking Age settlers.

LESSON 1

Ór *Gunnlaugs sǫgu ormstungu* (1. kap.)
(From the *Saga of Gunnlaug Serpent-Tongue*, Chap. 1)

Þorsteinn hét maðr; hann var Egilsson, Skalla-Grímssonar, Kveld-Úlfssonar, hersis ór Nóregi; en Ásgerðr hét móðir Þorsteins ok var Bjarnardóttir. Þorsteinn bjó at Borg í Borgarfirði; hann var auðigr at fé ok hǫfðingi mikill, vitr maðr ok hógværr ok hófsmaðr um alla hluti.

A man was named Thorstein; he was the son of Egil, the son of Skalla-Grim, son of Kveld-Ulf, a chieftain from Norway; and Thorstein's mother was named Asgerd and was the daughter of Bjorn. Thorstein lived at Borg in Borgarfjord; he was wealthy and a great leader, a wise man and gentle and a man of moderation in all respects.

1.1. Stems and Endings.

Most words in Old Norse are composed of two primary parts, a **stem** and an **ending**. The stem can also have two parts, a **root** and a **suffix**. The root is the most basic part of the word. If no suffix is attached to the root, then the stem is the same as the root.

$$\text{word} = \underbrace{\text{root (+ suffix)}}_{\text{stem}} + \text{ending}$$

1.2. Cases of Old Icelandic.

Cases play a large role in Old Icelandic. An easy way to understand cases is to consider English pronouns. Today's English inherited its pronouns from Old English (Anglo-Saxon), which was closely related to Old Norse.[1] Take for example English 'I' and 'me'. Both refer to the **first person**, that is the person who is currently speaking or writing, but they cannot be used in the same contexts. You say '**I** hit the ball' but not '**Me** hit the ball', and you say 'John saw **me**', but not 'John saw **I**'.

'I' can only be used as the subject of a sentence, and 'me' can only be used as an object. 'I' and 'me' show different cases of the same word: 'I' is in the **subject case** and 'me' is in the **object case**. Other subject-object pronoun pairs are 'he/him', 'she/her', 'we/us', and 'they/them'.

In addition to subject and object cases, English pronouns have a **possessive** case, which indicates belonging.[2] Hence, the possessive

---

[1] Medieval speakers of these two languages could, with some effort, understand each other.

[2] The term "possessive" does not necessarily indicate literal ownership, but some sort of special association. For example, when you say "**my** clothes", you

pronoun 'my' corresponds to the first person 'I/me', and likewise the other possessive pronouns 'his', her', 'our', and 'their'.

These series of subject, object, and possessive pronouns ('I/me/my', 'he/him/his', etc.) illustrate the case system of modern English. Nouns in English also have cases. Nouns do not show any difference in form between subjects and objects, but have a distinct possessive form spelled with -'s: f.ex., 'ship**'s**', 'Thorstein**'s**'.

In Old Icelandic, every pronoun, noun, and adjective must be in one of four cases: nominative (nom.), accusative (acc.), dative (dat.), or genitive (gen.). Principal uses of the four Old Icelandic or Old Norse cases are the following:

- **Nominative case** is used for the **subject** of a sentence. For example, in the sentence *Þórólfr sýndi Eiríki skip* '**Thorolf** showed (to) Eirik a ship', *Þórólfr* is the subjxect and in the nominative case.

- **Accusative case** distinguishes the **direct object** of a verb. In the sentence *Þórólfr sýndi Eiríki **skip*** 'Thorolf showed (to) Eirik a **ship**', *skip* is the direct object of the action of the verb *sýndi* 'showed' and is in the accusative case.

- **Dative case** designates the **indirect object** of a verb. For example, in *Þórólfr sýndi **Eiríki** skip* 'Thorolf showed (to) **Eirik** a ship', *Eiríki* '(to) Eirik' is the indirect object of the verb *sýndi* 'showed' and is in the dative case. As this example implies, the preposition 'to' or 'for' sometimes accompanies the indirect object in English, but not in Old Icelandic.

- **Genitive case** signals belonging. For example, if the ship belongs to Thorstein, it would be *Þorsteins skip* '**Thorstein's** ship'. The Icelandic genitive *Þorsteins* corresponds to the English possessive 'Thorstein**'s**'. Both Icelandic *-s* and English -'s are the same ending in origin. They are inherited from their common ancestor, Northwest Germanic.[3] (The apostrophe in English is merely a spelling convention to distinguish the possessive from the plural in writing.)

As a rule, whenever you see a noun, pronoun or adjective in Old Icelandic, it is best to determine its case in order to understand its role in the sentence. For example, consider the sentence *Í þann tíma réð fyrir Danmǫrku Sigurðr hringr.*

---

may mean that you "own" your clothes, but when you say "**my** boss", you do not mean you "own" your boss.

[3] The separation between the western group of Northwest Germanic dialects, from which Old English arose, and the northern group, from which Old Icelandic arose, began to be distinguishable around the year 200 CE. The separation was complete by around 500 CE.

Even if you do not understand the meaning, you can quickly determine that the phrase *Sigurðr hringr* (Sigurd Ring) is the subject of the sentence (in spite of the fact that it is placed at the end). This is because *Sigurðr* and *hringr* are both in the nominative case. The sentence means 'At that time Sigurd Ring ruled over Denmark.'

The chart below gives the singular declension of the masculine noun *hestr* 'horse' and the masculine forms of the adjective *góðr* 'good'.

	hestr (masc. noun)	góðr (adj. in masc.)
Sg *nom*	hestr	góðr
acc	hest	góðan
dat	hesti	góðum
gen	hests	góðs

Such charts illustrate the pattern, or **paradigm** (from a Greek word for 'model'), that these words follow in forming their cases. The paradigm of *hestr* is typical of many masculine nouns such as *hringr* 'ring' and *úlfr* 'wolf', and the paradigm of *góðr* is typical of adjectives such as *ágætr* 'excellent' and *hvítr* 'white'.

1.3. No Indefinite Article.

There is no indefinite article in Icelandic. When translating into English, the indefinite article, if it is necessary, must be supplied. For example, the sentence *Hann var hǫfðingi mikill ok vitr maðr* is translated 'He was **a** great leader and **a** wise man.'

1.4. Strong Nouns and Adjectives: Masculine Nominative Singular.

The nominative singular of one group of masculine nouns and adjectives (traditionally called **strong** masculine nouns and adjectives) is formed with the ending *-r*. This ending is added directly to the stem of the noun or adjective: hence *auðig-**r***.

Some masculine nouns such as *Þorsteinn* and *Egill* double the final stem consonant instead of adding *-r*. This doubling is the result of predictable rules discussed in section 2.1.

1.5. Strong Nouns: Masculine Genitive Singular.

The genitive singular of strong masculine nouns is formed with either the ending *-s* (as mentioned earlier) or the ending *-ar*. The ending *-s* is by far the more common of the two. As in the case of the nominative ending, the genitive endings are added directly to the stem: *Gunnlaug-**s***, *Egil-**s***, *Þorstein-**s***, *son-**ar***, *Bjarn-**ar***.

The genitive can be expressed in two different ways in English, by adding the ending *-'s* or by using the preposition 'of': For example, *Gunnlaugs saga* means both 'Gunnlaug's saga' and 'the saga of Gunnlaug'. Old Icelandic, however, has only one way to make a genitive, always adding a genitive ending like -*s* and -*ar* in the singular and -*a* in the plural: *Gunnlaugs saga* 'Gunnlaug's Saga', *Hávarðar saga* 'Havard's Saga', *Fóstbrœðra saga* 'Saga of the Foster-Brothers'.

1.6. Strong Adjectives: Genitive Singular Masculine.

Adjectives describe people and things. As descriptive words, Old Norse adjectives themselves do not belong to a specific gender class, but decline to match the noun they modify. The details of adjective declensions will be described in the coming lessons. In the case of masculine strong adjectives, -*s* is the only possible genitive singular ending, f.ex., *gǫfugs* and *ágæts* in the following passage:

Ór *Fóstbrœðra sǫgu* (2. kap.)
(From the *Saga of the Foster-Brothers*, Chap. 2)

Hon var dóttir Álfs, **gǫfugs** manns ok **ágæts**.

She was the daughter of Álf, a **noble** and **excellent** man.

1.7. Agreement of Adjectives with Nouns; Noun Apposition.

Adjectives agree (meaning they match) in case, number, and gender with the noun they modify. For example, in the phrase *dóttir Álfs, gǫfugs manns ok ágæts*, the two adjectives (*gǫfugs, ágæts*) are both in the genitive case, masculine gender, and singular. This is because they are in **agreement** with the noun *manns*, which is masculine, singular, and in the genitive case (the nominative is *maðr*). These properties of the noun determine the case, number and gender of the adjective. If the noun had been in the dative case, the adjectives would also be in the dative, and so on.

In the example above, the noun *maðr* is in the genitive case because it stands in the same relationship to the noun *dóttir* as does the personal name *Álfs* (nom. *Álfr*). This woman was the daughter of a man about whom three things are told: (a) he was named *Álfr* (so she is Alf's daughter); (b) he was a noble man (*gǫfugr maðr*); and (c) he was a famous man (*ágætr maðr*). These three pieces of information are expressed in three noun phrases that are in **apposition** to each other.

Appositive noun phrases are very common in all languages, including Old Norse. Noun phrases in apposition describe different features of the same person or thing. In our example, one noun phrase gives a man's name and the other two describe him as noble and famous. An important observation is that, in languages like Old Norse, all key nouns in an appositive phrase are always in the same case, because they all play the same syntactical role in a sentence.[4] Here, the noun phrases *Álfs*, *gǫfugs manns*, and *ágæts* [*manns*] all modify the same noun, *dóttir*, and hence are all in the genitive case.

Appositive noun phrases can also be **nested**, i.e., placed in a series where each is dependent on the previous one. A feature of Old Norse is that such nouns can join others in compounds. The first Reading Selection (R.S.) contains a typical example:

> *Þorsteinn var Egilsson, Skalla-Grímssonar, Kveld-Úlfssonar hersis.*

This complex sentence offers three pairs of appositive noun phrases with nouns nested into one another: (1) *Egils-* in **Egils**son and *-sonar* in *Skalla-Gríms***sonar**; (2) *Skalla-Gríms-* in **Skalla-Gríms**sonar and *-sonar* in *Kveld-Úlfs***sonar**; (3) *Kveld-Úlfs-* in **Kveld-Úlfs**sonar and *hersis*. The structure functions this way:

- *-sonar* (gen.) in *Skalla-Grímssonar* is in the same case as *Egils* (gen.), as both *Egils-* and this first *-sonar* are in apposition, modifying *-son* in *Egilsson*. Thorstein was the son of a man who (a) was called Egil, and who (b) was himself the son of another man, Skalla-Grim. Hence Thorstein is said to be the son 'of Egil' (*Egils-*) and 'of Skalla-Grim's son' (*Skalla-Grímssonar*).

- *-sonar* (gen.) in *Kveld-Úlfssonar* is in the same case as *Skalla-Gríms* (gen.), as both *Skalla-Gríms-* and this second *-sonar* are in apposition modifying *Egils-* (gen.). Egil is said to be a son of a man who (a) was called Skalla-Grim, and who (b) was himself the son of another man, Kveld-Ulf. To clarify, we are being told about Thorstein's father, grandfather, and great-grandfather.

- *hersis* (gen.) is in the same case as *Kveld-Úlfs-* (gen.) as both *hersis* and *Kveld-Úlfs-* are in apposition modifying *Skalla-Gríms-* (gen.). The father of Skalla-Grim was a man who (a) was called Kveld-Ulf and who (b) held the title of a *hersir*.

As mentioned in 1.5, *-s* and *-ar* are the two possible endings of masculine genitive singular nouns.

1.8. Review Paradigms: Nom. and Gen. Sing. of Strong Masc. Nouns and Adjectives.

	Noun	Adjective
nom	-r (for modifications see 2.1)	-r (for modifications see 2.1)
gen	-s, -ar	-s

---

[4] **Syntax** refers to rules, principles, and processes governing sentence structure in a language. In other words, it describes how words are put together into phrases and sentences.

1.9. Prepositions: A First Look.

Prepositions are small words such as 'to', 'from', 'with', 'of', etc. that precede a noun or pronoun and show how the noun or pronoun is related to the rest of the sentence. A preposition and its object (the noun or pronoun that follows) form a prepositional phrase. The preposition requires its object to be in a particular case: f.ex., *um* ('about') takes the accusative case, and *ór* ('from') takes the dative.

In the title to the R.S., the preposition *ór* changes the form of the noun from **saga** (nominative) to **sǫgu** (dative): *ór Gunnlaugs sǫgu* 'from the Saga of Gunnlaug'. Prepositions are found throughout the language and are discussed in later lessons.

EXERCISES

1. Identify the stem and ending of each of the following adjectives, nouns, and personal names.

Ex.: ágætr: stem _ágæt-_   ending _-r_

ágæts:	stem _____	ending _____
Gunnlaugr:	stem _____	ending _____
Gunnlaugs:	stem _____	ending _____
hersir:	stem _____	ending _____
hersis:	stem _____	ending _____
hógværr:	stem _____	ending _____
hógværs:	stem _____	ending _____
sonr:	stem _____	ending _____
sonar:	stem _____	ending _____

2. Identify the case (nom. or gen.) of the adjectives, nouns, and personal names indicated in bold type.

Sigurðr (_____) hét **maðr** (_____); hann var Bjarnarson, **Þorsteins- sonar** (_____), **hersis** (_____) ór Nóregi, en Ásgerðr hét móðir **Sigurðar** (_____). Hann var **ágætr** (_____) maðr og **hógværr** (_____).

3. Decline the masc. nouns *hringr* 'ring' and *úlfr* 'wolf' in the sing., and the adjectives *ágætr* 'excellent' and *hvítr* 'white' in the masc. sing., following the paradigms of *hestr* and *góðr* given in 1.2.

	Masc. nouns		Masc. adjectives	
nom	_hringr_	_úlfr_	_ágætr_	_hvítr_
acc	_____	_____	_____	_____
dat	_____	_____	_____	_____
gen	_____	_____	_____	_____

4. Vocabulary training.

Across
- 3 lived, dwelt
- 4 rich, wealthy
- 6 excellent
- 7 local chieftain
- 8 wise

Down
- 1 daughter
- 2 noble
- 3 brother
- 5 great
- 7 was named

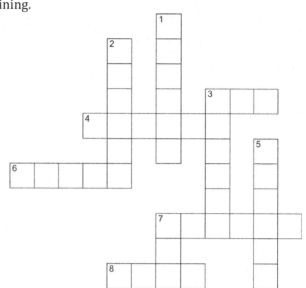

Supplementary Exercises for Old Norse – Old Icelandic

For those who want to sharpen their skills, we have assembled the workbook, *Supplementary Exercises for Old Norse – Old Icelandic.* This second volume in the Viking Language Old Norse Series offers a wealth of additional exercises along with an answer key and full vocabulary. There are also Old Norse readings drawn from the *Saga of Ragnar Lodbrok*, recounting Ragnar's attack on England and his death in the snake pit, as well as passages from *The Prose Edda*, telling of the Norse gods and the legendary hero Sigurd the Volsung, slayer of the dragon Fafnir.

Vocabulary

alla *acc pl masc of* **allr**
allr *adj* all
at *prep* [*w dat*] at; with respect to
auðigr *adj* rich, wealthy
ágætr *adj* excellent
Álfr *m* Alf ('Elf') (*personal name*)
Ásgerðr *f* Asgerd (*personal name*)

Bjarnardóttir *f* daughter of Bjorn
bjó (*inf* **búa**) *vb* lived, dwelt
Bjǫrn (*gen* Bjarnar) *m* Bjorn ('Bear') (*personal name*)
Borg *f* Borg (*place name*)
Borgarfjǫrðr *m* 'Borg's Fjord', a fjord in Western Iceland (*place name*)

bróðir *m* brother
búa (*past* bjó) *vb* live (in a place), dwell
Danmǫrk (*dat* Danmǫrku) *f* Denmark
dóttir *f* daughter
Egill (*gen* Egils) *m* Egil (*personal name*)
Egilsson *m* son of Egil
Eiríkr *m* Eirik (*personal name*)
en *conj* but; and (on the other hand)
fé *n* property, wealth; cattle
fóstbróðir *m* foster-brother
fóstbrœðra *gen pl* (*see* **fóstbróðir**) of the foster-brothers
góðr *adj* good
Gunnlaugr *m* Gunnlaug (*personal name*)
gǫfugr *adj* noble
hann *pron* he
heita (*past* hét) *vb* be named, called
hersir (*gen* -is) *m* local chieftain; a military leader with power from a king
hestr *m* horse
hét (*inf* **heita**) *vb* was named, called
hlutr (*acc pl* hluti) *m* part
hon *pron* she
hófsmaðr *m* man of moderation and restraint
hógværr *adj* gentle
hringr *m* ring
hvítr *adj* white
hǫfðingi *m* leader
í *prep* [*w dat*] in
kveld *n* evening

Kveld-Úlfr (*gen* Kveld-Úlfs) *m* Kveld-Ulf ('Evening-Wolf') (*personal name*)
Kveld-Úlfssonnar *gen* of the son of Kveld-Ulf
maðr (*gen* manns) *m* man; person
mikill *adj* great
móðir *f* mother
Nóregr *m* Norway
ok *conj* and (in addition)
ormr *m* serpent, snake
ormstunga *f* 'Serpent's Tongue' (*nickname*)
ór *prep* [*w dat*] out of, from
saga *f* story
sǫgu *dat sg of* **saga**
Sigurðr (*gen* -ar) *m* Sigurd (*personal name*)
Skalla-Grímr (*gen* Skalla-Gríms) *m* Skalla-Grim (*personal name*)
Skalla-Grímssonar *gen* of the son of Skalla-Grim
skip *n* ship
son(r) (*gen* sonar) *m* son
sýna (*past* sýndi) *vb* show
sýndi (*inf* **sýna**) *vb* showed
tunga *f* tongue
um *prep* [*w acc*] about, in regard to
úlfr *m* wolf
var (*inf* **vera**) *vb* was
vera (*past* var) *vb* be
vitr (*gen* vitrs) *adj* wise
Þorsteinn (*gen* Þorsteins) *m* Thorstein (*personal name*)
Þórólfr *m* Thorolf (*personal name*)

PHRASES

auðigr at fé wealthy
ór Nóregi from Norway
um alla hluti in all respects
í [__]firði in [__]fjord (f.ex., *í **Borgarfirði*** 'in Borgar Fjord')
ór [__] sǫgu from the saga of [__], from [__]'s saga (f.ex., *ór **Gunnlaugs** sǫgu* 'from the saga of Gunnlaug' or 'from Gunnlaug's saga')
[__]son the son of [__] (f.ex., ***Egils**son* 'the son of Egil')
[__]dóttir the daughter of [__] (f.ex., ***Bjarnar**dóttir* 'the daughter of Bjorn')

LESSON 2

Ór *Hrafnkels sǫgu Freysgoða* (2. kap.)
(From the *Saga of Hrafnkel the Priest of Frey*, Chap. 2)

En þá er Hrafnkell hafði land
numit á Aðalbóli, þá efldi hann
blót mikil. Hrafnkell lét gera
hof mikit. Hrafnkell elskaði
eigi annat goð meir en Frey.
Hrafnkell bygði allan dalinn
ok gaf mǫnnum land, en vildi
þó vera yfirmaðr þeira ok tók
goðorð yfir þeim. Við þetta
var lengt nafn hans ok
kallaðr Freysgoði, ok var
ójafnaðarmaðr mikill.

And when Hrafnkel had taken land
at Adalbol, then he performed great
sacrifices. Hrafnkel had a large
temple built. Hrafnkel loved
no other god more than Frey.
Hrafnkel occupied the whole valley
and gave land to people, and wanted
though to be their leader and
became a *goði* over them. With this
his name was lengthened and [he
was] called the *goði* of Frey, and [he]
was a very unjust man.

2.1. Special Stem Rules.

Two special stem rules affect the specific form of the nominative ending
-*r* of strong masculine nouns and pronouns. These rules reflect the
natural patterns of speech that occurred especially when people spoke
rapidly. The patterns simplify difficult sequences of
sound by smoothing out the articulation. The changes
depend on the length of the vowel (whether short or
long) that appears in the stem to which the ending is
added and whether the vowel is stressed.

Short		Long
i	—	í
y	—	ý
e	—	é
ø	—	œ
–		æ
a	—	á
ǫ		–
o	—	ó
u	—	ú

The table at right shows the short and long vowels
of Old Icelandic. The long vowel is simply a longer
version of the short vowel.[5] The short vowels are
represented each by a single, simple letter, while each
long vowel either has an acute accent (´) or is a
combination of two letters, called a **ligature** (æ and
œ).[6] There is no short equivalent of æ and no long equivalent of ǫ.

---

[5] Vowels in Modern Icelandic have changed somewhat; f.ex., *á* is no longer
simply a lengthened version of *a* as it was in the medieval period, but now
sounds similar to **ou** in English 'out'. Consonants have scarcely changed from
medieval to Modern Icelandic. Overall the changes in pronunciation from Old
to Modern Icelandic are relatively small for such a long period of time. (For
more information, see Appendix 1: Pronunciation Guide to Old Icelandic.)

[6] These ligatures were originally pronounced as single long vowels. In modern
Icelandic they have merged into a vowel sound similar to the **ai** of English
'**ai**sle'. This is a sequence of two vowel sounds, a short **a** (as in 'bar') which

Stress is much simpler in Icelandic than in English. In English, the stressed syllable (i.e., the most forcefully pronounced syllable) may be any syllable of a word; compare the words '**ta**-ble', 're-**spect**', '**au**-to-mo-bile', 'a-**part**-ment', 'o-ver-**whelm**'. In Icelandic, the stress almost always falls on the first syllable of the word stem: ***her**-sir*, ***mó**-ðir*, *hǫf-ðing-i*, ***hófs**-mað-r*, etc. A vowel will therefore generally be stressed if it is in the first syllable of the word, and unstressed if it is not. For example, the vowel *-i-* is stressed in ***vin**-r*, but unstressed in ***E**-gill*.

Now we can explain the two special stem rules that affect the nominative singular ending of strong masculine nouns and adjectives ending originally in *-r*.

Special Stem Rules:

1. If the stem ends in *-l-*, *-n-* or *-s-* preceded by a long vowel (or diphthong) or an unstressed short vowel, this final stem consonant is doubled, the second consonant taking the place of the ending *-r*: *ljós-**s*** (adj. 'light'), *væn-**n*** (adj. 'handsome'), *Þorstein-**n***, *mikil-**l***, *Egil-**l***. We say that the ending *-r* **assimilates** to the final consonant of the stem.

The *-r* does not change in the following situations:

- If *-l-*, *-n-* or *-s-* is preceded by a stressed short vowel, the ending *-r* is added as usual: *dal-**r*** 'valley,' *vin-**r*** 'friend.'

- If the stem ends in *-r-* preceded by a vowel, the ending *-r* is added as usual: *hógvær-**r***.

2. If the stem ends in *-r-* preceded by a consonant, the ending *-r* is not added. For example, the final *-r* of the adjective *vitr* 'wise' belongs to the stem, and is not the nominative singular masculine ending (which is dropped). That the *–r* belongs to the stem is illustrated by the genitive singular *vitr-**s***, which adds the genitive *–s*. Another example is the adjective *fagr* 'fair, beautiful' (with genitive singular *fagr-**s***). This rule simplifies consonant clusters (like *-trr* and *-grr*) that would be hard to pronounce.

2.2. Other Uses of the Genitive.

In addition to denoting possession or belonging (1.2), the genitive case in Old Icelandic has two other very important uses:

- Certain prepositions require that their object (the noun or pronoun that follows it) take the genitive case. Two such prepositions are *til* 'to' and *milli* 'between'. (The first of these is by far the more important.) If we wish to say 'to Thorstein' in Old Icelandic, we must use the genitive form of *Þorsteinn*: hence *til Þorsteins*.

---

glides to a short **i** (as in 'bid'), but it functions as a single vowel. Such vowel combinations are called **diphthongs**, and count the same as long vowels for the sake of these rules. Other examples of diphthongs in Old Icelandic are *au, ei, ey*.

- Certain verbs require that their direct objects take the genitive case instead of the accusative. For instance, the verb *þurfa* 'to need' takes the genitive: *þeir þurfa hersis* 'they need a chieftain'. The direct object *hersis* 'chieftain' must appear in the genitive, not the accusative. It is helpful to think of the meaning as 'have need of'.

It is important to know that verbs of asking require that the thing asked for must take the genitive, as in a marriage proposal, one person asking for the other. *Ásgerðr biðr Þorsteins* 'Asgerd asks for Thorstein'. This verb appears in a reading selection in Lesson 9.

2.3. Strong Nouns: Masculine Accusative and Dative Singular.

- The accusative singular of strong masculine nouns has no ending: *konung* 'king' (nom. *konungr*), *dal* 'valley, dale' (nom. *dalr*).

- The dative ending is usually *-i*: *konungi*; we have already encountered two datives in R.S. 1, *Nóregi* and *firði*. In some instances, there is no ending in the dative: *bekk* 'bench', *dal* 'valley, dale' (the acc. and dat. are the same).

2.4. Strong Adjectives: Accusative and Dative Singular Masculine.

- The accusative singular masculine ending of strong adjectives is *-an*: *ágætan, góðan*.

- The dative is *-um*: *ágætum, góðum*.

2.5. Review Paradigms: Endings of Masc. Sing. Strong Nouns and Adjectives (See 1.8).

	Noun	Adjective
nom	-r (see 2.1)	-r (see 2.1)
acc	–	-an
dat	-i, –	-um
gen	-s, -ar	-s

2.6. The Noun *maðr*.

The noun *maðr* is irregular in that its stem *mann-* changes to *mað-* in the nominative singular. This noun is also irregular in other cases. Since it is one of the most frequent nouns in Old Icelandic, its different forms are best learned early. Here is a complete paradigm in the singular and plural.

	Sg	Pl
nom	maðr	menn
acc	mann	menn
dat	manni	mǫnnum
gen	manns	manna

EXERCISES

1. Fill in the appropriate endings.

Grím__ var mikil__ mað__. Hann var Þorstein__son, Egil__son__.

2. Repeat the sentence from exercise **1**, with the following changes.

a. Make Grim the son of Egil and Egil the son of Thorstein.

_____

b. Change the sentence to be about Egil, and make Egil the son of Grim and Grim the son of Thorstein.

_____

c. Change the sentence to be about Thorstein, and make Thorstein the son of Egil and Egil the son of Grim.

_____

3. Fill in the appropriate endings.

Ásgerðr var dóttir Úlf__, mikil__ mann__ ok auðig__.

Hann var hersi__, ágæt__ mað__ ok gǫfug__.

4. Repeat the first sentence of exercise **3**, with the following changes.

a. Replace *mikill* with *hógværr* and *auðigr* with *vitr*.

_____

b. Replace *mikill* with *ríkr* 'powerful' and *auðigr* with *vænn* 'handsome'.

_____

5. Vocabulary training.

Across   10 make, build   5 give
  1 took, seized   11 name   6 land
  3 wished, wanted   12 valley, dale   7 they
  4 inhabit, dwell   **Down**   9 man, person
  8 fair, beautiful   2 call, name

VOCABULARY

Aðalból *n* Adalbol (*place name*)
allan *acc sg masc of* **allr**
allr *adj* all
annarr (*n* annat) *adj* other, another
á *prep* [*w dat*] on; at
blót (*pl* blót) *n* sacrifice
bygði (*inf* **byggja**) *vb* inhabited
byggja (*past* bygði) *vb* inhabit, dwell
dalr *m* valley, dale
dalinn = **dal** (*acc sg of* **dalr**) + **-inn**
  (*art*) the valley
efla (*past* efldi) *vb* make, perform
efldi (*inf* **efla**) *vb* made, performed
eigi *adv* not; no
elska (*past* elskaði) *vb* love; be fond of
elskaði (*inf* **elska**) *vb* loved
en *conj* but; and (on the other hand);
  w comp than
er *conj* when
fagr (*gen* fagrs) *adj* fair, beautiful
Freyr *m* Frey (*mythological name*, one
  of the Vanir)
Freysgoði *m* 'Frey's Chief' (*nickname*)
gaf (*inf* **gefa**) *vb* gave
gefa (*past* gaf) *vb* give
gera *vb* make, build
goð *n* god, one of the pagan gods
goði *m* chief (and priest)
goðorð *n* chieftainship, rank and
  authority of a **goði**
hafa (*past* hafði) *vb* have
hafði (*inf* **hafa**) *vb* had
hans *poss pron* his
hof *n* temple
Hrafnkell *m* Hrafnkel (*personal
  name*)
-inn *art* the (*suffixed to noun*)
kalla (*past* kallaði) *vb* call, name
kallaðr (*inf* **kalla**) *ppart* called (*nom
  sg masc*)
land *n* land
láta (*past* lét) *vb* let, allow; [*w inf*]
  have something done

lengja (*ppart* -dr) *vb* lengthen
lengt (*inf* **lengja**) *ppart* lengthened
  (*nom/acc sg neut*)
lét (*inf* **láta**) *vb* let, allowed; caused to
  be done
ljóss *adj* light
maðr (*gen* manns) *m* man; person,
  human being
meir *comp adv* (*see* **mjǫk**) more
mikill (*n sg* mikit; *n pl* mikil) *adj* big,
  great
milli *prep* [*w gen*] between
mjǫk (*comp* meir[r]) *adv* much
mǫnnum *dat sg and pl of* **maðr**
nafn *n* name
nema (*ppart* numit) *vb* take
numit (*inf* **nema**) *ppart* taken
  (*nom/acc sg neut*)
ok *conj* and (in addition)
ójafnaðarmaðr *m* unjust man, quarrelsome and overbearing, difficult to
  deal with
ríkr *adj* powerful, mighty
taka (*past* tók) *vb* take, seize
til *prep* [*w gen*] to
tók (*inf* **taka**) *vb* took, seized
var (*inf* **vera**) *vb* was
vera (*past* var) *vb* be
við *prep* [*w acc*] with, according to
vildi (*inf* **vilja**) *vb* wished, wanted
vilja (*past* vildi) *vb* wish, want
vinr (*gen* vinar) *m* friend
vænn *adj* fine, handsome, beautiful
yfir *prep* [*w acc/dat*] over, above
yfirmaðr *m* leader, chieftain
þá *adv* then
þeim *dat pl pron* (*see* **þeir**) them
þeir (*dat* þeim) *m pl pron* they
þeira *poss pron* their
þetta *dem pron* this (*nom/acc sg neut*)
þurfa *vb* [*w gen*] need, have need of
þó *adv* yet, though, nevertheless

PHRASES

lét gera had built   **þá er** *conj* when

LESSON 3

Ór *Egils sǫgu Skalla-Grímssonar* (50. kap.)
(From the *Saga of Egil Skalla-Grimsson*, Chap. 50)

Elfráðr inn ríki réð fyrir
Englandi; hann var fyrstr
einvaldskonungr yfir Englandi;
þat var á dǫgum Haralds ins
hárfagra, Nóregs konungs. Eptir
hann var konungr í Englandi
sonr hans Játvarðr; hann var
faðir Aðalsteins ins sigrsæla,
fóstra Hákonar ins góða.

Alfred the powerful ruled over
England; he was the first sole ruler
(monarch) over (all of) England;
that was in the days of Harald the
fair-haired, king of Norway. After
him his son Edward was king of
England; he was the father of
Athelstane the victorious, foster-
father of Hakon the good.

3.1. Definite Article: Singular Masculine.

The chart at right declines the def. art. in the sing.
masc. The nom. and gen. sing., *inn* and *ins*,
correspond to strong nouns and adjectives ending
in -*nn* (f.ex., *Þorsteinn, vænn*). The acc. and dat.,
however, are different from the acc. and dat. of

nom	inn
acc	inn
dat	inum
gen	ins

strong nouns and adjectives: the acc. is *inn* (identical to the nom.) and
the dat. is *inum*.

3.2. Weak Adjectives: Singular Masculine.

When an adj. is preceded by the def. art. or another limiting word (a
demonstrative pronoun or possessive adj.), it is traditionally called **weak**. The endings of weak adjectives
differ from those of strong adjectives. They are -*i* for the
nom. sing. masc. and -*a* for the other sing. masc. cases:
nom. *inn ríki*, acc. *inn ágæta*, dat. *inum fagra*, gen. *ins*
góða.

nom	-i
acc	-a
dat	-a
gen	-a

3.3. Weak Nouns: Masculine Singular.

Corresponding to the weak declension of adjectives is a
weak noun declension: nom. *hǫfðingi* (R.S. 1), *goði*
(R.S. 2), gen. *fóstra*. All three of these nouns are masc.
Many masc. names belong to the weak declension: *Helgi,*
Gísli, Ingi – acc./dat./gen. *Helga, Gísla, Inga*. Note that

nom	-i
acc	-a
dat	-a
gen	-a

the sing. endings of weak masc. nouns are identical with the
corresponding endings of weak adjectives.

Whereas adjectives vary between strong and weak forms depending on whether or not they are paired with an article or other determiner (3.2), nouns are either weak or strong by nature and do not alternate.

3.4. The Noun *sonr* (*-son*).

The nom. sing. of the word for 'son' is irregular. When it occurs attached to the gen. form of a name (*Egilsson,* etc.), it does not use the normal nominative singular masculine ending *-r*. When it occurs independently (as in R.S. 3), it usually has the ending *-r*. The gen. sing. is always *son**ar***.

3.5. Disyllabic Adjectives and Nouns.

When a disyllabic adj. takes an ending that contains a vowel, the vowel of the second syllable is lost. For example, the nom. sing. masc. weak form of *mikill* is *mikli*. This is true for all adjectives except those of participial form with the second syllable *-að-* (see 5.3.1, 8.7, 10.3.1). Disyllabic nouns also behave this way: f.ex., the dat. sing. of the neut. noun *sumar* 'summer' is *sumri* (R.S. 9).

3.6. Personal Pronouns: First and Second Persons.

Examples of the 1st person sing. pron. *ek* 'I' and the 2nd person sing. *þú* 'you' and *þér* '(to) you' will appear in R.S. 4. The full declensions are as follows.

	1st		2nd	
Sg nom	ek	'I'	þú	'you'
acc	mik	'me'	þik	'you'
dat	mér	'(to) me'	þér	'(to) you'
gen	mín	'of me'	þín	'of you'
Pl nom	vér	'we'	þér/ér	'you'
acc	oss	'us'	yðr	'you'
dat	oss	'(to) us'	yðr	'(to) you'
gen	vár	'of us'	yð(v)ar	'of you'

3.7. Preview of the Verb: The Infinitive.

Almost all Icelandic verbs form the infinitive by adding *-a* to the verb stem (i.e., the basic verb minus any endings): *gefa* 'give', *þiggja* 'accept'. The infinitve is used after modal auxiliary verbs:[7] *ek vil gefa* 'I will (= wish to) give', *ek vil þiggja* 'I will (= wish to) accept'. You will see these forms in R.S. 4.

---

[7] Modal auxiliary verbs, also called helping verbs, add qualities of meaning to the main verb to make it something other than a simple statement of fact. They express characteristics such as ability, possibility, necessity, intention, etc. Examples in English include 'can', 'could', 'may', 'might', 'must', 'shall', 'should, 'will', 'would', etc.

3.8. Infinitive Marker *at.*

When an infinitive appears in its own phrase (f.ex., *at segja* in *ok er frá honum gott **at segja*** 'and about him there is good **to tell**', R.S. 7), the infinitive is preceded by the particle *at*, which correspondes to English 'to'. Note that it is identical in form with the prep. *at* and the conj. *at.*

3.9. Additional Reading.

The following passage from the beginning of *Þorsteins þáttr Stangarhǫggs* (*Tale of Thorstein Staff-Struck*) is a typical opening to an Icelandic saga. The characters who appear at the start of the saga are introduced with a terse description of their background, where they lived, and a glimpse of their personal character.

Ór *Þorsteins þætti stangarhǫggs* (1. kap.)
(From the *Tale of Thorstein Staff-Struck*, Chap. 1)

Maðr hét Þórarinn, er
bjó í Sunnudal, gamall maðr
ok sjónlítill. Hann hafði verit
rauðavíkingr í œsku sinni. Hann
var eigi dældarmaðr, þótt hann
væri gamall. Son átti sér einn, er
Þorsteinn er nefndr. Hann var
mikill maðr ok ǫflugr ok vel
stilltr.

A man was named Thorarin, who
lived in Sunnudal, an old man
and of poor eyesight. He had been
a red viking in his youth. He
was not a gentle man, although he
was old. He had one son, who
is named Thorstein. He was
a big man and strong and very
calm.

Exercises

1. Fill in the appropriate endings.

   a. Mað__ hét Helgi. Hann var Hákon___son, Nóreg__ konung__.
      Helgi var væn__ mað__ ok vitr.

   b. Móðir Helg__ hét Ásgerðr, dóttir Þorstein__ in__ auðg__, rík__
      mann__ ok góð__.

   c. Aðalstein__ var son__ Harald__ in__ góð__, hersi__ rík__ í
      Nóreg__.

   d. Játvarð__ in__ góð__ var góð__ konung__ ok sigrsæl__. Hann réð
      fyrir England__ á dǫgum Harald__ in__ hárfagr__.

   e. Egil__ in__ mikl__ hét hersi__, son__ Þorstein__ in__ mikl__.

2. Supply suitable personal names, nouns, and adjectives.

    a. _____i (name)   inn   _____i (adj.)   hét

       _____r (noun). Hann var sonr _____s (name) ins

       _____a (adj.), _____s (adj.) _____s (noun) ok

       _____s (adj.).

    b. Repeat exercise **a**, interchanging the two names and using different adjectives.

    _____

    _____

    _____

3. Match the Old Norse infinitives with their English meanings by drawing a line between the two.

Old Norse	English
at búa	to love
at elska	to dwell
at gefa	to be named
at gera	to give
at hafa	to rule
at heita	to have
at kalla	to let
at láta	to be
at ráða	to make
at taka	to want
at vilja	to call
at vera	to take

4. Supply the Icelandic pronouns.

	1st		2nd	
Sg nom	_____ 'I'		_____ 'you'	
acc	_____ 'me'		_____ 'you'	
dat	_____ '(to) me'		_____ '(to) you'	
gen	_____ 'of me'		_____ 'of you'	
Pl nom	_____ 'we'		_____ 'you'	
acc	_____ 'us'		_____ 'you'	
dat	_____ '(to) us'		_____ '(to) you'	
gen	_____ 'of us'		_____ 'of you'	

VOCABULARY

Aðalsteinn *m* Athelstane (*personal name*)

at *inf marker* to

á *prep* [*w dat*] on, at, in (*location*)

Ásvaldr *m* Asvald (*personal name*)

dagr (*pl dat* dǫgum) *m* day

dalr (*dat* dal(i)) *m* valley, dale

dældarmaðr *m* gentle, easy man

dǫgum *dat pl of* **dagr**

eigi *adv* not

einn *num* one

einvaldskonungr *m* sole ruler

Elfráðr *m* Alfred (*personal name*)

England *n* England

eptir *prep* [*w acc*] after (*in time*)

er *rel pron* who

er (*inf* **vera**) *vb* is

faðir *m* father

fóstri *m* foster-father

fyrir *prep* [*w dat*] before, at the head of (leading)

fyrstr *superl adj* first

gamall *adj* old

Gísli *m* Gisli (*personal name*)

góðr *adj* good

hafa (*past* hafði) *vb* have

hafði (*inf* **hafa**) *vb* had

hann *pron* (*nom*) he; (*acc*) him

hans *poss pron* his

Haraldr *m* Harald (*personal name*)

Hákon (*gen* Hákonar) *m* Hakon (*personal name*)

hárfagr *adj* fair-haired

heita (*past* hét) *vb* be named, be called

Helgi *m* Helgi ('Holy') (*personal name*)

hét (*inf* **heita**) *vb* was named, called

honum *pron* (to) him (*dat sg of* **hann**)

hǫgg *n* stroke, blow

Ingi *m* Ingi (*personal name*)

inn *art* the

í *prep* [*w dat*] in (*location*)

Játvarðr *m* Edward (*personal name*)

konungr *m* king

maðr *m* man; person, human being

mikill *adj* big, great

nefna *vb* name, call

nefndr (*inf* **nefna**) *ppart* named

Nóregr *m* Norway

rauðavíkingr *m* 'red' viking, a particularly fierce and violent viking

rauðr *adj* red

ráða (*past* réð) *vb* rule, govern

réð (*inf* **ráða**) *vb* ruled, governed

ríkr *adj* powerful, mighty

segja *vb* say, tell

sér *dat refl pron* (for) himself

sigrsæll *adj* victorious

sinn (*dat fem* sinni) *refl poss adj* his (own)

sjónlítill *adj* having poor eyesight

sonr (*gen* sonar) *m* son

stangarhǫgg *n* Staff-Struck (*nickname*)

stilltr *adj* calm, composed

stǫng (*gen* stangar) *f* pole, staff

sunna *f* sun

Sunnudalr (*dat* Sunnudal(i)) *m* Sunnudal ('Sun Dale') (*place name*)

var (*inf* **vera**) *vb* was

vel *adv* well, very

vera (*past* var) *vb* be

verit (*inf* **vera**) *ppart* been

víkingr *m* a viking, sea-raider

væri (*inf* **vera**) *vb* was (*subjunct*)

yfir *prep* [*w acc/dat*] over, above

þat *dem pron* that

þáttr (*dat* þætti) *m* short story, tale

Þórarinn *m* Thorarin (*personal name*)

þótt = **þó at** *conj* [*w subjunct*] although, even though

þætti *dat sg of* **þáttr**

œska (*dat* œsku) *f* youth, childhood

ǫflugr *adj* strong, powerful

PHRASES

á dǫgum in the days (of)

átti sér had for himself = had

í Englandi in England

konungr yfir king of

hann réð fyrir he ruled over

LESSON 4

Ór *Egils sǫgu Skalla-Grímssonar* (36. kap.)
(From the *Saga of Egil Skalla-Grimsson*, Chap. 36)

Þat var einn dag, er þeir Þórólfr ok Bjǫrn gengu ofan til skipsins; þeir sá, at Eiríkr konungsson var þar, gekk stundum á skipit út, en stundum á land upp, stóð þá ok horfði á skipit.

It was one day when (they) Thorolf and Bjorn went down to the ship; they saw that Prince Eirik was there, [that he] went at times out onto the ship, and at times up onto land, then stood and looked at the ship.

Þá mælti Þórólfr: "Vandliga hyggr þú at skipinu, konungsson; hversu lízk þér á?"

Then Thorolf spoke: "Carefully you consider the ship, prince; how do you like it?"

"Vel," segir hann, "it fegrsta er skipit," segir hann.

"Very much," he says, "the ship is the most beautiful," he says.

"Þá vil ek gefa þér," sagði Þórólfr, "skipit, ef þú vill þiggja."

"Then I wish to give you," said Thorolf, "the ship, if you wish to accept."

"Þiggja vil ek," segir Eiríkr.

"I wish to accept," says Eirik.

4.1. Strong Nouns: Neuter Singular.

The singular declension of a strong neut. noun can be illustrated by the word *skip*. Note:

nom	skip
acc	skip
dat	skipi
gen	skips

- There is no ending in the nom., differing in this respect from strong masc. nouns.

- The nom. and acc. are identical.

- The dat. ending is -*i*, in common with the majority of strong masc. nouns.

- The gen. ending is -*s*, as in the case of many masc. nouns.

4.2. Review Paradigms: Masc. and Neut. Sing. Strong Noun Endings (See 2.5).

	Masc	Neut
nom	-r (see 2.1)	–
acc	–	–
dat	-i, –	-i
gen	-s, -ar	-s

4.3. Definite Article: Singular Neuter.

The nom. form of the neut. sing. art. occurs in the R.S.: *it fegrsta* 'the fairest'. The complete paradigm is shown in the table at right. Note:

nom	it
acc	it
dat	inu
gen	ins

- The nom. and acc. forms are identical (this is a characteristic of the neut. declension in general).

- The gen. form *ins* is identical with the gen. sing. masc. (3.1).

4.4. Review Paradigms: Masc. and Neut. Sing. Forms of the Article (See 3.1, 4.3).

	Masc	Neut
nom	inn	it
acc	inn	it
dat	inum	inu
gen	ins	ins

4.5. Strong and Weak Adjectives: Singular Neuter.

The strong neut. declension of adjectives has the endings shown in the box at right. Note:

nom	-t
acc	-t
dat	-u
gen	-s

- The nom. and acc. are identical.

- The gen. ending is -*s*, in common with masc. strong adjectives.

- The endings match those of the article: *it, it, inu, ins* (4.3).

Weak neut. adjectives have the ending -*a* in all cases of the singular. The nom. sing. neut. weak adj. ending was seen in R.S. 4: *it fegrsta*. The dat. sing. *sama* '[the] same' appears in the following reading example:

nom	-a
acc	-a
dat	-a
gen	-a

Ór *Magnúss sǫgu Erlingssonar* (16. kap.)
(From the *Saga of Magnus Erlingsson*, Chap. 16)

Eysteinn var vígðr á **sama**	Eystein was ordained in [the] same
ári ok Ingi konungr fell.	year that ('as') King Ingi fell.

4.6. Review Paradigms: Sing. Masc. and Neut. of Strong and Weak Adjectives (See 2.5, 3.2, 4.5).

	Strong		Weak	
	Masc	Neut	Masc	Neut
nom	-r (see 2.1)	-t	-i	-a
acc	-an	-t	-a	-a
dat	-um	-u	-a	-a
gen	-s	-s	-a	-a

4.7. Weak Nouns: Neuter Singular.

A weak neut. noun declension exists, but it has only a few members, none of which have occurred in the reading selections so far. Most of them refer to parts of the body; the main ones are: *auga* 'eye', *eyra* 'ear', *hjarta* 'heart', *lunga* 'lung'.

As with adjectives (4.5), neut. weak nouns end in -*a* in all cases of the singular.

4.8. Suffixed Definite Article.

The article is suffixed to the noun when the noun is not modified by an adj., as illustrated by the forms *skipit* (nom./acc.), *skipinu* (dat.), and *skipsins* (gen.) in the R.S.

	Strong		**Weak**	
	Masc	**Neut**	**Masc**	**Neut**
nom	konungr-inn	skip-it	goði-nn	auga-t
acc	konung-inn	skip-it	goða-nn	auga-t
dat	konungi-num	skipi-nu	goða-num	auga-nu
gen	konungs-ins	skips-ins	goða-ns	auga-ns

Note:

- The article is added after the appropriate case ending: *konungrinn = konung-r + -inn*; *konungsins = konung-s + -ins*; *skipsins = skip-s + -ins*.

- When the noun ends in a vowel, the initial *i*- of the article is dropped: strong dat. *konungi + -inum = konunginum*; *skipi + -inu = skipinu*; weak nom. *goði + -inn = goðinn*; *auga + -it = augat*; gen. *goða + -ins = goðans*; *auga + -ins = augans*.

- Although the masc. nom. and acc. forms of the article are identical, the two cases are distinguishable when the article is suffixed to the noun, because the forms of the noun differ: strong *konungrinn* (nom.), *konunginn* (acc.); weak *goðinn* (nom.), *goðann* (acc.).

4.9. More on the Accusative and Dative Cases.

As explained in 1.2, the acc. is generally used for direct objects and the dat. for indirect objects. For example: *Þá vil ek gefa **þér** (dat.) **skipit** (acc.).* 'Then will I give (to) you the ship'.

It is not necessary for a sentence to contain both a direct object and an indirect object. Sometimes only the direct object appears: *Þeir sá **skipit** (acc.)* 'They saw the ship'.

Old Icelandic sentences can also contain only an indirect object: *Þá vil ek gefa **þér** (dat.)* 'Then will I give (to) you'. Here the direct object is understood, and not made explicit.

Like the gen., the dat. is also required by certain prepositions and verbs:

- The following **prepositions** require the noun that goes with them to take the dat. case: *af, at, frá, hjá, móti, nær, ór, undan.* For example, *ór Nóregi* (dat.) 'from Norway'.

- Certain **verbs** require that their direct objects take not the acc. case but the dat. These are usually verbs whose direct objects can be understood as "instruments" of the action. An instrument is, as you might imagine, an object used deliberately to cause some effect. *Halda* 'hold,' *kasta* 'throw' and *skjóta* 'shoot' take the dat. in this way. For example, *Hann kastar sverði* (dat.) 'He throws a sword'.

We can see here that the subject is really using the direct object (the sword) as an instrument to cause some effect, probably on another person or thing.

Most prepositions in Old Icelandic can take either the acc. or the dat., depending on their meaning. Examples are: *á, eptir, í, fyrir, með, of, um, undir, við, yfir.* In general, these prepositions take the dat. when they express a position in space or time (or refer to an "instrument"), and take the acc. when they express motion with respect to a place or duration of time. For example:

> *Hann gekk á skip* (acc.) 'He went **onto a ship**'
> *Hann stóð á skipi* (dat.) 'He stood **on a ship**'

In the first example, *á* means 'onto', implying motion with respect to the ship, and requires the noun that goes with it to take the acc.; in the second example, *á* means 'on', implying a stationary position with respect to the ship, and requires the dat.

EXERCISES

1. Fill in the appropriate endings.

    a. Egil__ gekk til konung_____. "Ek vil gef__ þér land____," sagði konung_____. (all def.)

    b. Kveld-Úlf__ gekk ofan til skip_____ (def.).

    c. Þorgerðr var dóttir Egils. Hon var stór__ barn ok fagr__. (*stórr* adj. 'big'; *barn* neut. 'child')

    d. It stór__ sverð Egils var skarp__ ok lang__. (*skarpr* adj. 'sharp'; *langr* adj. 'long')

    e. Helg__ in__ vitr hét konungsson__; hann gekk á skip__ (def.) út ok á land__ (def.) upp.

    f. Konung__ stóð á inu fegrst__ skip__ ok horfð__ á land__.

2. Decline the independent def. art. in the masc. and neut. singular.

masc. nom. _____   neut. nom. _____

      acc. _____   acc. _____

      dat. _____   dat. _____

      gen. _____   gen. _____

3. Decline the def. art. suffixed to the nouns *úlfr* 'wolf', *sverð* 'sword', *fóstri* 'foster-father', and *hjarta* 'heart'.

nom. úlfr_____   sverð_____   fóstri_____   hjarta_____

  acc. úlf_____   sverð_____   fóstra_____   hjarta_____

  dat. úlfi_____   sverði_____   fóstra_____   hjarta_____

  gen. úlfs_____   sverðs_____   fóstra_____   hjarta_____

4. Vocabulary training.

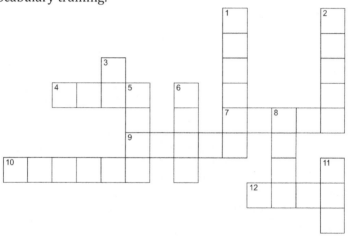

Across
4 be
7 said (*sg*)
9 went (*pl*)
10 accept

12 ship
Down
1 how
2 spoke (*sg*)
3 year

5 eye
6 one
8 went (*sg*)
11 up, upwards

VOCABULARY

at *conj* that
auga *n* eye
á *prep* [*w acc*] onto (motion), toward (*direction*); [*w dat*] on (*location*)
ár *n* year
barn *n* child
einn *num* (*m nom*) one
Eiríkr *m* Eirik (*personal name*)
ek *pron* I
ef *conj* if
er *conj* when

er (*inf* **vera**) *vb* is
Erlingr *m* Erling (*personal name*)
eyra *n* ear
Eysteinn *m* Eystein (*personal name*)
fagr *adj* fair, beautiful
falla (*past* fell) *vb* fall
fegrstr *superl adj* fairest, most beautiful (*see* **fagr**)
fell (*inf* **falla**) *vb* fell
ganga (*past* gekk, gengu) *vb* go, walk
gefa (*past* gaf) *vb* give

gekk (*inf* **ganga**) *vb* went (*sg*)
gengu (*inf* **ganga**) *vb* went (*pl*)
halda *vb* [*w dat*] hold
hjarta *n* heart
horfa (*past* horfði) *vb* (turn so as to) look on
horfði (*inf* **horfa**) *vb* looked on (*sg*)
hversu *int adv* how
hyggja (*pres* hyggr) *vb* think; give heed
kasta (*past* kastaði) *vb* [*w dat*] throw
konungsson(r) *m* prince
land *n* land; estate
langr *adj* long
lunga *n* lung
Magnús *m* Magnus (*personal name*)
mæla (*past* mælti) *vb* say, speak
mælti (*inf* **mæla**) *vb* said, spoke (*sg*)
ofan *adv* down, downwards
ok *conj* as
sagði (*inf* **segja**) *vb* said (*sg*)
samr *adj* same
sá (*inf* **sjá**) *vb* saw
segir (*inf* **segja**) *vb* says
segja (*past* sagði) *vb* say
sjá (*past* sá) *vb* see
skarpr *adj* sharp
skip *n* ship
skjóta *vb* [*w dat*] shoot

standa (*past* stóð, stóðu) *vb* stand
stóð (*inf* **standa**) *vb* stood (*sg*)
stórr *adj* big
stund *f* length of time, a while
stundum *adv* sometimes, at times (*dat pl of* **stund**)
sverð *n* sword
til *prep* [*w gen*] to
upp *adv* up (*motion*), upwards
út *adv* out (*motion*), outwards
vel *adv* well, very much
vera (*pres* er) *vb* be
vil (*inf* **vilja**) *vb* (I) want, wish
vilja (*1sg pres* vil, *2/3sg pres* vill) *vb* wish, want
vill (*inf* **vilja**) *vb* (you *sg*) want, wish
vígðr (*inf* **vígja**) *ppart* ordained (*nom sg masc*)
vígja (*ppart* vígðr) *vb* ordain, consecrate
þar *adv* there
þat *pron* it
þá *adv* then
þeir *pron* they (*m*)
þér *pron* (*dat of* **þú**) you (*sg*)
þiggja *vb* accept
Þorgerðr *f* Thorgerd (*personal name*)
Þórólfr *m* Thorolf (*personal name*)
þú *pron* you (*sg*)

PHRASES

einn dag one day (*definite time*)
horfa á look at
hversu lízk þér á how do you like, what do you think of
þú hyggr at you (*sg*) pay attention to, consider

From this point on, only new words are given in the lesson vocabularies. The rear of the book contains a full vocabulary.

Notes

_____

_____

_____

_____

_____

_____

LESSON 5

Ór *Snorra Eddu, Gylfaginning* (6. kap.)

(From *Snorri's Edda* [*The Prose Edda*], *The Beguiling of Gylfi*, Chap. 6)

Þá mælti Gangleri: "Hvar bygði Ymir? eða við hvat lifði hann?"

Hár svarar: "Næst var þat, þá er hrímit draup, at þar varð af kýr sú er Auðhumla hét, en fjórar mjólkár runnu ór spenum hennar, ok fœddi hon Ymi."

Þá mælti Gangleri: "Við hvat fœddisk kýrin?"

Hár segir: "Hon sleikti hrímsteina, er saltir váru, ok hinn fyrsta dag, er hon sleikti steina, kom ór steininum at kveldi manns hár, annan dag manns hǫfuð, þriðja dag var þar allr maðr. Sá er nefndr Buri."

Then said Gangleri: "Where did Ymir dwell? or on what did he live?"

Har answers: "Next it was, when the rime dripped, that there appeared the cow that was called Audhumla, and four milk-streams ran from her teats, and she fed Ymir."

Then said Gangleri: "With what did the cow feed herself?"

Har says: "She licked [the] rime stones, which were salty; and the first day, when she licked [the] stones, came from the stone at evening the hair of a man, [the] second day a man's head, [the] third day [the] whole man was there. That one is named Buri."

5.1. Personal Pronouns: 3rd Person.

We have already encountered several 3rd person pronouns ('he/she/it/they') in the readings. The full declension is as follows.

	Masc		Fem		Neut	
Sg nom	hann	'he/it'	hon	'she/it'	þat	'it'
acc	hann	'him/it'	hana	'her/it'	þat	'it'
dat	honum	'him/it'	henni	'her/it'	því	'it'
gen	hans	'his/its'	hennar	'her(s)/its'	þess	'its'
Pl nom	þeir	'they'	þær	'they'	þau	'they'
acc	þá	'them'	þær	'them'	þau	'them'
dat	þeim	'them'	þeim	'them'	þeim	'them'
gen	þeir(r)a	'their(s)'	þeir(r)a	'their(s)'	þeir(r)a	'their(s)'

Points to note:

- Noun gender in Old Norse is largely arbitrary. Old Norse requires that a pronoun always reflect the noun's gender, whether masc., fem., or neut. For example, *fjǫrðr* 'fjord' is a masc. noun and is therefore referred to by the pronoun *hann* 'he', *mjólk* 'milk' (fem.)

is referred to as *hon* 'she', and *skip* 'ship' (neut.) is referred to as *þat* 'it'. All these words are translated 'it' in English.

- In the plural, where English has 'they', Old Norse distinguishes all three genders: *þeir* (masc.), *þær* (fem.), and *þau* (neut.).

5.2. Verbs: Weak and Strong Verbs.

Some verbs (traditionally called **weak** verbs) form their past tense by adding a dental suffix (-*ð*- and its variants -*d*- and -*t*-, described below) to the verb stem (f.ex., *hafði* 'had', past tense of *hafa*). Another group (traditionally called **strong** verbs) form their past tense by changing the root vowel without the addition of a dental suffix (f.ex., *tók* 'took', past tense of *taka*).

The same distinction between weak and strong verbs exists in English. Weak verbs form their past tense by adding the dental suffix -**ed** ('walk/walk**ed**') or a variant ('hear/hear**d**', 'dwell/dwel**t**'). Strong verbs form their past tense by changing the root vowel without the addition of a dental suffix ('r**u**n/r**a**n', 's**i**ng/s**a**ng', 'take/t**oo**k').

This lesson presents the past-tense formation of weak verbs, and Lesson 6 presents the strong verbs.

5.3. Weak Verbs: Formation of the Past Tense.

As noted, weak verbs form their past tense by adding a dental suffix (-*ð*- or a variant, -*d*- or -*t*-) to the verb stem.

1. Weak Verbs with Vocalic Link -a-.

One large group of weak verbs is characterized by the presence of a vocalic link -*a*- suffixed to the verb root. These verbs form the largest group of weak verbs by far, and the conjugation is highly regular.

In this group of weak verbs, the vocalic link -*a*- forms part of the stem. (Recall from 1.1 that the stem of a word equals the root plus any suffixes that are added to it.) Additional suffixes, such as the past-tense dental suffix -*ð*-, are added after the vocalic link. Personal endings (f.ex., 3 sing. -*i*, 5.5) are added after the dental suffix. For example:

> *elsk-* + -*a*- + -*ð*- + -*i* → *elskaði* '(he) loved'
> *kall-* + -*a*- + -*ð*- + -*i* → *kallaði* '(he) called'

2. Weak Verbs without Vocalic Link.

Weak verbs that do not have the vocalic link -*a*- described above attach the past-tense dental suffix -*ð*- directly to the root. For example:

> *horf-* + -*ð*- + -*i* → *horfði* '(he) looked'
> *lif-* + -*ð*- + -*i* → *lifði* '(he) lived'
> *sag-* + -*ð*- + -*i* → *sagði* '(he) said'

5.4. Weak Verbs: Variation in the Dental Suffix.

The dental suffix *-ð-* sometimes changes to *-t-*, *-d-*, or zero (i.e., it disappears), depending on the sound that immediately precedes it. Several rules help to explain when the changes occur.

1. Change of Dental Suffix: Predictable Rules.

Following are three rules that are predicatable:

- **When the root ends in *-t-* or *-s-*,** *-ð-* becomes *-t-*.

    flut- + *-ð-* + *-i* → *flutti* '(he) conveyed'

- **When the root itself ends in *-ð-*,** the dental suffix *-ð-* becomes *-d-*, and the stem-final *-ð-* also becomes *-d-*.

    kvað- + *-ð-* + *-i* → *kvaddi* '(he) greeted'
    fœð- + *-ð-* + *-i* → *fœddi* '(he) fed'

- **When the root ends in *-d-* or *-t-* preceded by another consonant,** *-ð-* becomes zero, i.e., disappears.

    skipt- + *-ð-* + *-i* → *skipti* '(he) divided'
    send- + *-ð-* + *-i* → *sendi* '(he) sent'

2. Change of Dental Suffix: Less Predictable Rules.

In other environments, the patterns are less predicable, and there is considerable variation in the manuscripts. The following guidelines help to recognize the variations.

- **When the root ends in *-f-*,** the suffix *-ð-* usually remains unchanged:

    horf- + *-ð-* + *-i* → *horfði* '(he) looked'
    lif- + *-ð-* + *-i* → *lifði* '(he) lived'

    More rarely, *-ð-* changes to *-t-*:

    þurf- + *-ð-* + *-i* → *þurfti* '(he) needed'

- **When the root ends in *-p-* or *-k-*,** the suffix *-ð-* often becomes *-t-*.

    vak- + *-ð-* + *-i* → *vakti* '(he) woke'
    sleik- + *-ð-* + *-i* → *sleikti* '(he) licked'
    keyp- + *-ð-* + *-i* → *keypti* '(he) bought'

    In other instances *-ð-* remains unchanged:

    þak- + *-ð-* + *-i* → *þakði* '(he) thatched'
    glap- + *-ð-* + *-i* → *glapði* '(he) confused'

- **When the root ends in *-n-* or *-m-*** (nasal sounds), *-ð-* generally becomes *-d-*.

    mun- + *-ð-* + *-i* → *mundi* '(he) remembered'
    nefn- + *-ð-* + *-i* → *nefndi* '(he) named'

tam- + *-ð-* + *-i* → *tamdi* '(he) tamed'

But *-ð-* may also remain unchanged:

van- + *-ð-* + *-i* → *vanði* or *vandi* '(he) trained'

- **When the root ends in** *-l-*, the suffix *-ð-* sometimes becomes *-t-*, sometimes becomes *-d-*, and sometimes does not change.

  mæl- + *-ð-* + *-i* → *mælti* '(he) spoke'
  mul- + *-ð-* + *-i* → *muldi* '(he) crushed'
  val- + *-ð-* + *-i* → *valði* '(he) chose'

5.5. Weak Verbs: 3rd Person Past-Tense Endings.

The 3rd person sing. ending of weak verbs in the past tense is *-i* (compare the examples given in 5.3). The 3rd person pl. ending is *-u*. Personal endings are added after the dental suffix; f.ex.:

horfð- + *-i* → *horfði* '(he) looked'
horfð- + *-u* → *horfðu* '(they) looked'
lifð- + *-i* → *lifði* '(he) lived'
lifð- + *-u* → *lifðu* '(they) lived'

5.6. Weak Verbs: Vowel Alternation in Short Roots with *j*-Suffix.

Some weak verbs that add the dental suffix directly to the stem (5.3.2) have a different root vowel in the pres. tense.[8] The verbs of this group all have a **short** root followed by a *-j-* suffix in the infinitive: *kveðja*, *vekja*, *flytja*, and *spyrja*. A short root is one that contains a short vowel (see 2.1) followed by a single consonant; f.ex., the roots of the above verbs are *kvað-*, *vak-*, *flut-*, and *spur-*. These verbs are explained in greater detail in 14.2.

Two changes are the most important:

- If *a* in the past, then *e* in the pres.; f.ex.:

  kvaddi 'greeted' – *kveðja* 'greet'
  vakti 'woke' – *vekja* 'wake'

- If *u* in the past, then *y* in the pres.; f.ex.:

  flutti 'conveyed' – *flytja* 'convey'
  spurði 'asked' – *spyrja* 'ask'

Here are further examples:

sagði 'said' – *segja* (root *sag-*) 'say'
muldi 'crushed' – *mylja* (root *mul-*) 'crush'

---

[8] Modern English verbs such as 'sell/sold', 'tell/told', 'seek/sought', and 'teach/taught', show a similar type of sound change inherited from Old English.

Note the *-j-* before the infinitive ending *-a*. The stem-vowel changes are the result of an **umlaut**[9] process caused by the influence of this *-j-* in the pres. forms. This will be explained in 11.2.1.

EXERCISES

1. Fill in the appropriate endings. (NB: All verbs are weak verbs in the past tense.)

  a. Þeir Þorstein__ ok Grím__ horf____ á land____ (def.).

  b. Hrafnkel__ elsk____ goð____ (def.) Frey ok efl__ blót mikit.

  c. Gangleri mæl___: "Við hvat lif__ Ymi__?"

  d. Hár sag___: "Auðhumla sleik__ steininn, ok kom ór stein_____ (def.) at kveld__ mann__ hár."

2. Supply the Icelandic pronouns.

	Masc	Fem	Neut
Sg *nom*	_____ 'he'	_____ 'she'	_____ 'it'
acc	_____ 'him'	_____ 'her'	_____ 'it'
dat	_____ '(to) him'	_____ '(to) her'	_____ '(to) it'
gen	_____ 'his'	_____ 'her(s)'	_____ 'its'
Pl *nom*	_____ 'they'	_____ 'they'	_____ 'they'
acc	_____ 'them'	_____ 'them'	_____ 'them'
dat	_____ '(to) them'	_____ '(to) them'	_____ '(to) them'
gen	_____ 'their(s)'	_____ 'their(s)'	_____ 'their(s)'

3. Give the 3 sing. past form of the following verbs.

  a. Weak verbs with vocalic link *-a-*:

  Ex.: at kalla (*past* -að-):   hann _*kallaði*_

    at elska (*past* -að-):   hon _____

    at kasta (*past* -að-):   þat _____

  b. Weak verbs without vocalic link:

  Ex.: at mæla (*past* -t-):   hon _*mælti*_

    at fœða (*past* -dd-):   þat _____

    at lifa (*past* -ð-):   hann _____

    at sýna (*past* -d-):   hon _____

---

[9] Umlaut, a term borrowed from German, refers to the change in pronunciation that some vowels undergo due to the influence of other vowels or vowel-like sounds in the following syllable. Umlaut originally arose in rapid speech as speakers, anticipating the next syllable, would slightly alter the vowel to bring it closer in pronunciation to the upcoming sound.

c. Weak verbs with vowel alternation (see 5.6):

Ex.: at flytja (*past* flutt-): þat ___*flutti*___

at kveðja (*past* kvadd-): hann _____

at segja (*past* sagð-): hon _____

at spyrja (*past* spurð-): þat _____

4. The following 3 sing. past-tense weak verbs appeared in R.S. 5. Supply the 3 pl. past-tense form of each.

bygði: þeir _____   fœddi: þær _____

lifði: þau _____   mælti: þeir _____

sleikti: þær _____

VOCABULARY

af *adv* off, away
allr *adj* all, whole
annan *acc sg masc of* **annarr**
annarr (*acc m* annan) *adj* other, another; second
Auðhumla *f* Audhumla (*mythological name*, the primeval cow)
á (*pl* ár) *f* river
Buri *m* Buri (*personal name*)
draup (*inf* **drjúpa**) *vb* dripped
drjúpa (*past* draup, drupu) *vb* drip
eða *conj* or
efla (*past* -d-) *vb* make, perform
elska (*past* -að-) *vb* love; be fond of
fjórar *fem of* **fjórir**
fjórir *num* four
flutti (*inf* **flytja**) *vb* conveyed
flytja (*past* flutt-) *vb* convey
fyrstr *superl adj* first
fœða (*past* -ddi) *vb* feed
fœddi (*inf* **fœða**) *vb* fed
fœddisk (*inf* **fœða-sk**) *vb* fed itself, was fed
Gangleri *m* Gangleri (*personal name*)
glepja (*past* glapð-) *vb* confuse
hár *n* hair
Hár *m* Har ('High') (*mythological name*, pseudonym of Odin)
hennar *poss pron* her
hinn *var of art* **inn**
hrím *n* hoar-frost, rime
hrímsteinn *m* rime-stone
hvar *int adv* where
hvat *int pron* what
hǫfuð *n* head

kaupa (*past* keypt-) *vb* buy
kom (*inf* **koma**) *vb* came (*sg*)
koma (*past* kom, kómu) *vb* come
kvaddi (*inf* **kveðja**) *vb* greeted (*sg*)
kveðja (*past* kvadd-) *vb* greet
kveld *n* evening
kýr *f* cow
kýrin = **kýr** + **-in** (*art*) the cow
lifa (*past* -ð-) *vb* live
lifði (*inf* **lifa**) *vb* lived
mjólk *f* milk
mjólk-á *f* milk-stream, river of milk
muldi (*inf* **mylja**) *vb* crushed
mylja (*past* muld-) *vb* crush
muna (*past* -d-) *vb* remember
næst *adv* next (following)
renna (*past* rann, runnu) *vb* run
runnu (*inf* **renna**) *vb* ran (*pl*)
saltir *nom pl masc of* **saltr**
saltr *adj* salt(y)
sá (*f* sú) *dem pron* that (one)
senda (*past* -nd-) *vb* send
skipta (*past* -pt-) *vb* divide
sleikja (*past* -t-) *vb* lick
sleikti (*inf* **sleikja**) *vb* licked
Snorri *m* Snorri (*personal name*); Snorri Sturluson, author of *The Prose Edda*
speni *m* teat
spenum *dat pl of* **speni**
spurði (*inf* **spyrja**) *vb* asked
spyrja (*past* spurð-) *vb* ask
steina *acc pl of* **steinn**
steinn *m* stone
sú *dem pron* that (one) (*fem of* **sá**)

vakti (*inf* **vekja**) *vb* woke
valði (*inf* **velja**) *vb* chose
varð (*inf* **verða**) *vb* became
váru (*inf* **vera**) *vb* were
vekja (*past* vakt-) *vb* wake
velja (*past* valð-) *vb* choose
vera (*past* var, váru) *vb* be
verða (*past sg* varð) *vb* become; come
  to pass

við *prep* [*w acc*] with, by
Ymir *m* Ymir, the first giant (*mytho-logical name*)
þekja (*past* þakð-) *vb* cover, thatch
þriði *ord num* third
þriðja *acc sg masc of* **þriði**
þurfa (*past* þurft-) *vb* [*w gen*] need,
  have need of

PHRASES

hinn fyrsta dag ... annar dag ... þriðja dag (*acc*) on the first day ... on the second day ... on the third day

lifa við [*w acc*] live on, feed on
verða af come about, appear

Notes

_____

_____

_____

_____

_____

_____

_____

_____

_____

_____

_____

_____

_____

_____

_____

_____

_____

_____

_____

_____

LESSON 6

Ór *Ragnars sǫgu loðbrókar* (3. kap.)
(From the *Saga of Ragnar Lodbrok*, Chap. 3)

that   time   Denmark   Ring
Í þann tíma réð fyrir Danmǫrku Sigurðr hringr. Hann var ríkr konungr

('is famous become')
has become famous   from that   battle   which   fought
ok er frægr orðinn[10] af þeiri orrostu, er hann barðisk við Harald

Wartooth   Bravoll   fell   as   known
hilditǫnn á Brávelli,[11] ok fyrir honum fell Haraldr, sem kunnigt

('is')
[it] has become over all northern region of the world   had   who
er   orðit[9] of alla norðrálfu heimsins. Sigurðr átti einn son, er

                       in size   of appearance   intelligent
Ragnarr hét; hann var mikill vexti, vænn   yfirlits   ok vel viti borinn,

magnanimous   his   fierce   to his enemies
stórlyndr   við sína menn, en grimmr sínum óvinum.

6.1. Strong Verbs: Formation of the Past Tense.

Strong verbs form their past tense without a dental suffix (*-ð/d/t-*). Instead, they change the root vowel (sometimes with accompanying change in consonant structure of the stem). The R.S. above has four past-tense strong verbs: *réð* 'ruled', *hét* 'was named', *fell* 'fell', and *var* 'was'. In addition to these, the following strong verb forms have occurred in other Reading Selections:

> *hét* (R.S. 1, 3.9, 5) from *heita*
> *lét* (R.S. 2) from *láta*
> *tók* (R.S. 2) from *taka*
> *réð* (R.S. 3) from *ráða*
> *gekk* and *gengu* (R.S. 4) from *ganga*
> *sá* (R.S. 4) from *sjá*
> *stóð* (R.S. 4) from *standa*
> *draup* (R.S. 5) from *drjúpa*

---

[10] *Hann er orðinn* 'he has become', (*þat*) *er orðit* '(it) has become': lit., 'is become'. Past participles such as *orðinn/orðit* 'become' are verbal adjectives and agree in gender, number, and case with the noun they modify. See 8.7, 10.3.
[11] The legendary Battle of Bravoll is described in several sagas and in the Danish history *Gesta Danorum*. In this battle, Sigurd Ring, king of Sweden, defeated Harald Wartooth, king of Denmark, on the plain of Brávǫllr (modern Bråvalla) in Sweden.

runnu (R.S. 5) from *renna*.
var (R.S. 1, 1.6, 2, 3, 3.9, 4, 4.5, 5) and *váru* (R.S. 5) from *vera*
varð (R.S. 5) from *verða*

Many Old Icelandic strong verbs have corresponding strong verbs in English. For example, English equivalents of some of the verbs listed above are 'fall' – 'fell', 'run' – 'ran', 'see' – 'saw', 'stand' – 'stood', 'take' – 'took'.

6.2. Verbs: 3rd Person Past-Tense Endings.

Strong verbs regularly have no ending in the 3rd person sing. past. As in the case of weak verbs, the ending is *-u* in the 3rd person pl. The ending *-u*, however, is not added when the past-tense verb stem ends in *-á* or *-ó*, f.ex., *þeir sá*.

6.3. Review Paradigms: 3rd Person Past-Tense Endings of the Verb.

	Weak	Strong
3sg	(-a)-ð/d/t-i	–
3pl	(-a)-ð/d/t-u	-u

6.4. Strong Verbs: Singular and Plural Past-Tense Stems (See 6.1).

Many strong verbs have different stems in the sing. and pl. of the past tense:

vera 'be':	*hann **var***	– *þeir **váru*** (R.S. 5)
koma 'come':	*hon **kom***	– *þær **kómu***
renna 'run':	*hon **rann***	– *þær **runnu*** (R.S. 5)
skjóta 'shoot':	*hann **skaut***	– *þeir **skutu***
búa 'dwell':	*hon **bjó***	– *þær **bjoggu***
ganga 'go':	*hann **gekk***	– *þeir **gengu*** (see R.S. 4)

In some instances, the vowel in the past pl. stem is the long variant of the vowel in the past sing.: *hann var – þeir váru* (from *vera*); *hann kom – þeir kómu* (from *koma*). More often, however, the sing. and pl. of strong verbs have radically different vowels: *hann rann – þeir runnu* (from *renna*); *hann skaut – þeir skutu* (from *skjóta*). Some verbs have different consonant structures in the past sing. and pl. stems: *hann gekk – þeir gengu* (from *ganga*); *hann bjó – þeir bjoggu* (from *búa*).

Not all strong verbs show such alternation in the past stems, however. Some have the same vowel in both past sing. and pl.: *hann hét – þeir hétu* (from *heita*); *taka – hann tók – þeir tóku* (from *taka*).

6.5. The Verbs *vera* and *hafa*.

Two of the most common verbs are *vera* 'be' and *hafa* 'have'. They are conjugated as follows:

vera 'be'

	Pres.			Past		
1sg	ek	em	'I am'	ek	var	'I was'
2sg	þú	ert	'you are'	þú	vart	'you were'
3sg	hann hon þat }	er	'he/she/it is'	hann hon þat }	var	'he/she/it was'
1pl	vér	erum	'we are'	vér	várum	'we were'
2pl	þér	eruð	'you are'	þér	váruð	'you were'
3pl	þeir þær þau }	eru	'they are'	þeir þær þau }	váru	'they were'

hafa 'have'

	Pres.			Past		
1sg	ek	hef(i)	'I have'	ek	hafða	'I had'
2sg	þú	hef(i)r	'you have'	þú	hafðir	'you had'
3sg	hann hon þat }	hef(i)r	'he/she/it has'	hann hon þat }	hafði	'he/she/it had'
1pl	vér	hǫfum	'we have'	vér	hǫfðum	'we had'
2pl	þér	hafið	'you have'	þér	hǫfðuð	'you had'
3pl	þeir þær þau }	hafa	'they have'	þeir þær þau }	hǫfðu	'they had'

6.6. Additional Reading.

The following passage is from the opening of *Vápnfirðinga saga* ('Saga of the Families of Weapon's Fjord'). In common with many sagas, the story begins with genealogical details, telling of family history and placing the family in geographical settings.

Ór *Vápnfirðinga sǫgu* (1. kap.)

(From the *Saga of the Families of Weapon's Fjord*, Chap. 1)

begin we this tale where   Hof Weapon's Fjord who
Þar hefjum vér þenna þátt, er sá maðr bjó at Hofi í Vápnafirði,[12] er

Helgi hét. Hann var sonr Þorgils Þorsteinssonar, Ǫlvis sonar, Ásvalds

---

[12] *Vápnafjǫrðr* (modern Icelandic *Vopnafjörður*) is a fjord in northeastern Iceland, named after one of its first settlers, Eyvindr Vápni (Eyvind the Weapon). Hence the name means 'Vápni's (or Weapon's) Fjord'.

          landed man   in [the] days
sonar, Øxna-Þóris sonar. Ǫlvir var lendr maðr[13] í Nóregi um daga
     earl
Hákonar jarls Grjótgarðssonar.

     [the] White   Iceland of those forefathers
Þorsteinn   hvíti kom fyrst út til Íslands þeira langfeðga ok bjó
   Toptavoll   out beyond
at Toptavelli fyrir útan Síreksstaði. En Steinbjǫrn bjó at Hofi, sonr
        Red   when his wealth was squandered because of open-handedness
Refs ins rauða. Ok er   honum eyddisk fé   fyrir þegnskapar sakar,
  bought   the Hof estate   sixty (of) winters
þá keypti Þorsteinn Hofsland ok bjó þar sex tigu   vetra.   Hann
was married to   White
átti   Ingibjǫrgu Hróðgeirsdóttur ins hvíta.

6.7. Additional Adjectives.

Adjectives are indispensable for describing people and things, and at this point in the lessons, it would be helpful to introduce a few more. Below are some of the most common adjectives found in the sagas. The basic declension may be illustrated by *stórr* 'big':

	Strong				**Weak**		
	Masc	**Fem**	**Neut**		**Masc**	**Fem**	**Neut**
nom	stór-r	stór	stór-t		stór-i	stór-a	stór-a
acc	stór-an	stór-a	stór-t		stór-a	stór-u	stór-a
dat	stór-um	stór-ri	stór-u		stór-a	stór-u	stór-a
gen	stór-s	stór-rar	stór-s		stór-a	stór-u	stór-a

The following adjectives decline according to the paradigm above. The example sentences below are taken from various sagas:

fullr 'full':   ***fullr** af silfri* 'full of silver'
illr 'bad, evil':   *til góðs ok **ills*** 'for good and **bad**'
kyrr 'still, quiet': *er nú **kyrt** þar* 'it is now **quiet** there'
sterkr 'strong':} *hann smíðaði honum boga **stóran** ok **sterkan***
stórr 'big':   }   'he made for him a bow **big** and **strong**'
ungr 'young':   *menn á **ungum** aldri* 'men of a young age'

When the stem ends in a dental (-*t*-, -*d*-, -*ð*-), this dental assimilates with the ending -*t* in the neut. nom./acc. sing. (see 7.4). *Dauðr* 'dead' shows this assimilation:

---

[13] *Lendr maðr* 'landed man' is the Old Icelandic form of Norw. *lendmann*, the title of a medieval Norwegian nobleman whose lands and income were granted by the king in return for enforcement of the king's will. A *lendr maðr* (or *lendmann*) was roughly equivalent to an English baron, with a rank below *jarl* (earl) but above the *hǫldr* (Norw. *hauldr*), a free farmer holding ancestral land.

	Strong			Weak		
	Masc	**Fem**	**Neut**	**Masc**	**Fem**	**Neut**
nom	dauð-r	dauð	daut-t	dauð-i	dauð-a	dauð-a
acc	dauð-an	dauð-a	daut-t	dauð-a	dauð-u	dauð-a
dat	dauð-um	dauð-ri	dauð-u	dauð-a	dauð-u	dauð-a
gen	dauð-s	dauð-rar	dauð-s	dauð-a	dauð-u	dauð-a

The following adjectives demonstrate this pattern.

> *dauðr* 'dead' (neut. nom./acc. *dautt*): *eftir þat mun dýrit **dautt** upp koma* 'after that the beast will come up **dead**'
>
> *fríðr* 'beautiful, fine' (neut. nom./acc. *frítt*): *hann var mikill vexti ok **fríðr** sýnum* 'he was great in stature and **fine** in appearance'
>
> *reiðr* 'angry' (neut. nom/acc. sing. *reitt*): *í **reiðum** hug* 'in an **angry** mood'
>
> *vándr* 'bad, wretched' (neut. nom./acc. *vánt*): *ór húsi litlu ok **vándu*** 'from a little and **wretched** house'

The paradigm of *heill* 'healthy, well; whole' shows assimilation of *-r-* to stem-final *-l-* according to the Special Stem Rule (2.1.1): *er Eymundr var **heill** orðinn* 'when Eymund had become **well**'.

	Strong			Weak		
	Masc	**Fem**	**Neut**	**Masc**	**Fem**	**Neut**
nom	heil-**l**	heil	heil-t	heil-i	heil-a	heil-a
acc	heil-an	heil-a	heil-t	heil-a	heil-u	heil-a
dat	heil-um	heil-**l**i	heil-u	heil-a	heil-u	heil-a
gen	heil-s	heil-**l**ar	heil-s	heil-a	heil-u	heil-a

Vinsæll 'popular' follows the same pattern: *han var vitr og **vinsæll*** 'he was wise and **popular**'.

The paradigm of *lítill* 'little' is similar in many ways to *mikill* 'great', with assimilation of *-r-* (*mikill*, 2.1.1), nom./acc. neut. ending in *-it* (*mikit*, R.S. 2), and loss of the second syllable when the ending contains a vowel (*mikli*, 3.5): *ór húsi **litlu** ok vándu* 'from a house **little** and wretched'. (NB: The the long *-í-* of *lítill* is shortened when the second syllable is dropped.)

	Strong			Weak		
	Masc	**Fem**	**Neut**	**Masc**	**Fem**	**Neut**
nom	lítil-**l**	lítil	líti-t	litl-i	litl-a	litl-a
acc	litl-an	litl-a	líti-t	litl-a	litl-u	litl-a
dat	litl-um	lítil-li	litl-u	litl-a	litl-u	litl-a
gen	lítil-s	lítil-lar	lítil-s	litl-a	litl-u	litl-a

EXERCISES

1. Fill in the appropriate endings.

a. Harald__ hersi__ stóð ok horf____ á skip____ (def.).

b. Bjǫrn ok Þórólfr geng__ á skip____ (def.) út. Þeir stóð__ þá þar.

    c. Þeir hét___ Þórólfr ok Egill.

    d. Þeir Harald___ ok Álf___ réð___ fyrir Vínland___.

2. Give the 3 sing. and 3 pl. past forms of the following strong verbs:

    Ex.: at vera: hon _*var*_____   þær _*váru*_____

        at bera: hann _____   þeir _____

        (NB: *bera* follows the pattern of *vera* in the past tense.)

        at ganga: hann _____   þeir _____

        at heita: hon _____   þær _____

        at koma: þat _____   þau _____

        at renna: hann _____   þeir _____

        at taka: þat _____   þau _____

3. Translate the following phrases.

    ***vera* 'be'**

    I am _____   I was _____

    you (sing.) are _____   you (sing.) were _____

    he is _____   she was _____

    we are _____   we were _____

    you (pl.) are _____   you (pl.) were _____

    they (neut.) are _____   they (fem.) were _____

    ***hafa* 'have'**

    I have _____   I had _____

    you (sing.) have _____   you (sing.) had _____

    it has _____   he had _____

    we have _____   we had _____

    you (pl.) have _____   you (pl.) had _____

    they (masc.) have _____   they (neut.) had _____

4. The noun-adjective phrases *boga stóran ok sterkan* and *húsi litlu ok vándu* appeared in the examples in 6.7. Based on the noun and adj. declensions that you have learned (see especially 3.3, 4.2, and 4.6), answer the following:

    a. What is the gender of *boga*? _____

    b. What is the gender of *húsi*? _____

    c. Complete the charts below:

        nom.   _____

        acc.   boga stóran ok sterkan

        dat.   _____

        gen.   _____

d. nom. _____

acc. _____

dat. húsi litlu ok vándu

gen. _____

5. Vocabulary training.

Across

1 begin
4 size, stature
5 known
7 bear, carry

8 day
9 enemy
11 time

Down

2 earl

3 had, was married to
4 become
6 north (adv.)
10 winter

6. Translate the Reading Selections.

a. Í þann tíma réð fyrir Danmǫrku Sigurðr hringr. Hann var ríkr konungr ok er frægr orðinn af þeiri orrostu, er hann barðisk við Harald hilditǫnn á Brávelli, ok fyrir honum fell Haraldr, sem kunnigt er orðit of alla norðrálfu heimsins. Sigurðr átti einn son, er Ragnarr hét; hann var mikill vexti, vænn yfirlits ok vel viti borinn, stórlyndr við sína menn, en grimmr sínum óvinum.

_____

_____

_____

_____

_____

_____

b. Þar hefjum vér þenna þátt, er sá maðr bjó at Hofi í Vápnafirði, er Helgi hét. Hann var sonr Þorgils Þorsteinssonar, Ǫlvis sonar, Ásvalds sonar, Øxna-Þóris sonar. Ǫlvir var lendr maðr í Nóregi um daga Hákonar jarls Grjótgarðssonar.

Þorsteinn hvíti kom fyrst út til Íslands þeira langfeðga ok bjó at Toptavelli fyrir útan Síreksstaði. En Steinbjǫrn bjó at Hofi, sonr Refs ins rauða. Ok er honum eyddisk fé fyrir þegnskapar sakar, þá keypti Þorsteinn Hofsland ok bjó þar sex tigu vetra. Hann átti Ingibjǫrgu Hróðgeirsdóttur ins hvíta.

VOCABULARY

af *prep* [*w dat*] out of, from; of

aldr *m* age

alla *acc sg fem of* **allr**

allr *adj* all

átti (*inf* **eiga**) *vb* had; was married to

barðisk (*inf* **berjask**, *see* **berja**) *refl vb* fought (*sg*)

bera (*past* bar, báru; *ppart* borinn) *vb* carry, bear

berja (*past* barð-) *vb* beat, strike, smite; *refl* **berjask** fight

bogi *m* bow

borinn (*inf* **bera**) *ppart* borne; endowed

Brávǫllr (*dat* Brávelli) *m* Bravoll, a plain in Sweden (*place name*)

brók (*gen* -ar) *f* pants-leg; breeches

búa (*past* bjó, bjuggu) *vb* dwell

dagr (*pl acc* daga) *m* day

Danmǫrk (*dat* Danmǫrku) *f* Denmark

dauðr (*n* dautt) *adj* dead

dýr *n* animal, beast

eiga (*past* átti) *vb* own, have; be married to

er *rel pron* who, which, that

er *conj* when; where

eyða (*past* -dd-) *vb* lay waste; spend up, squander; *refl* **eyðask** (*past* eyddisk) be squandered, come to naught

eyddisk (*inf* **eyðask**, *see* **eyða**) *refl vb* was squandered

Eymundr *m* Eymund (*personal name*)

falla (*past* fell, fellu) *vb* fall

fell (*inf* **falla**) *vb* fell

frægr *adj* famous

fríðr (*n* frítt) *adj* beautiful, handsome, fine

fullr *adj* full

fyrir *prep* [*w acc*] for, because of; [*w dat*] before, in front of

fyrst *superl adv* first

ganga (*past* gekk, gengu) *vb* go, walk

grimmr *adj* grim, fierce, savage

Grjótgarðr *m* Grjotgard ('Stone-Fence') (*personal name*)

hálfa *f* region, part

hefja (*1pl* hefjum) *vb* begin

heill *adj* healthy, well, 'hale'; whole

heimr *m* world; land, region of the world

heita (*past* hét, hétu) *vb* be named, be called

hilditǫnn *f* 'War Tooth' (*nickname*)

hildr *f* battle, war (*poetic*)

Hof *n* Hof ('Temple') (*place name*)

Hofsland *n* the Hof estate

hringr *m* ring

Hróðgeirr *m* Hrodgeir (*personal name*)

hugr (*dat* hug(i), *gen* -ar) *m* mind; mood

hús *n* house

hvítr *adj* white

illr *adj* bad, evil, 'ill'

Ingibjǫrg *f* Ingibjorg (*personal name*)

Ísland *n* Iceland

jarl *m* earl

kaupa (*past* keypt-) *vb* buy

keypti (*inf* **kaupa**) *vb* bought

koma (*past* kom, kómu) *vb* come

kunnigr *adj* known

kyrr *adj* still, quiet

langfeðgar *m pl* forefathers, ancestors (through the father's line)

lendr *adj* 'landed', having lands

lítill (*n* lítit) *adj* little, small

loðbrók (*gen* -ar) *f* 'Hairy Breeches' (*nickname*)

munu (*pres* mun) *vb* will, shall

norðr *adv* north

norðrálfa = **norðrhálfa** (*acc* norðr-(h)álfu) *f* northern region

nú *adv* now

of *prep* [*w acc/dat*] over

orðinn (*inf* **verða**) *ppart* become

orrosta (*dat* orrostu) *f* battle

óvinr (*gen* -ar) *m* enemy

óvinum *dat pl of* **óvinr**

Ragnarr *m* Ragnar (*personal name*)

Refr *m* Ref ('Fox') (*personal name*)

reiðr (*n* reitt) *adj* angry, wrathful

renna (*past* rann, runnu) *vb* run

sakar *acc pl of* **sǫk**

sem *conj* as

sex *num* six; **sex tigir** *num* [*w gen*] sixty

silfr *n* silver

sinn *refl poss adj* his (own)

sína *acc pl of* **sinn**

sínum *dat pl of* **sinn**

Síreksstaðir *m pl* Sireksstadir ('Sirek's Farmstead') (*place name*)

skjóta (*past* skaut, skutu) *vb* shoot

smíða (*past* -að-) *vb* work in wood or metals, make, build

staðr (*pl* staðir) *m* stead, parcel of land

Steinbjǫrn *m* Steinbjorn ('Stone-Bear') (*personal name*)

sterkr *adj* strong

stórlyndr *adj* magnanimous

stórr *adj* big

sýn *f* sight, appearance

sǫk (*pl acc* sakar) *f* cause, reason, sake

taka (*past* tók, tóku) *vb* take

tigr (*pl nom* tigir, *acc* tigu) *m* [*w gen*] ten, a group of ten

tími *m* time

topt *n* toft, site of a house; foundation or bare walls, ruins of a house

Toptavǫllr (*dat* Toptavelli) *m* Topta-voll ('Field of Ruined Walls') (*place name*)

um *prep* [*w acc*] during, in (*time*)

ungr *adj* young

útan *adv* from without, from outside

vándr (*n* vánt) *adj* bad, wretched

Vápnafjǫrðr (*dat* -firði) *m* Vápna-fjord ('Weapon's Fjord') (*place name*)

verða (*ppart* orðinn) *vb* become

vetr (*pl gen* vetra) *m* winter; year (*in reckoning time*)

vinsæll *adj* popular

vit *n* good sense, wit, intelligence

vǫllr *m* field

vexti *dat of* **vǫxtr**

vér *pron* we

vǫxtr (*dat* vexti) *m* size, stature

yfirlit *n* look, personal appearance

þann *acc sg masc of* **sá**

þegnskapr (*gen* -ar) *m* generosity, open-handedness

þeira *gen pl of* **sá** (of) those

þeiri *dat sg fem of* **sá**

þenna *acc sg masc of* **þessi**

þessi *dem pron* this, these

Þorgils *m* Thorgils (*personal name*)

Ǫlvir (*gen* Ǫlvis) *m* Olvir (*personal name*)

Øxna-Þórir *m* Thorir 'of the Oxen' (*personal name*)

Phrases

er frægr orðinn has become famous

fríðr sýnum handsome, fine in appearance

fyrir ... sakar on account of, because of

fyrir útan [*w acc*] outside; out beyond

í þann tíma at that time, then

koma út til Íslands come out to Iceland (usually from Norway)

lendr maðr 'landed man' (= Norw. *lendmann*), a Norwegian nobleman whose lands and income were granted by the king

mikill vexti big, great in stature

sex tigu vetra for sixty years (lit. winters)

vel viti borinn intelligent, endowed with good sense

Notes

_____

_____

_____

_____

_____

_____

_____

_____

_____

_____

_____

_____

_____

_____

_____

_____

_____

_____

LESSON 7

Ór *Snorra Eddu, Gylfaginning* (22. kap.)

(From *Snorri's Edda* [*The Prose Edda*], *The Beguiling of Gylfi*, Chap. 22)

[there] is about   good
Annarr sonr Óðins er Baldr, ok   er frá honum gott at segja. Hann

best   praise all   so   handsome   radiant so
er beztr, ok hann lofa allir. Hann er svá fagr álitum ok bjartr, svá at

[it] shines   one plant   so white   likened [it] is   eyelash
lýsir   af honum, ok eitt gras er svá hvítt, at jafnat   er til Baldrs brár.

that   of all plants [the] whitest   from this can   infer beauty
Þat er allra grasa   hvítast, ok þar eptir mátt þú marka fegrð hans,

                     ('fairest spoken')
both of hair   of body   wisest of the gods   most eloquent
bæði á hár ok á líki. Hann er vitrastr ásanna ok fegrst talaðr ok

             ('there')
most gracious   lives in the place that is called   that   heaven
líknsamastr. Hann býr   þar,   sem heitir Breiðablik. Þat er á himni.

7.1. Strong Nouns: Neuter Nouns with Stem-Final -*i*.

Líki 'body' in the the above reading illustrates a class of neut. strong nouns that have final -*i* in the nom./acc. This final -*i* is not an ending. Instead, it belongs to the stem, to which the gen. ending -*s* is added (gen. *líkis*). The stem-final -*i* is dropped when

nom	líki
acc	líki
dat	lík-i
gen	líki-s

an ending beginning with a vowel is added. Hence dat. sing. *líki* (= *líki* + -*i*) resembles the nom./acc., but the final -*i* is the dat. ending.

    The common word *ríki* 'realm, kingdom; power' also belongs to this class.

7.2. Nouns and Adjectives: Genitive Plural.

The gen. pl. of all nouns ends in -*a*: *grasa* from *gras* (neut.) and *ásanna* (= *ása* + *inna* with the loss of the initial *i*- of the article *inna* after a vowel) from *áss* (masc.).

    The gen. pl. of all strong adjectives ends in -*ra*: *allra grasa;* similarly *allra ása, góðra ása,* etc. This ending is added to the stem of the adj. according to the same rules that apply to the nom. sing. masc. ending -*r* (see 2.1, Special Stem Rules): *mikilla ása, vænna ása, fagra grasa,* etc.

7.3. Definite Article: Genitive Plural.

The following passage illustrates the detached gen. pl. art. *inna* (the same for all genders). *Inna* offers another example of the assimilation of *-r* to stem-final *-n-* (2.1): *in-* + *-ra* = *inna*.

Ór *Egils sǫgu Skalla-Grímssonar* (20. kap.)
(From the *Saga of Egil Skalla-Grimsson*, Chap. 20)

of the
Maðr hét Yngvarr, ríkr ok auðigr; hann hafði verit lendr maðr **inna**
former
fyrri konunga.

7.4. Strong Adjectives: Nominative/Accusative Singular Neuter Stem Rules (See 4.5).

As explained in 4.5, the basic ending of nom./acc. sing. neut. strong adjectives is *-t*, added directly to the stem of the adj.: masc. *hvít-r* – neut. *hvít-t*. Two special stem rules affect this ending.

Special Stem Rules:

1. If the stem ends in *-ð-*, it is changed to *-t-*: *góð-r* – *got-t*.
2. If the stem ends in *-t-* preceded by another consonant, a second *-t* is not added: *hvítast-r* – *hvítast*, *bezt-r* – *bezt*, *bjart-r* – *bjart*.

7.5. Superlative Adjective Formation.

Superlative adjectives are formed by adding either *-ast-* or *-st-* to the stem of the basic adj. In the latter instance, the root vowel is often changed: *fagr* – *fegrstr*. (The retention of the final *-r* of *fagr* in the superl. *fegr-str* shows that this final *-r* is not the nom. sing. masc. ending, but belongs to the stem [see 2.1.2]. Similarly, *vitr* – *vitr-astr*, but *hvít-r* – *hvít-astr*.)

7.6. Adverb Formation.

Adverbs comprise a broad class of descriptive words that express manner (how), time (when), place (where), and degree (how much): f.ex., 'carefully', 'today', 'here', 'greatly'. Many adverbs are directly related to a corresponding adj., but whereas adjectives describe nouns, adverbs describe verbs, adjectives and other adverbs. Examples of adj./ adv. pairs are 'good/well', 'careful/carefully', 'great/greatly'. As the last two examples show, adverbs are frequently formed in English by adding the suffix '-ly' to an adj.

In Old Icelandic, adverbial forms of adjectives are identical with the nom. sing. neut. form: f.ex., *fegrst* 'most beautifully' in the phrase *fegrst talaðr*, lit. 'most beautifully spoken.' Adverbs are also formed from adjectives by means of suffixes: f.ex., *vand-liga* 'careful-**ly**' from *vandr* 'careful'.

7.7. Verbs: 3rd Person Singular Present-Tense Endings.

The 3 sing. pres. of most verbs ends in -*r*, sometimes preceded by the vowel -*a*- or -*i*-. The following guidelines will help you determine when the 3 sing. pres. ending is -*ar*, -*ir*, or -*r*.

- Section 5.3.1 described weak verbs that employ the vocalic link -*a*- before the dental suffix of the past tense. These verbs also insert -*a*- before the 3 sing. pres. ending -*r*: *kall-ar* 'calls', from *kalla* (3 sing. past *kall-aði*).

- Section 5.3.2 described weak verbs that form their past by adding the dental suffix directly to the root of the verb. The majority of these verbs insert -*i*- before the 3 sing. pres. ending -*r*: *lýs-ir* 'shines' (R.S. 7), from *lýsa* (3 sing. past *lýs-ti*).

- Section 5.6 described weak verbs with vowel alternation between the present and the past. These verbs usually do not insert -*i*-; instead they add the 3 sing. pres. ending -*r* directly to the stem: *spyr-r* 'asks' (R.S. 8), from *spyrja* (3 sing. past *spur-ði*).

- Strong verbs regularly add the 3 sing. pres. ending -*r* directly to the verb stem: *bið-r* 'asks, bids' and *get-r* 'gets' (R.S. 9.3), from *biðja* and *geta* (3 sing. past *bað* and *gat*).

Some common verbs do not adhere to the above patterns.

- Several verbs with 3sg. pres. -*r* show no vowel alternation:
  selja 'deliver' – *sel-r* – *seldi*
  setja 'set' – *set-r* – *setti*
  skilja 'separate' – *skil-r* – *skildi*.

- The weak verb *segja* 'say' undergoes vowel alternation (3 sing. past *sagði*) but also inserts -*i*- in the pres. tense (3 sing. pres. *seg-ir*).

- The weak verb *hafa* 'have' frequently appears in Old Norse texts in two forms. One adds -*r* directly to the stem in the pres. sing. (3 sing. *hef-r*). The other inserts -*i*- (3 sing. *hef-ir*) (see 6.5).

- The strong verb *heita* 'be called' also inserts an -*i*- in the pres. sing.: 3 sing. *heit-ir*.

7.8. Verbs: Assimilation of the 3rd Person Singular Present-Tense Ending -*r*.

The ending -*r* of the 3 sing. pres. tense of the verb regularly assimilates to a final -*s* of the verb root: *blæs-s* 'blows', *rís-s* 'rises'. Assimilation to -*l* or -*n* also sometimes occurs: the example of *þú vil-l* was seen in R.S. 4;

another common verb is *skín-n* 'shines'. Often, however, assimilation does not occur after *-l-* or *-n-*: *myl-r* 'crushes', *ven-r* 'trains'.

7.9. Verbs: 3rd Person Plural Present-Tense Endings.

The 3 pl. pres. form of the verb (with the exception of some preterite-present verbs, see 15.1) is identical to the infinitive. Both forms end in *-a*, added to the pres. stem. Examples appear in R.S. 7: *lofa* (3 pl. pres.); *marka*, *segja* (inf.).

7.10. Review Paradigms: 3rd Person Endings (Past and Pres.) of Weak and Strong Verbs (See 6.3).

	Pres.		Past	
	Weak	Strong	Weak	Strong
3sg	(-a/i/–)-r	-r	(-að/ð/d/t)-i	–
3pl	-a	-a	(-að/ð/d/t)-u	-u

EXERCISES

1. Fill in the appropriate endings.

    a. Konung__ var in__ fegrst__ mað__ í England__.

    b. Skip____ (def.) var fagr__ ok hvít__. Þat var all__ skip__ bezt.

    c. Baldr hét in__ hvít__ ás__. Hann var all__ ás__ bezt__ ok fegrst__.

    d. Konung__ gekk til in__ bezt__ skip__. Þat var i__ vænst__ skip.

    e. Yngvar__ var vitrast__ konung_____ (pl. def.). Hann var son__ Egil__, líknsam__ mann__ ok fagr__.

2. Supply suitable personal names, nouns and adjectives.

    a. _____r var _____astr _____anna, _____r ok _____n.

    b. Skipit var _____ra skipa _____ast ok _____st.

3. Write the 3 sing. pres. and 3 pl. pres. forms of the following verbs.

    a. Weak verbs with vocalic link *-a-*:

        Ex.: at kalla (*past* -að-): hann <u>*kallar*</u> þeir <u>*kalla*</u>

        at elska (*past* -að-): hon _____ þær _____

        at lofa (*past* -að-): þat _____ þau _____

        at tala (*past* -að-): hann _____ þeir _____

    b. Weak verbs without vocalic link:

        Ex.: at mæla (*past* -t-): þat <u>*mælir*</u> þau <u>*mæla*</u>

        at lifa (*past* -ð-): hann _____ þeir _____

        at senda (*past* -nd-) hon _____ þær _____

at sýna (*past* -d-):   hon _____ þær _____

c. Weak verbs with vowel alternation (5.6):

Ex.: at flytja (*past* flutt-):   hann _*flytr*____ þeir _*flytja*____

   at berja (*past* barð-):   hon _____ þær _____

   at kveðja (*past* kvadd-):   hon _____ þær _____

   at spyrja (*past* spurð-):   þat _____ þau _____

d. Strong verbs:

Ex.: at gefa (*past* gaf, gáfu):   hann _*gefr*____ þeir _*gefa*____

   at bera (*past* bar, báru):   þat _____ þau _____

   at renna (*past* rann, runnu): hann _____ þeir _____

   at rísa (*past* reis, risu):   hon _____ þær _____

   at skína (*past* skein, skinu): hann _____ þeir _____

4. Translate the Reading Selections.

a. Annarr sonr Óðins er Baldr, ok er frá honum gott at segja. Hann er beztr, ok hann lofa allir. Hann er svá fagr álitum ok bjartr, svá at lýsir af honum, ok eitt gras er svá hvítt, at jafnat er til Baldrs brár. Þat er allra grasa hvítast, ok þar eptir mátt þú marka fegrð hans, bæði á hár ok á líki. Hann er vitrastr ásanna ok fegrst talaðr ok líknsamastr. Hann býr þar, sem heitir Breiðablik. Þat er á himni.

_____

_____

_____

_____

_____

_____

_____

_____

_____

_____

b. Maðr hét Yngvarr, ríkr ok auðigr; hann hafði verit lendr maðr inna fyrri konunga.

_____

_____

_____

_____

Vocabulary

á *prep* [*w acc*] with respect to
álit *n pl* appearance, countenance
áss *m* god
Baldr *m* Baldr (*mythological name*)
beztr *superl adj* (*see* **góðr**) best
biðja (*pres* biðr, *past sg* bað) *vb* ask
bjartr *adj* bright, radiant
blása (*pres* blæss) *vb* blow
brá (*gen* brár) *f* eyelash
Breiðablik *n* Breidablik ('Broad Gleam') (*mythological place name*)
búa (*pres* býr) *vb* live (in a place), dwell
býr (*inf* **búa**) *vb* dwells
bæði *adv* both
eitt *num* one (*neut*)
eptir *prep* [*w dat*] after, according to
fagr (*superl* fegrstr) *adj* fair, beautiful
fegrð *f* beauty
fegrstr *superl adj* (*see* **fagr**) fairest, most beautiful
frá *prep* [*w dat*] from; about
fyrri *comp adj* former
geta (*pres* getr, *past* gat) *vb* get
gott *nom/acc sg neut of* **góðr**
góðr (*n* gott; *superl* beztr) *adj* good
gras *n* grass, plant, herb
heita (*pres* heitir) *vb* be named, be called
heitir (*inf* **heita**) *vb* is named
himinn (*dat* himni) *m* sky; heaven
hvítastr *superl adj* (*see* **hvítr**) whitest
hvítr (*superl* hvítastr) *adj* white
jafna (*past* -að-) *vb* compare, liken
jafnat (*inf* **jafna**) *ppart* compared,

likened
líki (*gen* -is) *n* body
líknsamastr *superl adj* (see **líknsamr**) most gracious, most merciful
líknsamr (*superl* líknsamastr) *adj* gracious, merciful
lofa (*past* -að-) *vb* praise
lýsa *vb* shine
lýsir (*inf* **lýsa**) *vb* shines
marka (*past* -að-) *vb* notice; infer
mátt (*inf* **mega**) *vb* (you *sg*) can
mega (*pres* má) *vb* can, may
Óðinn *m* Odin (*mythological name*), the chief god
ríki *n* realm, kingdom; power
rísa (*pres* ríss) *vb* rise
sá (*f* sú, *n* þat) *dem pron* that (one)
segja (*past* sagð-) *vb* say, tell
sem *rel pron* who, which, that
skína (*pres* skínn) *vb* shine
svá *adv* so, thus, in this way
tala (*past* -að-) *vb* speak
talaðr (*inf* **tala**) *ppart* spoken
venja (*past* vanð-/vand-) *vb* accustom, train
vera (*ppart* verit) *vb* be
verit (*inf* **vera**) *ppart* been (*nom/acc sg neut*)
vitr (*superl* vitrastr) *adj* wise
vitrastr *superl adj* (*see* **vitr**) wisest
Yngvarr *m* Yngvar (*personal name*)
þar *adv* there
þat *dem pron* that (*nom/acc sg neut of* **sá**)

Phrases

at segja frá to tell about
á himni in heaven
bæði... ok *conj* both... and
fagr álitum beautiful (in appearance), handsome

fegrð á hár/líki beauty of hair/body
fegrst talaðr most eloquent
hann hafði verit he had been
þar eptir accordingly, from this
þar, sem in the place that

The North Atlantic World of the Medieval Icelanders.

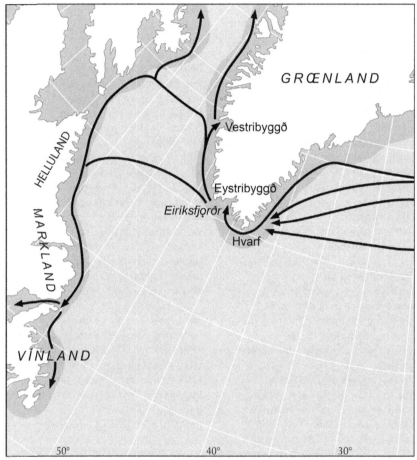

"Wise men report that from Stad in Norway it is a voyage of seven days west to Horn in eastern Iceland, and from Snæfellsnes [in western Iceland] it is four days' sail west to Greenland at the point where the sea is narrowest. It is said that if one sails due west from Bergen to Cape Farewell in Greenland, one passes a half day's sail to the south of Iceland. From Reykjanes in southern Iceland it is five days south to Slyne Head in Ireland, and from Langanes in northern Iceland it is four days northward to Svalbard in the Arctic Sea." (*The Book of Settlements*)

"Svá segja vitrir menn, at ór Nóregi frá Staði sé sjau dœgra sigling í vestr til Horns á Íslandi austanverðu, en frá Snæfellsnesi, þar er skemmst er, er fjǫgurra dœgra haf í vestr til Grœnlands. En svá er sagt, ef siglt er ór Bjǫrgyn rétt í vestr til Hvarfsins á Grœnlandi, at þá mun siglt vera tylft fyrir sunnan Ísland. Frá Reykjanesi á sunnanverðu Íslandi er fimm dœgra haf til Jǫlduhlaups á Írlandi (í suðr; en frá Langanesi á norðanverðu Íslandi er) fjǫgurra dœgra haf norðr til Svalbarða í hafsbotn." (*Landnámabók*)

VOCABULARY

austanverðr *adj* eastern

Bjǫrgyn (*dat* Bjǫrgyn) *m* Bergen, Norway (*place name*)

dœgr *n* a day (of 24 hours); **fjǫgurra (fimm) dœgra haf**, a sail of four (five) days; **sjau dœgra sigling** a sail of seven days

fimm *num* five

fjórir (*gen* fjǫgurra) *num* four

fjǫgurra *gen of* **fjórir**

Grœnland *n* Greenland

haf *n* sea; **fjǫgurra (fimm) dœgra haf** a sail of four (five) days

hafsbotn (*gen* -botns) *m* gulf; the Arctic Ocean (*place name*)

Hvarf *n* 'Disappearance', Cape Farewell in Greenland (*place name*)

Írland *n* Ireland

Jǫlduhlaup *n* 'Mare's Leap', Slyne Head in Ireland (*place name*)

Langanes *n* Langanes ('Long Headland'), peninsula in Northeast Iceland (*place name*)

nes (-j-) *n* headland, peninsula

norðanverðr *adj* northern

Reykjanes *n* Reykjanes ('Smoky Headland'), peninsula in Southwest Iceland (*place name*)

rétt *adv* straight

sé *vb* is (*3sg pres subjunct of* **vera**)

sigla (-d-) *vb* sail

sigling *f* sailing; voyage by sail; **sjau dœgra sigling** a sail of seven days

siglt *n ppart of* **sigla**

sjau *num* seven

skammr (*superl* skem(m)str) *adj* short, brief

skemmstr *superl adj, see* **skammr**

Snæfellsnes *n* Snæfellsnes ('Snow Mountain's Headland'), peninsula in Western Iceland (*place name*)

Staðr *m* Stad, a peninsula in Western Norway (*place name*)

suðr *n* the south; *adv* southwards; **í suðr** south(wards)

sunnan *adv* from the south; on the south side; **fyrir sunnan** [*w acc*] to the south of

sunnanverðr *adj* southern

Svalbarði *m* Svalbard ('Cold Coast'), archipelago in the Arctic Ocean (*place name*)

tylft *f* dozen, group of twelve; a half day's sail

vera (*3sg pres subjunct* sé) *vb* be

vestr *n* the west; *adv* west, westwards; **í vestr** west(wards)

vitr (*pl m* vitrir) *adj* wise

vitrir *m nom pl of* **vitr**

Notes

_____

_____

_____

_____

_____

_____

_____

_____

_____

_____

LESSON 8

Ór *Gunnlaugs sǫgu ormstungu* (9. kap.)
(From the *Saga of Gunnlaug Serpent-Tongue*, Chap. 9)

at this time   Sweden   [the] Swede
Þenna tíma réð fyrir Svíþjóð Óláfr konungr sœnski, sonr Eiríks

the   Ambitious
konungs sigrsæla ok Sigríðar innar stórráðu; hann var ríkr konungr

man of ambition   near
ok ágætr, metnaðar maðr mikill. Gunnlaugr kom til Uppsala nær

('during')
[the] assembly of (them) [the] Swedes   in   the spring   reached
þingi   þeira   Svía   um   várit, ok er hann náði

('meeting')
audience greeted   received
konungs   fundi, kvaddi hann konunginn. Hann tók honum vel ok

asks   who   was   said he was Icelandic
spyrr, hverr hann væri. Hann kvazk vera íslenzkr maðr. Þar var þá

með Óláfi konungi Hrafn Ǫnundarson.

('what of men')
what sort of man   Iceland
Konungr mælti: "Hrafn," segir hann, "hvat manna er hann á Íslandi?"

the   lower bench   valiant   before
Maðr stóð upp af inum óœðra bekk, mikill ok vaskligr, gekk fyrir

master   of the best family
konung ok mælti: "Herra," segir hann, "hann er innar beztu ættar ok

himself   bravest
sjálfr inn vaskasti maðr."

let him go   sit with
"Fari hann þá ok siti hjá þér," sagði konungr.

8.1. Definite Article: Singular Feminine.

(1) Ór *Landnámabók (Sturlubók)* (112. kap.)
(From the *Book of* Settlements [*Sturla's Book*], Chap. 112)

king of Hordaland   Æsa the fair
Hjǫrleifr Hǫrðakonungr átti Æsu **ina** ljósu.

(2) Ór *Egils sǫgu Skalla-Grímssonar* (55. kap.)
(From the *Saga of Egill Skalla-Grimsson*, Chap. 55)

parted   with the greatest friendship
Skildusk þeir Aðalsteinn konungr ok Egill með **inni** mestu vináttu.

- The nom. sing. fem. form of the art. is *in*, as in the name of the heroine of *Gunnlaugs saga*: *Helga **in** fagra*. It appeared suffixed in *kýr-**in*** 'the cow', R.S. 5.

- The acc. sing. fem. is *ina*: *Æsu **ina** ljósu* 'Æsa the fair'.

- The dat. sing. fem. is *inni*: ***inni** mestu vináttu*.

- The gen. sing. fem. is *innar*: *Sigríðar **innar** stórráðu*, ***innar** beztu ættar*.

(For the declension of weak feminine adjectives, f.ex., *fagra, ljósu*, etc. in these examples, see 9.1.)

8.2. Definite Article: Complete Declension (See 4.4, 7.3, 8.1).

At this point we have covered all the forms of the sing. def. art., as well as the gen. pl. Here is the full declension in both singular and plural:

	Masc	Fem	Neut
Sg *nom*	inn	in	it
acc	inn	ina	it
dat	inum	inni	inu
gen	ins	innar	ins
Pl *nom*	inir	inar	in
acc	ina	inar	in
dat	inum	inum	inum
gen	inna	inna	inna

8.3. Pronouns: Apposition.

In Icelandic a pers. pron. is often placed in apposition to a following noun or nouns. For example, *þeir Þórólfr ok Bjǫrn* (R.S. 4), *þeir Aðalsteinn konungr ok Egill* (R.S. 8.1(2)), *þeira Svía* (R.S. 8). (Note that the gen. form of the pl. pron. *þeir* also ends in *-a*: see 7.1). In these instances, the apposition is complete, i.e., the pron. is in apposition with only the stated nouns that follow.

In other instances, the apposition can be partial. For example, when paired with a single noun: *þeir Þórólfr* would mean 'Thorolf and his companions.' When paired with more than one noun, the apposition may be either complete, as above, or partial; hence *þeir Þórólfr ok Bjǫrn* could also mean 'Thorolf and Bjorn and their companions'. One relies on the context in the sentence to decide which meaning fits best.

8.4. Verbs: 1ˢᵗ and 2ⁿᵈ Person Past-Tense Endings.

1. First Person Singular.

The 1 sing. past ending of weak verbs is *-a*: *ek gerð-**a*** (from *gera* 'make, do'), *ek vild-**a*** (from *vilja* 'want, wish'). Like the 3 sing. ending, it is added after the dental suffix.

The 1 sing. past of strong verbs has no ending; it is identical to the 3 sing. past: *ek var, ek bað, ek gekk.*

2. Second Person Singular.

The 2 sing. past ending of weak verbs is -*ir*, added after the dental suffix: *þú gerð-ir, þú vild-ir.*

The 2 sing. past ending of strong verbs is -*t*. The following stem rules apply to this ending.

Special Rules Affecting the 2 Sing. Past Stem of Strong Verbs:

- If the 1/3 sing. past form ends in -*t* or -*tt* preceded by a vowel, this changes to -*z* before the addition of the 2 sing. ending -*t*: f.ex., the 1/3 sing. past of *heita* is *hét*, so the 2 sing. past is *hét + t → hézt.*

- If the 1/3 sing. past form ends in -*ð*, it changes to -*t* before the addition of the 2 sing. ending -*t*: f.ex., the 1/3 sing. past of *ráða* is *réð*, so the 2 sing. past is *réð + t → rétt.*

- A dental consonant preceded by -*r*-, -*l*-, or -*s*- changes to -*t* and no ending is added: f.ex., the 1/3 sing. past of *verða* is *varð*, so the 2 sing. past is *varð + t → vart.*

- After a long vowel, the ending -*t* doubles: f.ex., the 1/3 sing. past of *sjá* is *sá*, so the 2 sing. past is *sátt.*

3. First Person Plural.

The 1 pl. past ending of the verb is -*um*. It is added to the past-tense stem: *vér gerð-um, vér vár-um.* When the 1 pl. pron. follows the verb, the -*m* of the ending can be (but is not always) dropped: *gerðu vér, váru vér.*

4. Second Person Plural.

The 2 pl. past verb ending (used with all verbs) is -*uð*: *þér gerð-uð, þér vár-uð.* As with the 1 pl., the final consonant of the ending can be dropped when the pron. follows: *gerðu þér, váru þér.* Usage in different Old Icelandic texts varies widely in this respect.

8.5. Verbs: Moods and the Subjunctive.

In grammatical terms, the **mood** of a verb indicates the speaker's intention, not his or her emotional state. While "mood" is the accepted grammatical term, "mode" is a more accurate description of the concept.[14] There are three moods (or modes) in Old Norse: indicative, subjunctive, and imperative.

---

[14] The grammatical term "mood" derives from Lat. *modus* meaning 'manner' or 'mode'.

Statements that are presented as being true or factual are in the **indicative mood.** This is by far the most common mood, and most of the verbs in the previous lessons have been in the indicative.

When the verb expresses some degree of uncertainty, potentiality, or wish (something that might be, could be, or would be), it appears in the **subjunctive mood.**

In Old Norse the subjunctive mood is often used in dependent clauses, especially indirect speech. Indirect speech is presented in the subjunct. because it is reported or summarized rather than quoted exactly. Three subjunctives occur in R.S. 8: *hann spyrr, hverr hann* **væri** 'he asks who he **was'** (reporting indirect speech), and *fari hann þá ok siti hjá þér* '**let him go** then and **let him sit** with you' (both expressing a wish). Certain conjunctions are also regularly followed by the subjunctive, f.ex., *þótt* 'athough': *þótt hann* **væri** *gamall* '**although** he **was** (subjunct.) old' (R.S. 3.9).

Commands are in the **imperative mood** (which will be discussed in 10.1).

8.6. Verbs: 3ʳᵈ Person Singular Subjunctive Endings.

The 3 sing. subjunct. forms, both pres. and past, have the ending *-i* in all verbs: f.ex., 3 sing. pres.: *fari, siti,* 3 sing. past: *væri.*

8.7. Participles: A First Look.

A **participle** is a verbal adjective, and all participles are formed from verbs. Old Norse has two types of participles: present and past.

Present participles are easily recognized. They employ the suffix *-and-,* which corresponds to English '-ing': f.ex., ON *verðandi* 'becoming', from the verb *verða.* (*Verðandi* [R.S 17] is the name of one of the three Norns, the Norse version of the Fates. See 17.4 for more on pres. participles.)

Past participles are very common and have already appeared in the reading selections: *kallaðr* 'called', *lengt* 'lengthened', *numit* 'taken' (in R.S. 2), *nefndr* 'named' (R.S. 3.9, 5), *verit* 'been' (R.S. 3.9, 7.2), *vígðr* 'ordained' (R.S. 4.5), *orðinn* and *orðit* 'become' (R.S. 6), *jafnat* 'likened', and *talaðr* 'spoken' (R.S. 7).

In addition to being used as adjectives, past participles also have a specialized function in compound tenses. This section looks at the adjectival usage of past participles. The next section considers past participles in compound tenses.

When used as adjectives, past particples take regular adjectival endings, which are added to the ppart. stem. In weak verbs, the ppart. stem is identical to the past-tense stem: *kallað-, nefnd-, talað-, vígð-.* In strong verbs, the ppart. has a special stem (see 10.3.2).

For example, the two past participles that appear in R.S. 7 are *talaðr* (nom. sing. masc. modifying *hann* 'he') and *jafnat* (nom. sing. neut. modifying *gras* 'grass'). Both of these verbs, *tala* 'speak' and *jafna* 'liken', are weak verbs with vocalic link -*a*- (5.3.1), hence the ppart. stem ends in -*að*-: *talað*- and *jafnað*-. As illustrated by *jafnat* and *lengt*, the dental suffix of the stem assimilates to the ending when neut. nom. -*t* is added:

jafnað- + -*t* → *jafnat*.
lengd- + -*t* → *lengt*.

8.8. Participles: Past Participles in Compound Tenses.

The nom./acc. neut. ppart. is also used with *hafa* to form compound tenses, similar to English 'have called', 'have taken', etc. These occur frequently. Below are examples of with past participles of weak verbs:

hann hafði sagt 'he had said' (stem *sagð*- w. dental suffix -*ð*-);
hann hafði mælt 'he had spoken' (stem *mælt*- w. dental suffix -*t*-);
hann hafði dæmt 'he had judged' (stem *dæmd*- w. dental suffix -*d*-);
hann hafði kastat 'he had thrown' (stem *kastað*- w. dental suffix -*ð*- preceded by linking vowel -*a*-).

We have seen two examples of such compound tenses in the reading selections, both with the ppart. of strong verbs:

hann hafði numit 'he had taken' (R.S. 2) (inf. *nema*),
hann hafði verit 'he had been' (R.S. 7.2) (inf. *vera*).

Present and Past Perfect

These compound tenses are called **perfect** tenses. The term "perfect" derives from Latin *perfectum* meaning 'completed', because the action is finished with respect to the time of the verb 'have'.

The **present perfect** (*hefir sagt* '**has** said', etc.) employs 'have' in the present tense.

The **past perfect** (*hafði sagt* '**had** said', etc.) employs 'have'in the past tense.

EXERCISES

1. Fill in the appropriate endings.

   a. Þeir Egil__ geng__ til Uppsala ok spurð__, hverr in__ sœnsk__ maðr vær__.

   b. Gunnlaug__ var kalla___ Ormstunga ('Serpent's Tongue').

   c. Skip___ (def.) hafð__ ver__ kalla___ Ormrinn langi ('The Long Serpent').

2. Conjugate the following verbs in the past tense. The 3 sing. and 3 pl. forms are supplied.

a. Weak verbs:

Ex: gera (-ð-):   ek _gerða_____, þú _gerðir_____, hann gerði

vér _gerðum_____, þér _gerðuð_____, þeir gerðu

lifa (-ð-):   ek _____, þú _____, hann lifði

vér _____, þér _____, þeir lifðu

mylja (mulð-):   ek _____, þú _____, hann mulði

vér _____, þér _____, þeir mulðu

mæla (-t-):   ek _____, þú _____, hann mælti

vér _____, þér _____, þeir mæltu

senda (-nd-):   ek _____, þú _____, hann sendi

vér _____, þér _____, þeir sendu

b. Strong verbs:

Ex: heita: ek _hét_____, þú _hézt_____, hann hét

vér _hétum_____, þér _hétuð_____, þeir hétu

bera: ek _____, þú _____, hann bar

vér _____, þér _____, þeir báru

ganga: ek _____, þú _____, hann gekk

vér _____, þér _____, þeir gengu

skjóta: ek _____, þú _____, hann skaut

vér _____, þér _____, þeir skutu

standa: ek _____, þú _____, hann stóð

vér _____, þér _____, þeir stóðu

verða: ek _____, þú _____, hann varð

vér _____, þér _____, þeir urðu

3. Write the following verbs in the 3 sing. pres. perfect and the 3 sing. past perfect tenses. Each verb is given in the 3 sing. past.

	Pres. perf.	Past perf.
Ex.: hann horfði:	_hann hefr horft_	_hann hafði horft_
hon lýsti:	_____	_____
hon svaraði:	_____	_____
hann sagði:	_____	_____
þat nefndi:	_____	_____
hann hafði:	_____	_____
hon mælti:	_____	_____
hon vígði:	_____	_____

4. Write the nom. sing. masc. form of the past participles of the weak verbs in exercise **3**.

---

5. Translate the Reading Selections.

    a. Þenna tíma réð fyrir Svíþjóð Óláfr konungr sœnski, sonr Eiríks konungs sigrsæla ok Sigríðar innar stórráðu; hann var ríkr konungr ok ágætr, metnaðar maðr mikill. Gunnlaugr kom til Uppsala nær þingi þeira Svía um várit, ok er hann náði konungs fundi, kvaddi hann konunginn. Hann tók honum vel ok spyrr, hverr hann væri. Hann kvazk vera íslenzkr maðr. Þar var þá með Óláfi konungi Hrafn Ǫnundarson.

    Konungr mælti: "Hrafn," segir hann, "hvat manna er hann á Íslandi?"

    Maðr stóð upp af inum óœðra bekk, mikill ok vaskligr, gekk fyrir konung ok mælti: "Herra," segir hann, "hann er innar beztu ættar ok sjálfr inn vaskasti maðr."

    "Fari hann þá ok siti hjá þér," sagði konungr.

---

b. Hjǫrleifr Hǫrðakonungr átti Æsu ina ljósu.

_____

_____

c. Skildusk þeir Aðalsteinn konungr ok Egill með inni mestu vináttu.

_____

_____

VOCABULARY

bekkr (*dat* bekk) *m* bench
bók *f* book
fara *vb* go, travel
fundr *m* meeting
fyrir *prep* [*w acc*] before, in front of (*motion*)
herra *m* master, sir (NB: *nom ends in* -a)
hjá *prep* [*w dat*] by, beside, with
Hjǫrleifr *m* Hjorleif (*personal name*)
Hrafn *m* Hrafn ('Raven') (*personal name*)
hvat *int pron* what
hverr *int pron* who
Hǫrðakonungr *m* king of Hǫrðaland (in Western Norway)
íslenzkr *adj* Icelandic
kvaddi (*inf* kveðja) *vb* greeted (*sg*)
kvazk *refl vb* said of himself (*3sg past of* kveðask)
kveða (*past sg* kvað) *vb* say; *refl* kveðask (*past sg* kvazk) say of oneself [*w inf*]
kveðja (*past* kvadd-) *vb* greet
landnám *n* 'land-taking', settlement
Landnámabók *f* Book of Settlements
ljóss *adj* light, fair
ljósu *adj* fair (*wk acc sg fem of* ljóss)
manna *gen pl* of **maðr**
með *prep* [*w dat*] with (accompanying)
mestr *superl adj* greatest (*see* mikill)
mikill (*superl* mestr) *adj* great

ná (*past* -ð-) *vb* [*w dat*] reach
nær *prep* [*w dat*] near (to)
Óláfr *m* Olaf (*personal name*)
óœðri *comp adj* lower
Sigríðr *f* Sigrid (*personal name*)
sitja *vb* sit
sjálfr *adj* self; oneself, himself
skildusk (*inf* skiljask, *see* skilja) *refl vb* parted from each other
skilja (*past* -d-) *vb* separate, divide; *refl* skiljask part from each other
Sturlubók *f* 'Sturla's Book', version of the **Landámabók** made by Sturla Thordarson
Svíar *m pl* the Swedes
Svíþjóð *f* Sweden
sœnskr *adj* Swedish
taka (*past sg* tók) *vb* take, receive
tók (*inf* taka) *vb* received ('took') (*sg*)
Uppsalir *m pl* Uppsala ('Upper Halls'), a town in Sweden (*place name*)
vaskastr *superl adj* (*see* vaskr) bravest
vaskr *adj* brave, valiant
vár *n* spring (season)
vera *vb* be
væri (*inf* vera) *vb* was (*subjunct*)
þeira *pron* of them (*gen of* þeir)
þér *pron* you (*pl*)
þing *n* assembly
Æsa *f* Æsa (*personal name*)
ætt *f* family
Ǫnundr *m* Onund (*personal name*)

PHRASES

hann kvazk vera he said he was
hann tók honum vel he received him well
hvat manna what sort of man
um várit in the spring
þenna tíma at this time

LESSON 9

Ór *Egils sǫgu Skalla-Grímssonar* (32. kap.)
(From the *Saga of Egil Skalla-Grimsson*, Chap. 32)

Bjǫrn hét hersir ríkr í Sogni, er bjó á Aurlandi; hans son var Brynjólfr,

inheritance   father his   sons
er   arf   allan tók eptir fǫður sinn. Synir Brynjólfs váru þeir Bjǫrn

                      age   of news
ok Þórðr; þeir váru menn á ungum aldri, er þetta var tíðenda.

[sea-]farer   [engaged] in raiding
Bjǫrn var farmaðr mikill, var stundum   í víking, en stundum

trading trips   most accomplished
í kaupferðum; Bjǫrn var inn   gǫrviligsti   maðr.

it happened   one   certain summer   present [the] Fjords
Þat barsk at á einu hverju sumri, at Bjǫrn var staddr í Fjǫrðum

party   certain   well-attended   girl   whom
at veizlu nǫkkurri fjǫlmennri; þar sá hann mey fagra, þá er

    he liked very much   asked about of what
honum fannsk mikit um. Hann spurði eptir, hverrar ættar hon var;

honum var þat sagt, at hon var systir Þóris hersis Hróaldssonar ok hét

         (i.e. proposed)
      raised up petition his   requested   refused
Þóra. Bjǫrn hóf upp bónorð sitt ok   bað   Þóru, en Þórir synjaði

   the match   thus   autumn
honum ráðsins, ok skildusk þeir at svá gǫrvu. En þat sama haust fekk

   for himself band of men   went   boat full-manned north into
Bjǫrn sér   liðs   ok fór með skútu alskipaða norðr í

[the] Fjords   at home   took
Fjǫrðu   ok kom til Þóris ok svá, at hann var eigi heima. Bjǫrn nam

   away   brought [her] home   him(self)   they
Þóru á brott ok hafði   heim með sér á Aurland; váru þau þar

         ('make wedding to')
  the winter   marry   her
um vetrinn, ok vildi Bjǫrn gera brúðlaup til hennar.

9.1. Weak Nouns and Adjectives: Feminine Singular.

Most weak fem. nouns and all weak fem. adjectives end in -a in the nom. sing., -u in the other cases of the sing. Note that, as in the case of weak masc. and neut. nouns and adjectives, the fem. sing. declensions of weak nouns and adjectives are identical.

nom	-a
acc	-u
dat	-u
gen	-u

Examples of weak nouns from R.S. 9 are nom. *Þóra*, acc. and gen. *Þóru* (NB: the verb *biðja* takes a gen. object); acc. *skútu* (nom. *skúta*); and dat. *veizlu* (nom. *veizla*). In addition, nom. *kona* 'woman, wife' and gen. *konu* appear below in R.S. 9.3.

Examples of adjectives are: nom. *Helga in fagra* 'Helga the fair'; acc. *Æsu ina ljósu* 'Æsa the fair' (R.S. 8.1(1)); dat. *inni mestu vináttu* 'with the greatest friendship' (R.S. 8.1(2)); gen. *innar beztu ættar* 'of the best family' (R.S. 8).

A small number of weak fem. abstract nouns end in *-i*, f.ex., *elli* 'old age', *ævi* 'time, lifetime, age', *gremi* 'wrath'. These nouns are indeclinable, having *-i* throughout the singular. For example, acc. *goðagremi* 'wrath of the gods' appears in R.S. 13(3). No weak adjectives end in *-i*.

nom	-i
acc	-i
dat	-i
gen	-i

9.2. Review Paradigms: Complete Weak Noun and Adj. Endings in the Sing. (See 4.7, 9.1).

	Masc	Fem	Neut
nom	-i	-a, (-i)	-a
acc	-a	-u, (-i)	-a
dat	-a	-u, (-i)	-a
gen	-a	-u, (-i)	-a

9.3. Strong Nouns: Feminine Singular.

Ór *Gísla sǫgu Súrssonar* (5. kap.)
(From the *Saga of Gisli Sursson*, Chap. 5)

'Seal-Cliff'
Þórbjǫrn hét maðr ok var kallaðr selagnúpr; hann bjó í Tálknafirði at

wife
Kvígandafelli; Þórdís hét kona hans, en Ásgerðr dóttir.

                                 ('to have')
this   woman Þorkell requests   gets   in marriage
Þessarar konu biðr Þorkell Súrsson ok getr hana at eiga, en Gísli

      requested sister   got
Súrsson bað systur Vésteins, Auðar Vésteinsdóttur, ok fekk hana;

dwell now both together
búa nú báðir saman í Haukadal.

- Strong fem. nouns usually have no ending in the nom. sing.: f.ex., *Þórdís*; but the ending *-r* is quite common, especially in personal names: f.ex., *Ásgerðr, Auðr.*

nom	–,	-r
acc	–, (-u),	-i
dat	–, -u,	-i
gen		-ar

	'beauty'	'earth'	'Ingibjorg'	'Aud'
nom	fegrð	jǫrð	Ingibjǫrg	Auðr
acc	fegrð	jǫrð	Ingibjǫrgu	Auði
dat	fegrð	jǫrðu	Ingibjǫrgu	Auði
gen	fegrðar	jarðar	Ingibjargar	Auðar

- The acc. and dat. sing. forms of most strong fem. nouns have no ending: acc. *fegrð* (R.S. 7), *mey* (R.S. 9; nom. *mær*), dat. *Borg* (R.S. 1), *Svíþjóð* (R.S. 8).

  o A number of strong fem. nouns, however, end in -*u* in the dat. sing.: *jǫrð* 'earth' – acc. *jǫrð* (R.S. 12(2)), dat. *jǫrðu* (R.S. 17).

  o Some strong fem. nouns, mostly personal names, have -*u* in both the acc. and dat.: *Ingibjǫrg* – acc./dat. *Ingibjǫrgu* (R.S. 6).

  o Strong fem. nouns with nom. sing. -*r* regularly take the ending -*i* in both the acc. and dat. sing.: *Auðr* – acc./dat. *Auði*.

- The gen. sing. of strong fem. nouns ends in -*ar* in most instances: *Auðar, Sigríðar*.

  o When the root vowel is -*ǫ*- in the nom. sing., the vowel becomes -*a*- in the gen. sing.: *jarðar, Ingibjargar*. (The same alternation occurs in the masc. name *Bjǫrn* – gen. *Bjarnar*, R.S. 1. This vowel change will be explained in Lesson 11.)

  o If the stem of the noun ends in a vowel, the initial -*a*- of the gen. ending is omitted: f.ex., *brár* (R.S. 7) = *brá* + -*ar*.

9.4. Review Paradigms: Complete Strong Noun Endings in the Singular (See 4.2, 9.3).

	Masc	Fem	Neut
nom	-r (see 2.1)	–, -r	–
acc	–	–, -i, -u	–
dat	-i	–, -i, -u	-i
gen	-s, -ar	-ar	-s

9.5. Kinship Terms in -*ir*: Singular Declension.

A very small class of nouns consisting of family members (both masc. and fem.) has the ending -*ir* in the nom. sing. These nouns take -*ur* in the other cases of the singular:

  bróðir – acc./dat./gen. *bróður*

  dóttir – acc./dat/gen. *dóttur*

  faðir – acc./dat./gen. *fǫður*[15]

  móðir – acc./dat./gen. *móður*

  systir – acc./dat./gen. *systur*

---

[15] The change of root vowel from *faðir* to *fǫður* will be explained in 11.2.2.

9.6. Strong Adjectives: Singular Feminine.

(1) Ór *Hávarðar sǫgu* (1. kap.)
(From the *Saga of Havard*, Chap. 1)

young   of a great family
Hon var **ung** kona ok **stórrar** ættar.

(2) Ór *Snorra Eddu* (10. kap.)
(From *Snorri's Edda* [*The Prose Edda*], Chap. 10)

giant   Giant-Land   Night
Nǫrvi hét jǫtunn, er bygði í Jǫtunheimum. Hann átti dóttur, er Nótt

        black   dark   was characteristic of her family
hét. Hon var **svǫrt** ok **døkk** sem   hon átti ætt til.

- The nom. sing. fem. form of strong adjectives has no ending: *ung kona, svǫrt, døkk.*

- The acc. sing. fem. ends is *-a: mey fagra, skútu alskipaða.*

- The dat. sing. fem. ends is *-ri: veizlu nǫkkurri fjǫlmennri.*

nom	–
acc	-a
dat	-ri
gen	-rar

- The gen. sing. fem. ends in *-rar: stórrar ættar.*

The dat. and gen. endings are modified according to the same rules that apply to the nom. sing. masc. ending *-r* (2.1).

9.7. Review Paradigms: Complete Strong Adj. Endings in the Sing. (See 4.6, 9.6).

	Masc	**Fem**	**Neut**
nom	-r (see 2.1)	–	-t
acc	-an	-a	-t
dat	-um	-ri (see 2.1)	-u
gen	-s	-rar (see 2.1)	-s

9.8. Verbs: 1st and 2nd Person Present-Tense Endings.

1. First Person Singular.

The 1 sing. pres. of verbs has no ending. It is the same as 3 sing. pres. form (7.7) minus the ending *-r: ek kalla* (3 sing. pres. *kallar*), *ek segi* (3 sing. pres. *segir*, R.S. 4, 5, 8), *ek bið* (3 sing. pres. *biðr*, R.S. 9.3), *ek spyr* (3 sing. pres. *spyrr*, R.S. 8).

2. Second Person Singular.

The 2 sing. pres. of verbs is the same as the 3 sing. pres.: *þú kallar, þú segir, þú biðr, þú spyrr.*

3. First Person Plural.

The 1 pl. pres. verb ending is the same as the past, -*um*: *vér ger**um**, vér bið**um**.* It is added to the pres. stem of the verb.

- If the infinitve stem ends in -*j*-, this is retained in the 1 pl.: *vér spyr**j**um* (inf. *spyrja*), *vér seg**j**um* (inf. *segja*), *vér vil**j**um* (inf. *vilja*).

- As with the 1 pl. past (8.4.3), when the pron. follows the verb, the consonant of the ending can be dropped: *vil**j**u vér* for *vil**j**um vér*.

4. Second Person Plural.

The 2 pl. pres. verb ending is -*ið*: *þér bið**ið**, þér ger**ið**, þér spyr**ið**, þér seg**ið**.*

9.9. Review Paradigms: Pres. and Past-Tense Endings of Verbs (See 7.10, 8.4, 9.8).

	Pres. Weak	Strong	Past Weak	Strong
1sg	(-a/i/–)–	–	(-að/ð/d/t)-a	–
2sg	(-a/i/–)-r	-r	(-að/ð/d/t)-ir	-t
3sg	(-a/i/–)-r	-r	(-að/ð/d/t)-i	–
1pl	-um	-um	(-að/ð/d/t)-um	-um
2pl	-ið	-ið	(-að/ð/d/t)-uð	-uð
3pl	-a	-a	(-að/ð/d/t)-u	-u

EXERCISES

1. Fill in the appropriate endings.

    a. Þóra in auðg___ hét kon__. Hon var móðir Ásgerð___ in__ væn__ ok Harald__ in__ hárfagr__.

    b. Gísl__ bað Helg__ in__ auðg__ ok fekk h____ at eig__.

    c. I__ sœnsk__ þing var um vár__ (def.).

    d. Fegrð Helg__ in__ auðg__ var mikil. Hon var góð kon__ ok gofug__ ætt__.

    e. Auð__, kon__ Gísl__ in__ vitr__, var væn kon__ ok stórráð.

    f. Þeir Gunnlaugr ok Hrafn stóð__ upp af bekk____ (def.) ok geng__ fyrir konungsson____ (def.).

    g. Þeir Eirík__ náð__ fund__ Óláf__ konung__.

    h. Konung__ bjó í firð____ (def.).

    i. Þorstein__ in__ stór__ stóð á skip____ (def.) ok kvadd__ konung.

2. Fill in the appropriate endings.

    a. Maðr hét Gísli. Hann var sonr Ásgerð____, kon__ Þorkel__ in__ mikl__, auðig__ mann__ ok vaen__.

    b. Kon__ Gísl__ hét Auð__. Hon var syst___ Véstein__ in__ auðg__, mikil__ mann__ ok vaen__.

    c. Véstein__ bað Ásgerð__, dótt___ Gísl__ ok Auð__ ok syst__ Yngvar__.

    d. Gísl__ bað Auð__, ágaet__ kon__ ok vitr__.

    e. Egil__ var faðir Ásgerð__, væn____ kon__ ok mikil__.

3. Repeat exercise **2**, substituting all names of strong noun form with names of weak noun form. For example, interchange the forms of *Gísli* and *Vesteinn*, or use any other masc. names. For the replacements for the strong fem. names *Auðr* and *Ásgerðr*, use the weak fem. names *Helga* and *Þóra*.

    a. _____

    _____

    b. _____

    _____

    c. _____

    _____

    d. _____

    e. _____

4. Conjugate the following verbs in the pres. tense. The 3 sing. and 3 pl. forms are supplied.

    a. Weak verbs:

Ex: lifa:	ek _lifi_ ,	þú _lifir_ ,	hann lifir
	vér _lifum_ ,	þér _lifið_ ,	þeir lifa
elska:	ek ____ ,	þú ____ ,	hann elskar
	vér ____ ,	þér ____ ,	þeir elska
mæla:	ek ____ ,	þú ____ ,	hann mælir
	vér ____ ,	þér ____ ,	þeir mæla
spyrja:	ek ____ ,	þú ____ ,	hann spyrr
	vér ____ ,	þér ____ ,	þeir spyrja

    b. Strong verbs:

Ex: biðja:	ek _bið_ ,	þú _biðr_ ,	hann biðr
	vér _biðjum_ ,	þér _biðið_ ,	þeir biða

gefa: ek _____, þú _____, hann gefr

            vér _____, þér _____, þeir gefa

hefja: ek _____, þú _____, hann hefr

            vér _____, þér _____, þeir hefja

rísa: ek _____, þú _____, hann ríss

            vér _____, þér _____, þeir rísa

5. Translate the Reading Selections.

a. Bjǫrn hét hersir ríkr í Sogni, er bjó á Aurlandi; hans son var Brynjólfr, er arf allan tók eptir fǫður sinn. Synir Brynjólfs váru þeir Bjǫrn ok Þórðr; þeir váru menn á ungum aldri, er þetta var tíðenda. Bjǫrn var farmaðr mikill, var stundum í víking, en stundum í kaupferðum; Bjǫrn var inn gǫrviligsti maðr.

_____

_____

_____

_____

_____

_____

_____

_____

_____

Þat barsk at á einu hverju sumri, at Bjǫrn var staddr í Fjǫrðum at veizlu nǫkkurri fjǫlmennri; þar sá hann mey fagra, þá er honum fannsk mikit um. Hann spurði eptir, hverrar ættar hon var; honum var þat sagt, at hon var systir Þóris hersis Hróaldssonar ok hét Þóra. Bjǫrn hóf upp bónorð sitt ok bað Þóru, en Þórir synjaði honum ráðsins, ok skildusk þeir at svá gǫrvu.

_____

_____

_____

_____

_____

_____

_____

_____

En þat sama haust fekk Bjǫrn sér liðs ok fór með skútu alskipaða
norðr í Fjǫrðu ok kom til Þóris ok svá, at hann var eigi heima. Bjǫrn
nam Þóru á brott ok hafði heim með sér á Aurland; váru þau þar
um vetrinn, ok vildi Bjǫrn gera brúðlaup til hennar.

_____

_____

_____

_____

_____

_____

_____

_____

b. Þórbjǫrn hét maðr ok var kallaðr selagnúpr; hann bjó í Tálknafirði
at Kvígandafelli; Þórdís hét kona hans, en Ásgerðr dóttir. Þessarar
konu biðr Þorkell Súrsson ok getr hana at eiga, en Gísli Súrsson bað
systur Vésteins, Auðar Vésteinsdóttur, ok fekk hana; búa nú báðir
saman í Haukadal.

_____

_____

_____

_____

_____

_____

_____

_____

c. Hon var ung kona ok stórrar ættar.

_____

_____

d. Nǫrvi hét jǫtunn, er bygði í Jǫtunheimum. Hann átti dóttur, er Nótt
hét. Hon var svǫrt ok døkk sem hon átti ætt til.

_____

_____

_____

_____

VOCABULARY

aldr *m* age
alskipaðr *adj* fully manned
arfr *m* inheritance
Auðr *f* Aud (*personal name*)
Aurland *n* Aurland (*place name*)
átti (*inf* **eiga**) *vb* had, owned
bað (*inf* **biðja**) *vb* requested (*sg*)
barsk (*inf* **berask**, *see* **bera**) *refl vb*
  barsk at happened
báðir *pron* both (*masc*)
bera (*past sg* bar) *vb* carry, bear; *refl*
  berask at happen
biðja (*pres* biðr, *past sg* bað) *vb* ask;
  [*w gen*] ask for, request
biðr (*inf* **biðja**) *vb* requests
bónorð *n* request, petition
brott *adv* **á brott** away (*motion*)
brúðlaup *n* wedding
Brynjólfr *m* Brynjolf (*personal name*)
døkkr *adj* dark
eiga (*past* átti) *vb* own, have
elli *f* old age
faðir (*acc/dat/gen* fǫður) *m* father
fannsk (*inf* **finnask**, *see* **finna**) *refl vb*
  appeared
fara (*past sg* fór) *vb* travel, go
farmaðr *m* traveler, sea-farer
fá (*past sg* fekk) *vb* [*w gen*] get; marry
fekk (*inf* **fá**) *vb* got; married
fell *n* mountain
finna (*past sg* fann) *vb* find; *refl*
  finnask appear
Firðir *m pl* the Fjords (*place name*)
fjǫlmennr *adj* populous, with many
  people, well attended
fór (*inf* **fara**) *vb* traveled, went
fǫður *m* father (*acc of* **faðir**)
gera (-ð-) *vb* make, do
geta (*pres* getr) *vb* get
getr (*inf* **geta**) *vb* gets
gremi *f* wrath, anger
gǫrr (-v-) *adj* done
gǫrviligstr *superl adj* (*see* **gǫrviligr**)
  most accomplished
gǫrviligr *adj* accomplished, capable,
  enterprising
hana *pron* her (*acc of* **hon**)
haust *n* autumn, fall
Hávarðr *m* Havard (*personal name*)
hefja (*past sg* hóf) *vb* raise
heim *adv* (to) home (*motion*)
heima *adv* at home (*location*)

heimr *m* land, region of the world
hennar *pron* (of) her (*gen of* **hon**)
hon (*acc* hana, *gen* hennar) *pron* she
hóf (*inf* **hefja**) *vb* raised (*sg*)
Hróaldr *m* Hroald (*personal name*)
hverr *indef pron* any, anyone
Jǫtunheimar *m pl* Land of Giants
jǫtunn *m* giant
kaupferð *f* trading trip
kona *f* woman, wife
Kvígandafell *n* 'Heifer Mountain'
  (*place name*)
lið *n* troop, force, band of armed
  supporters; aid, assistance
mey *f* girl (*acc of* **mær**)
mikit *adv* much (*neut of* **mikill**)
mær (*acc* mey) *f* girl
nam (*inf* **nema**) *vb* took (*sg*)
nema (*past sg* nam) *vb* take
norðr *adv* north
nótt *f* night
nú *adv* now
nǫkkurr *indef pron* one, a certain
Norvi *m* Norvi (*personal name*)
ráð *n* match, marriage
saman *adv* together
selagnúpr *m* 'Seal-Cliff' (*nickname*)
sér *refl pron* to himself (*dat of* **sik**)
sik *refl pron* himself
sinn *refl poss adj* his (own) (*refers
  back to subject*)
sitt *refl poss adj* his (own) (*neut of
  sinn)
skúta *f* small boat, skiff
Sogn *n* Sogn, area in Western Norway
  (*place name*)
sonr (*gen* -ar; *pl* synir) *m* son
spyrja (spurð-) *vb* ask
staddr *adj* present; located
sumar (*dat* sumri) *n* summer
sú *dem pron* that (one) (*fem of* **sá**)
Súrr *m* Sur (*personal name*)
svartr (*fem* svǫrt) *adj* black
svǫrt *adj* black (*nom sg fem of* **svartr**)
synir *m* sons (*pl of* **sonr**)
synja (*past* -að-) *vb* [*w gen*] refuse,
  deny
systir (*acc/dat/gen* systur) *f* sister
Tálknafjǫrðr *m* Talknafjord, a fjord
  in Northwest Iceland
tíðenda *n pl* of news (*gen of* **tíðendi**)
tíðendi *n pl* news, tidings

ungr *adj* young
veizla *f* feast, party
Vésteinn *m* Vestein (*personal name*)
víking *f* sea-raiding
þau *pron* they (*n pl*)
þá *dem pron* that (one) (*acc of* **sú**)
þessarar *dem pron* (of) this (*gen sg fem of* **þessi**)
þessi (*n* þetta) *dem pron* this

þetta *dem pron* this (*neut nom/acc of* **þessi**)
Þorkell *m* Thorkel (*personal name*)
Þóra *f* Thora (*personal name*)
Þórbjǫrn *m* Thorbjorn (*personal name*)
Þórðr *m* Thord (*personal name*)
Þórir *m* Thorir (*personal name*)
ævi *f* time, lifetime, age

PHRASES

at svá gǫrvu thus, this being the case, as things stood
á ungum aldri young, of a young age
biðja konu (*gen*) ask for a woman in marriage
einn hverr one, a certain
er þetta var tíðenda when this happened (lit., 'was of news')
fá sér liðs gather a band of men, get support
gera brúðlaup til marry

geta hana at eiga get her in marriage, marry her
hafa heim með sér bring home with oneself
hefja upp bónorð propose
nema á brott take away, abduct
sem hon átti ætt til which was characteristic for her family
svá at so that
þá er honum fannsk mikit um whom he liked very much

A Small Icelandic Manuscript. The production of such books made from calfskin began in the century after the Icelandic conversion to Christianity around the year 1000. Christian missionaries and clerics introduced the technique of writing with ink and the use of vellum pages. (Photo Courtesy of Árni Magnússon Manuscript Institute, Reykjavík.)

Suggested Readings: *Viking Language 2*

At this stage, we suggest turning to the longer passages, complete short sagas, and Eddic and Skaldic poetry found in *Viking Language 2: The Old Norse Reader.*

Viking Language 2: The Old Norse Reader (ISBN 978-14-81175265) is a treasure trove of Scandinavian lore with a broad selection of Old Norse sources and runes. The learner chooses from myths, legends, sagas, and runic inscriptions. Several chapters delve deeply into the tales and poems of the Scandinavian gods and heroes. To assist the learner, *The Old Nores Reader* features a large vocabulary and a full reference grammar. Below is the Table of Contents.

www.oldnorse.org
www.juleswilliampress

Viking Language 2: The Old Norse Reader
Table of Contents

Chapter 1a, Readings from the Family Sagas (*Íslendinga-sögur*)[16]

London Bridge (*bryggja Lundúnar*) Pulled Down
Chieftains (*goðar*) and Families (*ættir*) from *Njáls saga* (*Njáls saga*)
Gift-Giving (*gjafaskipti*) in the Sagas
A Gift in *Njáls saga*, Gunnar's Faithful Hound: Four Sample Translations
King Harald Fairhair (*Haralds saga ins hárfagra*)
Egil's Bones – Saga and Archaeology (*Egils saga Skalla-Grímssonar*)

Chapter 2, Creation of the World: Ymir, Yggdrasill, and Ásgarðr

Creation: Ymir, Auðhumla, and Óðinn

---

[16] *Íslendingasögur* (*Sagas of the Icelanders* or *Family Sagas*) is a modern term, hence spelled with modern Icelandic -*ö*- rather than Old Icelandic -*ǫ*-. The same is true of the modern term *fornaldarsögur* (Legendary Sagas).

The Norse Cosmos and the World Tree (Yggdrasill)
Loki and Svaðilfari – The Walls of Ásgarðr

Chapter 3, Ragnarok: The Battle at the World's End

The Doom of the Gods (*Ragnarøkr*)

Chapter 4, Gods and Goddesses

The Æsir and the Vanir
Óðinn the All-Father
Þórr
Týr
Goddesses and Supernatural Women
Frigg and the Goddesses
Female Divinities and Valkyries (*Valkyrjur*)
Baldr
The Vanir – Njǫrðr, Frey, and Freyja
Loki

Chapter 5, Þórr and the Giant Útgarða-Loki

Þórr Meets Skrýmir in the Forest
Þórr Reaches the Giant's Stronghold
Útgarða-Loki Reveals the Truth

Chapter 6, Otter's Ransom: The Dwarves' Gold and the Ring

Why is Gold Called Otter's Ransom (*Otrgjǫld*)?
Sigurðr the Volsung, the Dragon Fáfnir, and the Ring (Andvaranaut)

Chapter 7, Settling the North Atlantic: Ísland

Sailing Routes
Directions and Time
Explorations West over the Atlantic
Iceland Settled
The Conversion of Iceland

Chapter 8, Grœnland and Vínland

Greenland Discovered and Settled
Greenland and Vinland Discovered
Seafaring in the North Atlantic
Greenlanders Sail to Vinland
The Greenland Seeress

Chapter 9, The Tale of Auðunn from the West Fjords

Auðunar þáttr vestfirzka (The Complete Tale)

Chapter 10, Hrafnkel's Saga

Hrafnkels saga Freysgoða (The Complete Saga)

Chapter 11, Runes (*Rúnar*) in Viking and Medieval Times

The Hørning Runestone from Jutland in Denmark, The Gratitude of a
Freed Man (*leysingi*)
Two Runestones from the Parish of Klepp
Runes in the Family Sagas (*Íslendingasögur*)
Runes in *Egils saga Skalla-Grímssonar*
Runes in the Legendary Sagas (*fornaldarsögur*)
Medieval Runes
Medieval Runes from Bergen
Medieval Runes in Commerce
Bryggen Love Runes
Runic Inscriptions in Latin
Key to the Rune Exercises

Chapter 12, Eddic Poetry

Eddic Verse and Its Sources
Eddic Titles
Eddic Tradition – Long Lines and Half Lines

Chapter 13, Eddic Meters

The Four Principal Eddic Meters
Eddic Examples from Mythic Poems

Chapter 14, *The Lay of Thrym* (*Þrymskviða*)

Poetic Devices
Poetic Grammar
Þrymskviða (*The Lay of Thrym*)

Chapter 15, Runes and Eddic Meter from Sweden (*Svíþjóð*)

Two Bällsta Runestones (From Uppland, Sweden)
The Carver and the Carving
A Suggested Translation

Chapter 16, Skaldic Poetry

Skaldic Composition
Heiti and Kennings
Kennings in *Háttatal*: A Series of Examples
Three Skaldic Fragments about Þórr
Classification: The Five Sievers Types
Húsdrápa (*Housepoem*), A Picture Poem of Praise

Chapter 17, The Karlevi Runestone: A Skaldic Poem Carved in Runes on a Baltic Island.

The Karlevi Stone

LESSON 10

Ór *Óláfs sǫgu Tryggvasonar* (108. kap.)
(From the *Saga of Olaf Tryggvason*, Chap. 108)

to   some   some
Þá mælti Eiríkr jarl við þann mann, er sumir nefna Finn, en sumir

Finnish   bowman shoot (you)
segja, at hann væri finnskr – sá var inn mesti bogmaðr: "Skjóttu mann

the bow-room
þann inn mikla í krapparúminu."

shot   the arrow struck [the] middle [of] Einar's bow at that moment
Finnr skaut, ok kom ǫrin á boga Einars miðjan í því bili, er

drew [for] the third time the bow broke   two pieces
Einarr dró it þriðja sinn bogann. Brast þá boginn í tvá hluti.

broke   loudly
Þá mælti Óláfr konungr: "Hvat brast þar svá hátt?"

answers   out of your hand
Einarr svarar: "Nóregr ór hendi þér, konungr."

not is likely   break [to have] happened   take
"Eigi mun svá mikill brestr orðinn," segir konungr, "tak

my   shoot with [it]   threw the bow
boga minn ok skjót af" – ok kastaði boganum til hans.

the bow drew at once beyond [the] point of the arrow
Einarr tók bogann ok dró þegar fyrir odd ǫrvarinnar ok mælti:

too weak   sovereign's bow   threw back the bow
"Of veikr, of veikr allvalds bogi" – ok kastaði aptr boganum, tók þá

shield his   sword
skjǫld sinn ok sverð ok barðisk.

10.1. Verbs: The Imperative.

The imperative is the form of the verb used to make commands or requests. The imperative tells someone what to do, f.ex., 'go!'. Expressing one's own intentions (f.ex., 'let's go') is also a type of imperative.

1. Second Person Singular

The 2 sing. imperative of the verb is the bare pres. stem, which takes one of three forms.

- For weak verbs vocalic link -a- (5.3.1), the imperative retains the vocalic link as part of the stem: *kalla* 'call!'. In these verbs the imperative looks like the infinitive.

- For most other weak verbs and for strong verbs, the imperative is the same as the bare root: *tak* 'take!' (inf. *taka*), *skjót* 'shoot!' (inf. *skjóta*).

- A few weak verbs have the suffix *-i* in the imperative: *þegi* 'be silent!' (inf. *þegja*).

The pron. *þú* often follows the imperative verb, without changing the meaning: *tak þú* = *tak* ('take!') *skjót þú* = *skjót* ('shoot!'). When the command is empatic (forceful), *þú* is left as a separate word, but in most instances *þú* behaves like a suffix and is joined to the verb in the shortened form *-ðu*: *kallaðu* = *kalla þú* ('call!'), *farðu* = *far þú* ('go!'), *gerðu* = *ger þú* ('do!').

When joined to the verb, the dental consonant of *-ðu* assimilates to the final consonant of the stem according to the same rules (5.4) that determine the form of the dental suffix *-ð-* in the past tense of weak verbs: *skjóttu, taktu*.

- When the stem ends in *-nd-*, *-ng-*, and *-ld-*, these consonant clusters sometimes change to *-tt*, *-kk*, and *-lt*. For example, *standa*, *ganga*, and *halda* in the imperative become *statt(u)*, *gakk(tu)*, and *halt(u)*.

2. Second Person Plural.

The 2 pl. imperative form is identical to the 2 pl. indic. (see 9.8). For example, *takið* can be either a simple statement 'you (pl.) are taking' or a command 'take!' (adressed to a group). Similarly, *skjótið* can mean either 'you (pl.) are shooting' or 'shoot! (pl.)'.

3. First Person Plural.

The 1 pl. imperative is the same as the 1 pl. indic.: *gerum* 'we do' or 'let's do', *skjótum* 'we shoot' or 'let's shoot'.

10.2. Stem Variation in *-j-* and *-v-*.

The stems of many Icelandic words end in either *-j-* or *-v-*, the presence of which is determined by the ending that follows. Examples are:

Nouns:

    masc. *leggr* (*-j-*) 'leg' – gen. sing. *leggjar*, gen. pl. *leggja*
    fem. *ey* (*-j-*) 'ísland' – dat. sing. *ey/eyju*, gen. sing. *eyjar*, gen. pl. *eyja*
    neut. *ríki* (*-j-*) 'power' – gen. pl. *ríkja*
    fem. *ǫr* (*-v-*) 'arrow' – gen. sing. *ǫrvar*, gen. pl. *ǫrva*

Verbs:

    segja 'say' – 3 sing. pres. *segir*
    biðja 'ask for' – 3 sing. pres. *biðr*
    syngja (older *syngva*) 'sing' – 3 sing. pres. *syngr*

Adjectives:

miðr (-*j*-) 'middle' – acc. sing. masc. *miðjan*, fem. *miðja*, dat. sing. masc. *miðjum*, dat. *miðju*, etc.

þriði (-*j*-) 'third' – (always weak) nom. sing. fem. *þriðja*, acc./dat./ gen. sing. masc. *þriðja*, fem. *þriðju*, etc.

døkkr (-*v*-) 'dark' – strong acc. sing. *døkkvan*; weak nom. sing. masc. *døkkvi*, fem. *døkkva*, etc.

Pronouns:

hverr (-*j*-) – dat. sing. masc. *hverjum*, neut. *hverju*

The presence of stem-final -*j*- and -*v*- is governed by the following rules:

- Both -*j*- and -*v*-, when present in the stem, appear before the ending -*a*.
- -*j*- does not appear before -*i*.
- -*v*- does not appear before -*u*.
- -*v*- appears before the ending -*i* (f.ex., weak masc. *døkkvi*) but does not appear before a suffixed article (f.ex., *ǫrin* 'the arrow').
- Neither -*j*- nor -*v*- appears before a consonantal ending.
- Neither -*j*- nor -*v*- appears when there is no ending.

10.3. Verbs: Past Participle Formation.

Weak verbs and strong verbs form their past participles in manners parallel to the formation of the past tense (5.2).

1. Weak Verbs.

The ppart. of weak verbs adds the same dental suffix as the past tense (-*ð*-, -*d*-, or -*t*-, see 5.4). Hence the two stems are the same: *kalla* – past/ppart. stem *kallað*-; *nefna* – past/ppart. stem *nefnd*-; *víga* – past/ppart. stem *vígð*-.

The ppart. adds regular adj. endings to this stem: nom. sing. masc. *kallað-r* (R.S. 2), *nefnd-r* (R.S. 3.9, 5), *vígð-r* (R.S. 4.5), *talað-r* (R.S. 7); and nom./acc. sing. neut. *lengt* (R.S. 2), *jafnat* (R.S. 7).

- A few verbs (f.ex., *lifa* 'live', *vaka* 'awaken', *vilja* 'want') behave differently from the general rule. They attach the dental suffix directly to the stem in the past tense, but insert -*a*- before the ending in the neut. ppart.: f.ex., *vaka* 'awaken': 3 sing. past *vak-ti*; ppart. masc. *vak-tr*, but neut. *vak-**a**-t*.

2. Strong Verbs.

Instead of adding a dental suffix, strong verbs form their past participles by changing the stem vowel. The ppart. stem is distinct from the past-tense stem: *taka* – past *tók, tóku* – ppart. *tekinn*. Another example is *syngja* 'sing' – past *sǫng, sungu* – ppart. *sunginn*. English strong verbs show a similar pattern: 'take' – 'took' – 'taken'; 'sing' – 'sang' – 'sung'.

The endings of Icelandic strong past participles are identical in form with the article (*tekinn, sunginn*).[17] Some examples from the reading selections are: nom. sing. masc. *borinn* (R.S. 6), from *bera* 'bear'; nom. sing. masc. *orðinn* (R.S. 6, 10) and nom. sing. neut. *orðit* (R.S. 6), from *verða* 'become'. Other common examples: *ganga* 'go, walk' – ppart. *genginn*; *gefa* 'give' – ppart. *gefinn*; *koma* 'come' – ppart. *kominn*.

The ppart. of *taka* shows the full pattern (compare the def. art., 8.2):

	Masc	Fem	Neut
Sg *nom*	tek-inn	tek-in	tek-it
acc	tek-inn	tek-ina	tek-it
dat	tek-inum	tek-inni	tek-inu
gen	tek-ins	tek-innar	tek-ins
Pl *nom*	tek-inir	tek-inar	tek-in
acc	tek-ina	tek-inar	tek-in
dat	tek-inum	tek-inum	tek-inum
gen	tek-inna	tek-inna	tek-inna

At this point you have learned all the principal parts of strong verbs. They are listed in the vocabulary as follows:

fá (fær; fekk, fengu; fenginn) *vb* get
liggja (liggr; lá, lágu, leginn) *vb* lie
ríða (ríðr; reið, riðu; riðinn) *vb* ride
standa (stendr; stóð, stóðu; staðinn) *vb* stand

10.4. Verbs: Function of Reflexive Verbs.

Reflexive verbs have four basic functions: reflexive, reciprocal, passive, and impersonal.

1. Reflexive Function.

The reflexive function is used when the action of the verb reflects back onto the subject, that is, when one is doing something to or for oneself. For example, *kýrin fœddisk* 'the cow fed herself' (R.S. 5), from *fœða* 'feed'.

A reflexive verb followed by an infinitive is the regular construction for indirect discourse when the person speaking is reporting something about him- or herself. For example, *hann kvazk vera* (R.S. 8) 'he said he was', lit. 'he said himself to be' (from *kvað*, 3 sing. past of *kveða* 'say'). Note the contrast between this construction and the subjunct. of

---

[17] Technically speaking, the strong ppart. adds the suffix *-in-* (*tek-in-, sung-in-*) followed by adjectival endings. Recall from 2.1 that the *-r-* of these endings assimilates to stem-final *-n-* according to the Special Stem Rules. The Icelandic suffix *-in-* comes from the same source as English '-en' found on past participles such as 'tak**en**' and 'giv**en**'.

indirect discourse (8.5), which is used when the person speaking is different from the one being spoken about: *hann spyrr, hverr hann væri* 'he (i.e., the king) asks who he (i.e., Gunnlaug) was' (R.S. 8).

2. Reciprocal Function.

The reciprocal function always involves a plural subject. It expresses an action that the verb's subjects perform with regard to each other. For example, *þeir skuldusk* 'they parted', lit. 'they parted from each other' (from *skilja* 'to part, separate'); also *hann barðisk* 'he fought' (R.S. 6, 10), from *berjask* 'to fight', lit. 'strike each other' (from *berja* 'to strike').

3. Passive Function.

Reflexive verbs are also used in a passive sense, that is, to indicate that something "is done" or "was done", without necessarily specifying who does or did it. For example: *hjósk skjǫldr Helga* 'Helgi's shield was struck' (*hjósk*, lit. 'struck itself', from *hjó*, 3 sing. past of *hǫggva* 'strike').

4. Use in Impersonal Constructions.

Reflexive verbs occur frequently in impersonal constructions where the original reflexive function is no longer always clear. These usages are often idiomatic and do not translate literally.

> *honum fannsk mikit um* (R.S. 9) 'he liked very much' (*fannsk* from *finna* 'find')
>
> *hversu lízk þér á* (R.S. 4) 'how do you like, what do you think of' (*lízk á* from *líta á* 'look at')

Note that in these constructions the logical subject appears in the dative case.

10.5. Reflexive Verbs: Formation of the 3rd Person.

Reflexive verbs in the 3rd person are formed with the ending *-sk*, a contraction the 3 sing. acc. refl. pron. *sik* (compare the dat. form *sér* in R.S. 9). The infinitive of a refl. verb ends in *-ask*: *berjask* 'fight.' When the verb is conjugated, the ending *-sk* is added to the personal ending of the verb (not to the stem), as the following examples illustrate:

> *barðisk* (R.S. 6, 10) = *barði* (3 sing. past of *berja*) + *-sk*
> *barsk* (R.S. 9) = *bar* (3 sing. past of *bera*) + *-sk*
> *fannsk* (R.S. 9) = *fann* (3 sing. past of *finna*) + *-sk*
> *skildusk* (R.S. 8.1(2), 9) = *skildu* (3 pl. past of *skilja*) + *-sk*

When *-sk* is added to the verb, the following modifications involving assimilation and loss regularly occur:

- Assimilation after a dental consonant.

  Dental consonant + -sk = -zk. For example, *kvazk* (R.S. 8) = *kvað-* + -sk. This is a general type of assimilation and is not limited to this ending; compare the superl. *beztr* 'best' (R.S. 7) = stem *bet-* + -str.

- Loss of final -r of the personal ending.

  A final -r of a personal ending is lost before the ending -sk. For example, *lízk* (R.S. 4) = *lítr* + -sk. In this case the final -r is first lost and the refl. ending is then assimilated to the stem-final -t.

EXERCISES

1. The phrase *kastaði boganum* appeared twice in the R.S.

  a. What is the grammatical case of *boganum*? _____

  b. Why is it in this case? _____

2. Fill in the appropriate endings and missing vowels.

  a. Eystein___ stóð á inu stór___ skip___ ok barðisk.

  b. Einar___ kast___ð___ in___ sam___ bog___ aptr til Óláf___ konung___.

  c. Óláf___ tók in___ veik___ bog___ ok dró h_____.

  d. In___ stór___ bog___ brast.

3. Fill in the appropriate endings.

  a. Kon___ hét Þór___ in ljós___. Hon bjó í stór___ firð___ á Ísland___ hjá Brynjólf___ in___ rík___, góð___ mann___ ok auðg___, ok Helg___ in___ stór___, ágæt___ kon___ ok væn___.

  b. Þór___ átti Gísl___ in___ mikl___, gǫfg___ mann ok vitr___. Bjǫrn in___ hvít___ var sonr Gísl___ ok Þór___ ok hann átti Ber___ in___ stórráð___, fagr___ kon___ ok ung___. Bjǫrn var ung___ mað___ ok góð_____ ætt___ ok átti stór___ skip. Hann var i víking á ein___ hverj___ haust___ ok fór með it stór___ skip til England___. Þar náði hann fund___ Óláf___ in___ góð___, konung___ England___, ok var með Óláf___ þetta sam___ haust.

4. Commands. Write the 2 sing. imperative of the following verbs. Give both the bare stem and the stem with suffixed -ðu.

  Ex: flytja (flutt-): _*flyt*____ / _*flyttu*_____

  a. Weak verbs:

  kasta (-að-): _____ / _____

  kveðja (kvadd-): _____ / _____

  mæla (-t-): _____ / _____

b. Strong verbs:

bera: _____ / _____

biðja: _____ / _____

þiggja: _____ / _____

5. Construct the reflexive form of the following verb forms:

a. at taka _____, hon tekr _____,

hon tók _____, þær tóku _____.

b. at mæla _____, hann mælir _____,

hann mælti _____, þeir mæltu _____.

c. at skjóta _____, þat skýtr _____,

þat skaut _____, þau skutu _____.

6. Translate the following reflexive expressions:

a. Þeir mæltusk við.

_____

b. Dagr sezk. (*at setja* 'to set'; 3 sing. pres. *hann setr*)

_____

7. Translate the following two sentences and explain the difference:

a. Konungrinn sagðisk vera ríkr maðr.

_____

_____

b. Konungrinn sagði, at hann væri ríkr maðr.

_____

_____

8. Translate the Reading Selection.

Þá mælti Eiríkr jarl við þann mann, er sumir nefna Finn, en sumir segja, at hann væri finnskr – sá var inn mesti bogmaðr: "Skjóttu mann þann inn mikla í krapparúminu."

Finnr skaut, ok kom ǫrin á boga Einars miðjan í því bili, er Einarr dró it þriðja sinn bogann. Brast þá boginn í tvá hluti.

_____

_____

_____

_____

_____

_____

Þá mælti Óláfr konungr: "Hvat brast þar svá hátt?"
Einarr svarar: "Nóregr ór hendi þér, konungr."
"Eigi mun svá mikill brestr orðinn," segir konungr, "tak boga minn
ok skjót af" – ok kastaði boganum til hans.

Einarr tók bogann ok dró þegar fyrir odd ǫrvarinnar ok mælti: "Of
veikr, of veikr allvalds bogi" – ok kastaði aptr boganum, tók þá skjǫld
sinn ok sverð ok barðisk.

VOCABULARY

Hereafter, verbs in the vocabularies are listed as follows:

Weak verbs: **infinitive** (dental suffix or past-tense stem) *vb* definition
Strong verbs: **infinitive** (3sg. pres.; 3sg. past, 3pl. past; ppart.) *vb* definition

aptr *adv* back
barðisk (*inf* **berjask**, *see* **berja**) *refl vb* fought (*sg*)
berja (barð-) *vb* beat, strike, smite; *refl* **berjask** fight
bil *n* moment
bogi *m* bow
bogmaðr *m* bowman, archer
bresta (brestr; brast, brustu; brostinn) *vb* break
brestr *m* break
draga (dregr; dró, drógu; dreginn) *vb* pull, draw
døkkr (-v-) *adj* dark
Einarr *m* Einar (*personal name*)
ey (*dat* ey/eyju, *gen* -jar; *pl* -jar) *f* island
fá (fær; fekk, fengu; fenginn) *vb* get
finnskr *adj* Finnish
Finnr *m* Finn (*personal name*)
hár *adj* loud
hátt *adv* loudly (*neut of* **hár**)
hendi *dat sg of* **hǫnd**
hǫnd (*dat* hendi) *f* hand
í *prep* [*w acc*] into
kasta (-að-) *vb* [*w dat*] throw
leggr (*gen* -jar; *pl* -ir) *m* leg, limb; hollow bone (of arm and leg)
liggja (liggr; lá, lágu, leginn) *vb* lie
miðr (-j-) *adj* middle
minn *poss adj* my, mine
munu (mun, munu; mundi) *vb* will,

shall (*futurity*), be likely
oddr *m* point
of *adv* too
orðinn (*inf* verða) *ppart* happened, taken place
ríða (ríðr; reið, riðu; riðinn) *vb* ride
ríki (-j-) *n* power
sinn *n* a time, instance
skjóta (skýtr; skaut, skutu; skotinn) *vb* shoot
skjǫldr *m* shield
setja (-tt-) *vb* set, put, place
standa (stendr; stóð, stóðu; staðinn) *vb* stand
sumir *adj* (*m pl*) some (people)
svara (-að-) *vb* answer

sverð *n* sword
syngja (*older* **syngva**) (syngr; sǫng, sungu; sunginn) *vb* sing
Tryggvi *m* Tryggvi (*personal name*)
tvá *num* two (*acc masc of* **tveir**)
tveir (*acc masc* tvá) *num* two
veikr *adj* weak
verða (verðr; varð, urðu; orðinn) *vb* become; happen, come to pass (NB: regular loss of initial *v*- before *-o-* and *-u-*)
þegar *adv* at once, immediately
þriði (-j-) *ord num* third
því *dem pron* (to) that (*dat of* **þat**)
ǫr (-v-) *f* arrow

PHRASES

eigi mun svá mikill brestr orðinn such a great break is not likely to have occurred
í því bili at that moment

koma á strike
mæla við [*w acc*] speak to
ór hendi þér out of your hand

Notes

_____

_____

_____

_____

_____

_____

_____

_____

_____

_____

_____

_____

_____

_____

_____

LESSON 11

Ór *Fóstbrœðra sǫgu* (23. kap.)
(From the *Saga of the Foster-Brothers*, Chap. 23)

tent
Egill mælti: "Ek var at búð Þorgríms Einarssonar, ok þar er nú mestr

part   of the assembly   tells   story
hluti þingheimsins. Þorgrímr segir þar sǫgu."

about   whom   story that
Þormóðr mælti: "Frá hverjum er saga sú, er hann segir?"

know   fully about   whom   the story   this
Egill svarar: "Eigi veit ek gǫrla frá hverjum sagan er, en hitt veit

entertainingly   chair set   under   out
ek, at hann segir vel frá ok skemmtilega, ok er stóll settr undir hann úti

the tent   around   listen to   the story
hjá búðinni, ok sitja menn umhverfis ok hlýða til sǫgunnar."

you are probably able   who
Þormóðr mælti: "Kunna muntu nǫkkurn mann at nefna, þann sem

('in is')
is in   the story   especially since   [it] is amusing
í er sǫgunni, allra helzt er þú segir svá mikit frá, at gaman sé at."

hero   the story
Egill mælti: "Þorgeirr nǫkkurr var mikill kappi í sǫgunni, ok svá

[it] seems to me   must have been   somehow [connected]
virðisk mér sem hann Þorgrímr myndi verit hafa nǫkkut   við

('gone very well forward')
the story   fought very well   likely   would like   go
sǫguna ok gengit mjǫk vel fram, sem líkligt er. Vilda ek, at þú gengir

to there
þangat."

maybe
"Vera má þat," sagði Þormóðr.

11.1. Strong Verbs: Present-Stem Vowel Alternation.

The pres. sing. stem of strong verbs frequently contains a different vowel from that of the pres. pl. stem. For example, *hann gengr – þeir ganga*. Since the 3 pl. pres. is always identical with the inf. (7.9), the vowel of the pres. pl. stem is also the vowel of the inf. stem.

The chart below shows the alternation between the vowels of the pres. sing. and pl. stems of strong verbs. One does not have to memorize every strong verb, only know the pattern of this sound change.

The Regular Stem Vowel Alternation in Strong Verbs

Alternation

Pl		Sing	Examples
a	–	e	at t**a**ka – hann t**e**kr
á	–	æ	at r**á**ða – hann r**æ**ðr
o	–	e	at k**o**ma – hann k**e**mr
ǫ	–	ø	at h**ǫ**ggva – hann h**ø**ggr ('strike')
ú	–	ý	at b**ú**a – hann b**ý**r
jú	–	ý	at dr**jú**pa – hann dr**ý**pr
jó	–	ý	at sk**jó**ta – hann sk**ý**tr
au	–	ey	at hl**au**pa – hann hl**ey**pr ('run')

No Alternation

Pl		Sing	Examples
e	–	e	at g**e**fa – hann g**e**fr
ø	–	ø	at s**ø**kkva – hann s**ø**kkr ('sink')
i	–	i	at b**i**ðja – hann b**i**ðr
í	–	í	at r**í**sa – hann r**í**ss
y	–	y	at s**y**ngja – hann s**y**ngr ('sing')
ý	–	ý	at sp**ý**ja – hann sp**ý**r ('spew')
æ	–	æ	at hl**æ**ja – hann hl**æ**r ('laugh')
ei	–	ei	at h**ei**ta – hann h**ei**tir
ey	–	ey	at d**ey**ja – hann d**ey**r ('die')

11.2. Umlaut: An Explanation.

The process that changes the vowel of the inf. and pl. stem into the vowel of the sing. stem in the table above is known as *i*-**umlaut** (also called *i*-**mutation** or **front mutation**). A few basic points of vowel phonetics make umlaut easy to understand.

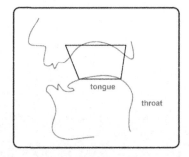

In all languages, two of the factors that differentiate one vowel from another are the position of the tongue in the mouth and the shape of the lips when the vowel is pronounced. Linguists use a space chart to illustrate the position of the vowels in the mouth.

The three cardinal vowels are **i** (as in 'machine'), **u** (as in 'sue'), and **a** (as in 'father'). They are placed in the vowel chart as follows.

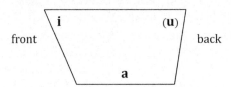

When you say these vowels, notice that the **i** of 'machine' is pronounced high in the mouth and toward the front; the **u** of 'su**e**' is pronounced high in the mouth and toward the back; and the **a** of 'father' is pronounced low in the mouth and near the center. Note too that the lips are somewhat rounded (indicated by parentheses) when you pronounce **u**, but are not rounded when you pronounce **a** and **i**.

Below are the short and long vowels of Old Icelandic:[18]

Short Vowels

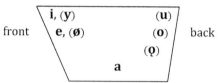

Long Vowels

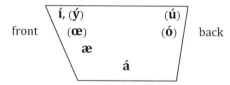

1. i-*Umlaut.*

i-umlaut is the result of a historical process in which a vowel was "pulled" forward (and often higher) in the mouth, toward the position of **i**, by an upcoming -*i*- or -*j*- in the next syllable.[19]

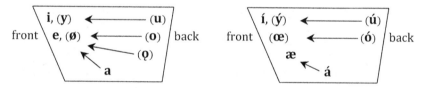

The -*i*- or -*j*- that caused the umlaut has sometimes disappeared by the time of Old Icelandic (although it was present in Proto-Norse, before approximately 700 CE), but its influence survives in the vowel change.

Look again at the above table of sing. and pl. stem vowels. When the vowels alternate, the sing. stem vowel in each instance is the result of moving the pl. stem vowel closer to the position of **i** on the mouth

---

[18] The vowels in these charts illustrate the pronunciation of Old Icelandic and not that of Modern Icelandic. For example, in Old Icelandic, *á* was essentially a longer version of *a*; whereas in Modern Icelandic, *á* is pronounced as a diphthong similar to the **ou** in 'h**ou**se'.

[19] The process of *i*-umlaut operated historically throughout the Northern and Western Germanic languages. Although it is no longer an active (productive) process in Modern English, many relics of Old English *i*-umlaut have been preserved: f.ex., man – men, **foot** – **feet**, m**ou**se – mice, etc. These often have direct parallels in Old Norse: *maðr* (*mann-*) – *menn, fótr – fœtr, mús – mýss*, etc.

chart.[20] The vowels that do not alternate are **front vowels** to start with, so *i*-umlaut has no effect on them.

2. u-*Umlaut* (*a~ǫ Alternation*)

The short vowel -*a*- is regularly replaced by -*ǫ*- when the next syllable contains -*u*- or -*v*-: *fara* 'travel' – *vér fǫrum* 'we travel'; *hafa* 'have' – *vér hǫfum* 'we have', *vér hǫfðum* 'we had', *þeir hǫfðu* 'they had'. This process is called *u*-**umlaut** or *a~ǫ* **alternation**.

Frequently, the original -*u*- or -*v*-[21] that triggered this sound change is no longer present in Old Icelandic, but the presence of the vowel -*ǫ*- shows that it existed at an earlier stage of the language. For example, *fǫr* (fem.) 'journey' is from earlier **fǫru*.

As the vowel chart shows, the sound of **ǫ** is the result of raising and backing of an **a** (that is, shifting it toward the position of **u**), and also acquiring lip rounding like **u**.

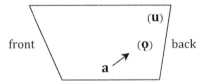

11.3. Weak Feminine Nouns: *a~ǫ* Alternation in the Singular.

The declension of the weak fem. noun *saga* illustrates the alternation of -*a*- with -*ǫ*-. In the acc., dat., and gen., the fem. sing. weak ending -*u* regularly triggers *u*-umlaut.

		Indef	Def
Sg *nom*		saga	saga-n
	acc	sǫgu	sǫgu-na
	dat	sǫgu	sǫgu-nni
	gen	sǫgu	sǫgu-nnar

The table at right shows the complete declension of *saga* in all cases of the singular. All of the forms with suffixed article appeared in the R.S. Recall from 4.8 that the article loses its initial *i*- when it is attached to a noun ending in a vowel.

11.4. Strong Feminine Nouns: *a~ǫ* Alternation in the Singular.

All strong fem. nouns with root vowel -*a*- also show *a~ǫ* alternation: the nom. and acc. forms, and usually also the dat., contain -*ǫ*-, whereas the gen. retains the original vowel -*a*-: nom./acc./dat. *fǫr* 'journey' – gen. *farar*; nom./acc. *jǫrð* 'earth', dat. *jǫrðu* – gen. *jarðar*. This is due to an ending -*u* that existed at an earlier stage of the language; in some nouns, the ending -*u* remains in the dat. sing. (*jǫrðu*). The complete sing. declension of such fem. nouns is as follows:

---

[20] Umlaut affects the vowels of dipthongs in the same way it affects individual vowels. For example, *au* → *ey* when affected by *i*-umlaut (*a* → *e* + *u* → *y*).

[21] In earlier Icelandic, *v* was pronounced like *w*.

	Indef	Def	Indef	Def
Sg nom	fǫr	fǫr-in	jǫrð	jǫrð-in
acc	fǫr	fǫr-ina	jǫrð	jǫrð-ina
dat	fǫr	fǫr-inni	jǫrðu	jǫrðu-nni
gen	farar	farar-innar	jarðar	jarðar-innar

11.5. Strong Masculine Nouns: *a~ǫ~e* Alternation in the Singular.

A number of strong masc. nouns show *a~ǫ~e* (or *ja~jǫ~i*) alternation in the singular. Several of these have occurred: nom. *Bjǫrn* (R.S. 4), gen. *Bjarnar* (R.S. 1); dat. *velli* (R.S. 6, 6.6) from *vǫllr* 'field'; *vexti* (R.S. 6) from *vǫxtr* 'growth'; dat. *firði* (R.S. 1, 6.6, 9.3) from *fjǫrðr* 'fjord'; acc. *skjǫld* (R.S. 10) from *skjǫldr* 'shield'.

The complete sing. declension of this type of strong masc. noun can be illustrated by the nouns *vǫllr*, *ǫrn* 'eagle', *Bjǫrn*, and *skjǫldr*:

	'field'	'eagle'	'Bjorn'	'shield'
Sg nom	vǫllr	ǫrn	Bjǫrn	skjǫldr
acc	vǫll	ǫrn	Bjǫrn	skjǫld
dat	velli	erni	Birni	skildi
gen	vallar	arnar	Bjarnar	skjaldar

Note that the nom. sing. masc. ending -*r* is not added after stem-final -*rn*: *ǫrn*, *Bjǫrn*.

With regard to strong masc. nouns with this three-way alternation *a~ǫ~e* (or *ja~jǫ~i*):

- the gen. retains the original vowel: *arnar*, *Bjarnar*, *skjaldar*;
- the nom. and acc. show the influence of *u*-umlaut (*ǫrn*, *Bjǫrn*, *skjǫldr*), but the original -*u* in the ending that triggered the *a~ǫ* alternation is no longer present;
- in contrast to the nom. and acc. which have lost their ending, the dat. preserves the ending -*i* causing *a~e* alternation (*arnar~erni*);
- *Bjǫrn* and *skjǫldr* have -*i*- as the stem vowel in the dat. (*Birni*, *skildi*), the result of *i*-umlaut on the root vowel -*ja*- (shown in the gen. *Bjarnar*, *skjaldar*).

11.6. Strong Feminine Noun *hǫnd*: *a~ǫ~e* Alternation in the Singular.

One fem. noun, *hǫnd* 'hand' (9.3), shows *a~ǫ~e* alternation in the singular. The declension is shown at right.

As in the case of the strong masc. nouns with three-way alternation, the original -*u* in the ending that triggered the *a~ǫ* alternation in the

	'hand'
Sg nom	hǫnd
acc	hǫnd
dat	hendi
gen	handar

nom. and acc. is no longer present, but the dat. ending -*i* that caused the *a~e* alternation is still preserved.

11.7. Strong Adjectives: *a~ǫ* Alternation in the Singular.

Strong adjectives with stem vowel -*a*- (f.ex., *svartr* 'black') show *u*-umlaut in three forms of the singular: the dat. masc. (which ends in -*um*, 2.4; f.ex., *svǫrtum*), the dat. neut. (which ends in -*u*, 4.5; f.ex., *svǫrtu*), and the nom. fem. (which has no ending, 9.6; f.ex., *svǫrt*). The following declentions of *svartr* 'black' and *fagr* 'fair' illustrate these *a~ǫ* alternations:

| | 'black' | | | 'fair' | | |
	Masc	Fem	Neut	Masc	Fem	Neut
Sg *nom*	svartr	svǫrt	svart	fagr	fǫgr	fagrt
acc	svartan	svarta	svart	fagran	fagra	fagrt
dat	svǫrtum	svartri	svǫrtu	fǫgrum	fagri	fǫgru
gen	svarts	svartrar	svarts	fagrs	fagrar	fagrs

- Recall (2.1.2) that the final -*r* of *fagr* belongs to the stem, and that the initial -*r*- of the ending is dropped: nom. masc. *fagr*, dat. fem. *fagri*, gen. fem. *fagrar*.

EXERCISES

1. Fill in the appropriate endings and missing vowels.

    a. Þeir Eiríkr kóm___ ok nám___ konu___ á brott, sem sagt er í sǫg_____. (all def.)

    b. Gísli var faðir Helg___ in_____ f__gr___, þeirar er átti Bjǫrn in___ vitr___.

    c. Bjǫrn kom ok nam Helg___ in___ f__gr___ á brott.

    d. Jǫrð___ (def.) er stór ok f__gr.

    e. Nótt___ (def.) er sv__rt, en dagr_____ (def.) bj__rt___.

    f. Brá Baldrs var hvít ok bj__rt.

2. Write the 3 sing. pres. form of the following strong verbs. (See 11.1. Note too that the 3 sing. pres. ending -*r* is added to the stem according to the rules given in 7.8).

Ex: fá 'get'   *fær*   hefja 'raise'   *hefr*

aka 'drive'	_____	halda 'hold'	_____
auka 'increase'	_____	liggja 'lie'	_____
bera' carry'	_____	ríða 'ride'	_____
binda 'bind'	_____	sitja 'sit'	_____
blása 'blow'	_____	sjóða 'boil'	_____
draga 'pull'	_____	skína 'shine'	_____

drepa 'kill'	_____	sofa 'sleep'	_____
fljúga 'fly'	_____	standa 'stand'	_____
frjósa 'freeze'	_____	svelgja 'swallow'	_____
geta 'get'	_____	sǫkkva 'sink'	_____
gráta 'cry'	_____	þiggja 'accept'	_____

3. Write the 1 pl. pres. form of the following verbs.

Ex: kalla 'call' <u>_kǫllum_</u>   hafa 'have'   <u>_hǫfum_</u>

banna 'forbid'   _____   skapa 'shape'   _____

falla 'fall'   _____   svara 'answer'   _____

halda 'hold'   _____   tala 'speak'   _____

4. Write the 3 pl. past form of the following verbs.

Ex: leggja (lagð-) <u>_lǫgðu_</u>   velja (valð-)   <u>_vǫlðu_</u>

berja (barð-)   _____   segja (sagð-)   _____

kveðja (kvadd-)   _____   vekja (vakt-)   _____

5. Give the title of the following sagas in the dat. (Remember that the preposition *ór* takes the dat.)

Ex.: Gunnlaugs saga ormstungu: ór <u>_Gunnlaugs sǫgu ormstungu_</u>

Fóstbrœðra saga: ór _____

Hrafnkels saga Freysgoða: ór _____

Magnúss saga Erlingssonar: ór _____

Ragnars saga loðbrókar: ór _____

Vápnfirðinga saga: ór _____

Gísla saga Súrssonar: ór _____

Hávarðar saga: ór _____

6. Translate the Reading Selection.

Egill mælti: "Ek var at búð Þorgríms Einarssonar, ok þar er nú mestr hluti þingheimsins. Þorgrímr segir þar sǫgu."

Þormóðr mælti: "Frá hverjum er saga sú, er hann segir?"

Egill svarar: "Eigi veit ek gǫrla frá hverjum sagan er, en hitt veit ek, at hann segir vel frá ok skemmtilega, ok er stóll settr undir hann úti hjá búðinni, ok sitja menn umhverfis ok hlýða til sǫgunnar."

_____
_____
_____
_____
_____
_____

_____

_____

_____

_____

_____

Þormóðr mælti: "Kunna muntu nǫkkurn mann at nefna, þann sem í er sǫgunni, allra helzt er þú segir svá mikit frá, at gaman sé at."

Egill mælti: "Þorgeirr nǫkkurr var mikill kappi í sǫgunni, ok svá virðisk mér sem hann Þorgrímr myndi verit hafa nǫkkut við sǫguna ok gengit mjǫk vel fram, sem líkligt er. Vilda ek, at þú gengir þangat."

"Vera má þat," sagði Þormóðr.

_____

_____

_____

_____

_____

_____

_____

_____

VOCABULARY

aka (ekr; ók, óku; ekinn) *vb* drive
búð *f* tent, booth
deyja (deyr; dó, dóu; dáinn) *vb* die
ekki *indef pron* nothing (*n of* **engi**)
en *conj* than (*w comp*)
engi *indef pron* no one, none (*n* **ekki**)
er *conj* since
fram *adv* forward
frjósa (frýss; fraus, frusu; frosinn) *vb* freeze
gaman *n* fun, amusement, pleasure
ganga (gengr; gekk, gengu; genginn) *vb* go, walk
gǫrla *adv* fully, quite
hafa (-ð-) *vb* have
hinn *pron* this (the other)
hitt *dem pron* this (the other) (*n of* **hinn**)
hlaupa (hleypr; hljóp, hljópu; hlaupinn) *vb* run
hluti *m* part

hlýða (-dd-) *vb* listen
hlæja (hlær; hló, hlógu; hleginn) *vb* laugh
hǫggva (hǫggr; hjó, hjoggu; hǫgg(v)inn) *vb* strike, hack, hew
jǫrð (*dat* -u) *f* earth
kappi *m* hero, champion, great fighter
koma (kemr; kom, kómu; kominn) *vb* come
kunna (kann, kunnu; kunni; kunnat) *vb* be able
líkligr *adj* likely, probable
mega (má, megu; mátti; mátt) *vb* be able
mjǫk *adv* very
munu (mun, munu; mundi) *vb* will, shall (*future*), be likely
myndi (*inf* **munu**) *vb* should, would be likely (*3sg past subjunct*)
nefna (-d-) *vb* name, mention by name

nǫkkut *adv* somewhat, in some degree

sé (*inf* **vera**) *vb* is (*3sg pres subjunct*; see 16.2)

sitja (sitr; sat, sátu; setinn) *vb* sit

skemmtiliga *adv* entertainingly

spýja (spýr; spjó, spjó; spúinn) *vb* spew

stóll *m* chair

svelgja (svelgr; svalg, sulgu; sólginn) *vb* swallow

syngja (syngr; sǫng, sungu; sunginn) *vb* sing

sǫkkva (søkkr; sǫkk, sukku; sokkinn) *vb* sink

umhverfis *adv* around, round about

undir *prep* [*w acc/dat*] under

úti *adv* outside (*location*)

vilja (vill; vildi; viljat) *vb* want, wish, will

virðask (-rð-) *refl vb* [*w dat*] seem, think (*impers*)

vita (veit, vitu; vissi; vitaðr) *vb* know

þangat *adv* (to) there, thither

þeira *poss pron* their

þingheimr *m* assembly (i.e., those in attendance at a **þing**)

Þorgeirr *m* Thorgeir (*personal name*)

Þorgrímr *m* Thorgrim (*personal name*)

Þormóðr *m* Thormod (*personal name*)

PHRASES

allra helzt especially, most of all

at gaman sé at that it is amusing

ganga vel fram fight well

hann segir vel frá he tells it well

kunna muntu at nefna you are probably able to name

myndi verit hafa was likely to have been, must have been

vera má þat maybe, perhaps

vera nǫkkut við be somehow connected with

virðisk mér it seems (seemed) to me

þangat til to there

Notes

_____

_____

_____

_____

_____

_____

_____

_____

_____

_____

_____

_____

_____

_____

_____

LESSON 12

(1) Ór *Ragnars sǫgu loðbrókar* (7. kap. 'Frá Ragnarssonum')
(From the *Saga of Ragnar Lodbrok*, Chap. 7 'About the Sons of Ragnar')

the boy   with water sprinkled
Var sveinninn vatni ausinn ok nafn gefit ok kallaðr Ívarr. En sá

boy   boneless   as if cartilage   bones should
sveinn var beinlauss ok sem brjósk væri þar, sem bein skyldu vera.

none
Ok þá er hann var ungr, var hann vexti svá mikill, at engir váru hans

equals   most handsome in appearance
jafningjar. Hann var allra manna   fríðastr   sýnum ok svá vitr,

certain   greater wise man
at eigi er víst, hverr meiri spekingr hefir verit en hann....

White-Shirt   fourth
Annarr sonr þeira hét Bjǫrn, inn þriði Hvítserkr, inn fjórði Rǫgnvaldr.

most valiant   as soon as
Þeir váru miklir menn allir ok inir frœknustu, ok þegar þeir máttu

something   undertake   of every kind skills   wherever
nǫkkut at hafask, námu þeir alls konar íþróttir. Ok hvert sem þeir

poles   because   walk
fóru, lét Ívarr bera sik á stǫngum, því at hann mátti eigi ganga, ok

should   plans   whatever   did
skyldi hann hafa ráð fyrir þeim, hvat sem þeir hǫfðusk at.

(2) Ór *Heimskringlu* (1. kap.)
(From *Heimskringla* or the *History of the Kings of Norway*, Chap. 1)[22]

orb   mankind   inhabits   scored with bays
Kringla heimsins, sú er mannfólkit byggvir, er mjǫk vágskorin;

seas large   the oceans into the earth   sea
ganga hǫf stór ór útsjánum inn í jǫrðina. Er þat kunnigt, at haf

the Straits of Gibraltar   all the way   Jerusalem's Land (i.e., Israel)
gengr frá Nǫrvasundum ok   alt   út til Jórsalalands.

12.1. Demonstrative Pronouns: *sá* 'that, that one' and *þessi* (*sjá*) 'this, this one'.

Sá. Individual forms of the dem. pron. *sá* 'that (one)' have appeared in the reading selections: *sá* (R.S. 5, 6.6, 10, 12(1)), *sú* (R.S. 5, 11, 12(2)),

---

[22] *Heimskringla* means 'Orb of the World' but is usually referred to as the *History of the Kings of Norway*.

þat (R.S. 3, 7, 9), *þann* (R.S. 6, 10, 11), *þá* (R.S. 9), *þeiri* (R.S. 6), *því* (R.S. 10, 12(1)). The neut. sing. forms (*þat*, etc.) are also employed as the neut. pron. 'it' (R.S. 4, 5, 9, 11, 12(2)).

Þessi. In addition to *sá*, 'that (one)', Old Norse has the dem. pron. *þessi* 'this (one)'. *Þessi* refers to an object that is close, while *sá* refers to an object that is further away. The acc. sing. masc. *þenna* appeared in R.S. 6.6 and R.S. 8, and neut. sing. *þetta* appeared in R.S. 2 and R.S. 9. Here are *sá* and *þessi* side by side.

		sá 'that'			þessi (sjá) 'this'	
	Masc	**Fem**	**Neut**	**Masc**	**Fem**	**Neut**
Sg nom	sá	sú	þat	þessi/sjá	þessi/sjá	þetta
acc	þann	þá	þat	þenna	þessa	þetta
dat	þeim	þeiri	því	þessum	þessari	þessu
gen	þess	þeirar	þess	þessa	þessarar	þessa
Pl nom	þeir	þær	þau	þessir	þessar	þessi
acc	þá	þær	þau	þessa	þessar	þessi
dat	þeim	þeim	þeim	þessum	þessum	þessum
gen	þeir(r)a	þeir(r)a	þeir(r)a	þessara	þessara	þessara

- The pl. forms of *sá* are identical in all genders with the pl. pers. pronouns (5.1).

- The dem. pronouns *sá* and *þessi* agree in gender and number with noun they modify: nom. *sá maðr* 'that man', *þessi maðr* 'this man'; acc. *þann mann* 'that man', *þessa mann*, etc.

- When *sá* and *þessi* are followed by an adj., the adj. is weak (3.2): nom. *sá/þessi góði maðr* 'that/this good man'; acc. *þann/þessa góða mann* 'that/this good man', etc.

12.2. Relative Particles *er* and *sem*.

A rel. clause is introduced by a rel. particle, which can be either *sem* or *er*. Often the rel. particle is preceded by a form of the dem. pron. *sá* in agreement with the noun to which it refers in the preceding clause. The rel. particles and the dem. pronouns are bolded in the following examples. Note that when the dem. pron. appears in these examples, it appears together with the rel. particle.

> Bjǫrn hét hersir ríkr í Sogni, **er** bjó á Aurlandi; hans son var Brynjólfr, **er** arf allan tók eptir fǫður sinn. (R.S. 9)
> Þar sá hann mey fagra, **þá er** honum fannsk mikit um. (R.S. 9)
> Kringla heimsins, **sú er** mannfólkit byggvir (R.S. 12(2))
> Kunna muntu nǫkkurn mann at nefna, **þann sem** í er sǫgunni. (R.S. 11)

In the following examples, the dem. pron. is part of the preceding clause:

> Frá hverjum er saga **sú**, **er** hann segir? (R.S. 11)

Þá mælti Eiríkr jarl við **þann** mann, **er** sumir nefna Finn. (R.S. 10)
Kom ǫrin á boga Einars miðjan í **því** bili, **er** Einarr dró it þriðja sinn bogann. (R.S. 10)

Er and *sem* as Conjunctions.

Er can also be used as a conjunction of time, meaning 'when':

Þeir váru menn á ungum aldri, **er** þetta var tíðenda. (R.S. 9)
Ok **er** hann náði konungs fundi, kvaddi hann konunginn. (R.S. 8)
Þat var einn dag, **er** þeir Þórólfr ok Bjǫrn gengu ofan til skipsins.
  (R.S. 4)

Both *er* and *sem* can also be used as other types of conjunctions (all examples are from R.S. 11):

allra helzt ***er*** 'especially **since'**
svá virðisk mér ***sem*** 'so it seems to me **as if'**
sem *líkligt er* '**as** is likely, **as** might be expected'

Sem also occurs with the adv. *þar* as a conjunction of place, meaning 'in the place that'.

Hann býr **þar**, **sem** heitir Breiðablik. (R.S. 7)

12.3. Strong Nouns: Plural of All Genders.

1. Masc. Nom. and Acc. Pl.

The nom. pl. of masc. strong nouns ends in -*ar* or -*ir*: *hestar* ('horses'), *vinir* ('friends').

Strong Noun Endings			
	Masc	**Fem**	**Neut**
Pl *nom*	-ar, -ir	-ar, -ir, -(i)r	(o)–
acc	-a, -i	-ar, -ir, -(i)r	(o)–
dat	-um	-um	-um
gen	-a	-a	-a

Superscript (i) or (o) indicates that the ending triggers *i*-umlaut or *u*-umlaut (11.2).

- In most instances, masc. nouns with gen. sing. -*s* take the nom. pl. ending -*ar* (gen. sing. *hests*, nom. pl. *hestar*), whereas masc. nouns with gen. sing. -*ar* take the nom. pl. ending -*ir* (gen. sing. *vinar*, nom. pl. *vinir*).

The acc. pl. has the same form as the nom. minus the final -*r*: acc. pl. *hesta* and *vini*.

- Three masc. nouns (in addition to the kinship nouns in 14.8 below) end in -*r* in both the nom. and acc. pl. These nouns are: *fótr* 'foot', nom./acc. pl. *fœtr* (the ending triggers *i*-umlaut; see 11.2.1); *fingr* 'finger', nom./acc. pl. *fingr*; *vetr* 'winter', nom./acc. pl. *vetr*.

2. Fem. Nom. and Acc. Pl.

The nom. and acc. pl. of the fem. declension are in all ways identical, including those of the article, strong adjectives, weak adjectives, nouns, and pronouns. In the strong noun declension, they end in -ar, -ir, or -r: *farar*, *ættir*, *bœkr* ('books').

- The nom./acc. pl. ending -r triggers *i*-umlaut (11.2.1): *bók*, pl. *bœkr*; *hǫnd* (stem *hand-*), pl. *hendr*.

3. Neut. Nom. and Acc. Pl.

The nom. and acc. pl. of strong neut. nouns are identical. They have no ending, and in most instances are the same as the nom. and acc. neut. sing.: *blót* 'a sacrifice' or 'sacrifices', *sverð* 'a sword' or 'swords'.[23] If the root vowel is -*a*-, it changes to -*ǫ*- in the nom./acc. pl. due to *u*-umlaut: *land*, pl. *lǫnd* ('lands'). Like strong fem. nouns (f.ex., *fǫr* 'journey', 11.2.2; 11.4), the *u*-ending that originally triggered the umlaut is no longer present.

4. Dat. and Gen. Pl. (all genders).

The dat. pl. ending is -*um* for nouns of all genders: *hestum*, *meyjum*, *hǫndum*, *sverðum*. The gen. pl. ending of all strong nouns is -*a* (see 7.1): *hesta*, *meya*, *handa*, *sverða*.

- Plural forms of monosyllabic nouns ending in -*á* show contraction in all forms: nom./acc. pl. *brár* (= brá-ar), dat. pl. *brám* (= brá-um), gen. pl. *brá* (= brá-a); so also nom./acc. pl. *ár*, dat. pl. *ám*, gen. pl. *á*.

12.4. Weak Nouns: Plural of All Genders.

The nom. pl. ending of weak masc. nouns is -*ar*. Like strong masc. nouns, the acc. pl. of weak masc. nouns is the same as the nom. without -*r*: nom. *góðar*, acc. *góða*.

The nom. and acc. pl. of weak fem. nouns both have the ending -*ur* (which triggers *u*-umlaut): *konur* (R.S. 13(2)), *sǫgur* (R.S. 16).

The nom. and acc. pl. of weak neut. nouns end in -*u* (which triggers *u*-umlaut): *hjǫrtu*.

Weak Noun Endings			
	Masc	**Fem**	**Neut**
Pl nom	-ar	-ur	-u
acc	-a	-ur	-u
dat	-um	-um	-um
gen	-a	-na	-na

The dat. pl. of weak nouns of all genders ends in -*um*: *góðum*, *sǫgum*, *hjǫrtum*.

The gen. pl. ending of weak masc. nouns is -*a*, but fem. and neut. weak nouns have a stem-final -*n*- before the gen. pl. -*a*: f.ex., *sagna* from fem. *saga*; *hjartna* from neut. *hjarta*.

- The gen. pl. of *kona* 'woman' is *kvenna*, with an irregular change in the root vowel; *hún var allra **kvenna** fríðust* 'she was of all women most beautiful'.

---

[23] Compare English words such as 'deer' and 'sheep', which are the same in the singular and plural. These were neut. nouns in Old English.

12.5. Review Paradigms: Noun Endings, Sing. and Pl.

	Strong			Weak		
	Masc	**Fem**	**Neut**	**Masc**	**Fem**	**Neut**
Sg *nom*	-r (see 2.1)	(ǫ)–, -r	–	-i	-a	-a
acc	–	(ǫ)–, -i, -u	–	-a	-u	-a
dat	-i	(ǫ)–, -i, -u	-i	-a	-u	-a
gen	-s, -ar	-ar	-s	-a	-u	-a
Pl *nom*	-ar, -ir	-ar, -ir, -(i)r	(ǫ)–	-ar	-ur	-u
acc	-a, -i	-ar, -ir, -(i)r	(ǫ)–	-a	-ur	-u
dat	-um	-um	-um	-um	-um	-um
gen	-a	-a	-a	-a	-na	-na

EXERCISES

1. Fill in the appropriate endings and missing vowels.

    a. Þeir tók__ skip___ (def.) sem váru þar ok fór__ á brott.

    b. Fǫr___ (def.) frá Nóreg__ til Ísland__ er l__ng ok h__rð. (*harðr* 'hard')

2. Fill in the missing forms of the dem. pron. *sá*.

	Masc	**Fem**	**Neut**
Sg *nom*	sá	_____	þat
acc	_____	þá	_____
dat	_____	_____	_____
gen	_____	_____	þess
Pl *nom*	_____	_____	_____
acc	_____	þær	þau
dat	_____	_____	þeim
gen	þeira	_____	_____

3. Fill in the missing forms of the dem. pron. *þessi*.

	Masc	**Fem**	**Neut**
Sg *nom*	þessi	_____	_____
acc	_____	_____	þetta
dat	þessum	_____	_____
gen	_____	_____	_____
Pl *nom*	_____	þessar	þessi
acc	þessa	_____	_____
dat	_____	_____	_____
gen	_____	þessara	_____

4. Strong nouns. Decline the following nouns in the singular and plural.

	Masc	Fem	Neut
Sg nom	hestr	fǫr	land
acc			
dat			
gen			
Pl nom			
acc			
dat			
gen			

5. Weak nouns. Decline the following nouns in the singular and plural.

	Masc	Fem	Neut
Sg nom	goði	saga	hjarta
acc			
dat			
gen			
Pl nom			
acc			
dat			
gen			

6. Translate the Reading Selections.

a. Var sveinninn vatni ausinn ok nafn gefit ok kallaðr Ívarr. En sá sveinn var beinlauss ok sem brjósk væri þar, sem bein skyldu vera. Ok þá er hann var ungr, var hann vexti svá mikill, at engir váru hans jafningjar. Hann var allra manna fríðastr sýnum ok svá vitr, at eigi er víst, hverr meiri spekingr hefir verit en hann....

_____

_____

_____

_____

_____

_____

_____

_____

_____

Annarr sonr þeira hét Bjǫrn, inn þriði Hvítserkr, inn fjórði
Rǫgnvaldr. Þeir váru miklir menn allir ok inir frœknustu, ok þegar
þeir máttu nǫkkut at hafask, námu þeir alls konar íþróttir. Ok hvert
sem þeir fóru, lét Ívarr bera sik á stǫngum, því at hann mátti eigi
ganga, ok skyldi hann hafa ráð fyrir þeim, hvat sem þeir hǫfðusk at.

_____

_____

_____

_____

_____

_____

b. Kringla heimsins, sú er mannfólkit byggvir, er mjǫk vágskorin;
ganga hǫf stór ór útsjánum inn í jǫrðina. Er þat kunnigt, at haf
gengr frá Nǫrvasundum ok alt út til Jórsalalands.

_____

_____

_____

_____

Vocabulary

alt *adv* all the way
ausa (eyss; jós, jósu/jusu; ausinn) *vb* sprinkle, pour
bein *n* bone
beinlauss *adj* boneless
brjósk *n* cartilage
byggva = **byggja** (bygð-) *vb* inhabit
engi *indef pron* no one; (*pl*) none
fjórði *adj* fourth
fríðastr *superl of* **fríðr**
fríðr *adj* beautiful, handsome, fine
frœkn *adj* bold, daring, valiant
frœknustu *wk m pl of* frœknastr, *superl of* **frœkn**
fǫr *f* journey
haf *n* sea
harðr *adj* hard
hvert *adv* to where

Hvítserkr *m* Hvitserk ('White-Shirt') (*personal name*)
hǫf *pl of* **haf**
inn *adv* in, into
Ívarr *m* Ivar (*personal name*)
íþrótt (*pl* -ir) *f* skill, feat, accomplishment
jafningi (*pl* -jar) *m* equal, match
Jórsalaland *n* 'Jerusalem's Land', Israel (*place name*)
konar *gen sg of obs* ***konr** *m* kind, sort
kringla *f* disc, circle
langr *adj* long
mannfólk *n* mankind
mikill (*comp* meiri) *adj* big, large, great
meiri *comp adj* greater (*see* **mikill**)
Njáll *m* Njal (*personal name*)

nǫkkurr (*n* nǫkkut) *indef pron* some, somebody; (*n*) something

Nǫrvasund *n pl* Straits of Gibraltar (*place name*)

ráð *n* plan

Rǫgnvaldr *m* Rognvald (*personal name*)

sem *conj* [*w subjunct*] as if

serkr *m* shirt

skarpr *adj* sharp

skera (skerr; skar, skáru; skorinn) *vb* cut, carve, 'shear'

skulu (skal, skulu; skyldi) *vb* shall (necessity)

skyldi, skyldu (*inf* **skulu**) *vb* should

spekingr *m* wise man, sage

sund *n* sound, strait, channel

sveinn *m* boy, lad

sýn *f* sight, appearance

útsjár *m* ocean

vatn *n* water

vágr *m* bay

vágskorinn *adj* scored with bays

víss *adj* certain, sure

þegar *conj* as soon as

Phrases

alls konar of every kind, of all kinds

fríðastr sýnum most handsome, finest in appearane

nǫkkut hafask at undertake ('have at') something

hvat sem whatever

hvert sem (to) wherever

inn í into

því at because

Notes

_____

_____

_____

_____

_____

_____

_____

_____

_____

_____

_____

_____

_____

_____

_____

_____

LESSON 13

(1) Ór *Egils sǫgu Skalla-Grímssonar* (25. kap.)
(From the *Saga of Egil Skalla-Grimsson*, Chap. 25)

      prepared for   trip   before   chose
Skalla-Grímr bjósk til ferðar þeirar, er fyrr var frá sagt; hann valði

            servants   his (own)   neighbors   strongest
sér menn af heimamǫnnum **sínum** ok nábúum þá er váru **sterkastir**

in strength   boldest   of them   were at hand twelve   for
at afli   ok **hraustastir** þeira, er til váru.... Tólf váru þeir til

               strongest   many   shapeshifters
fararinnar,[24] ok **allir** inir sterkustu menn ok **margir** hamrammir.

(2) Ór *Egils sǫgu Skalla-Grímssonar* (25. kap.)
(From the *Saga of Egil Skalla-Grimsson*, Chap. 25)

  early   prepared   their (own)
Snemma um várit bjuggu þeir Kveld-Úlfr skip   sín;   þeir hǫfðu[25]

  great   naval force   prepared   *knǫrr* (merchant ships)
mikinn skipakost ok góðan, bjuggu tvá knǫrru   **mikla** ok

        each   thirty   able-bodied
hǫfðu á hvárum þrjá tigu manna, þeira er **liðfœrir** váru, ok

in addition   young people   ready   sailed
um fram konur ok ungmenni.... En er þeir váru **búnir**, þá sigldu þeir

  away   sailed islands   many
í brott; þeir sigldu í eyjar þær, er Sólundir heita; þat eru **margar**

islands
eyjar ok **stórar** ok svá mjǫk **vágskornar**, at þat er mælt, at þar

are likely few   [the] harbors
munu **fáir** menn vita **allar**   hafnir.

(3) Ór *Egils sǫgu Skalla-Grímssonar* (57. kap.)
(From the *Saga of Egil Skalla-Grimsson*, Chap. 57)

  turned   back   I call to witness
Þá snerisk Egill aptr ok mælti hátt: "Þat skírskota ek undir þik,

                            hear   case
Arinbjǫrn, ok þik, Þórðr, ok þá menn **alla** er nú heyra mál mitt, **lenda**

      lawmen   common people   forbid   lands
menn ok lǫgmenn ok alla   alþýðu,   at ek banna jarðir þær **allar** er

---

[24] Hint: *farar-innar* is the gen. sing. of fem. *fǫr* with the suffixed def. art. (11.4).
[25] Hint: see 6.5 for the conjugation of *hafa*.

has owned   rent   work   profits from [them]
átt hefr Bjǫrn Brynjólfsson, at byggja ok vinna ok **allra** gagna af

make use of forbid   all   other
at   neyta.   Banna ek þér, Berg-Ǫnundr, ok **ǫllum ǫðrum** mǫnnum,

foreign   native   noble   common
útlenzkum ok **innlenzkum, tignum** ok **ótignum,** en hverjum er þat

does I charge with breaking the law of the land wrath of the gods   trucebreaking
gjǫrir legg ek við lagabrot landsréttar,   goðagremi ok griðarof."

(4) Ór *Egils sǫgu Skalla-Grímssonar* (66. kap.)
(From the *Saga of Egil Skalla-Grimsson*, Chap. 66)

all   children   promising   oldest
Ǫll váru bǫrn Egils **mannvæn** ok vel viti **borin**; Þorgerðr var ellzt
barna Egils.

13.1. Strong Adjectives: Plural.

Strong pl. adj. endings correspond to those of the article (8.2):

	Strong Adj Endings				**Article**		
	Masc	**Fem**	**Neut**		**Masc**	**Fem**	**Neut**
Pl *nom*	-ir	-ar	–(ǫ)		inir	inar	in
acc	-a	-ar	–(ǫ)		ina	inar	in
dat	-um	-um	-um		inum	inum	inum
gen	-ra (2.1)	-ra (2.1)	-ra (2.1)		inna	inna	inna

- The nom. pl. masc. of strong adjectives ends in -*ir*: *allir, margir, sterkastir, hraustastir* (R.S. 13(1) above).

- The acc. pl. masc. ending is -*a*: *alla, lenda* (R.S. 13(3) above).

- The nom. and acc. pl. fem. ending of strong adjectives is -*ar*: *allar, margar, stórar* (R.S. 13(2) and (3) above).

- Like the nom. and acc. pl. of strong neut. nouns (12.3.3), the neut. nom./acc. pl. of strong adjectives has no ending (*mannvæn, borin*), and adjectives with the stem vowel -*a*- (f.ex., *allr*) show *a~ǫ* alternation: *ǫll* (R.S. 13(4) above).

- The dat. pl. ending of all strong adjectives is -*um*: *innlenzkum, útlenzkum* (R.S. 13(3) above), *sínum* (R.S. 13(1) above), *góðum*. As expected, adjectives with the stem vowel -*a*- show *a~ǫ* alternation: *ǫllum, ǫðrum* (R.S. 13(3) above).

- Disyllabic adjectives (3.5) lose the vowel of the second syllable when the ending is added: *tignum, ótignum* (= (ó-)*tigin-* + -*um*) (R.S. 13(3) above). Note, however, that *mannvænn* in R.S. 13(4) is not a disyllabic adj. but a compound of *mann-* plus the monosyllabic adj. *vænn* 'promising', so the vowel -*æ*- in this word is not lost when the ending -*um* is added: *mannvænum*.

- Recall (7.1) that the gen. pl. ending of all strong adjectives is -*ra* (with regular assimilation after -*l*, -*n*, -*s* according to the Special Stem Rules of 2.1): *allra, góðra, mikilla, vænna, fagra*.

13.2. Review Paradigms: Complete Endings of Strong Adjectives (See 9.7, 13.1).

	Masc	Fem	Neut
Sg *nom*	-r (see 2.1)	–(ǫ)	-t
acc	-an	-a	-t
dat	-um	-ri (see 2.1)	-u
gen	-s	-rar (see 2.1)	-s
Pl *nom*	-ir	-ar	–(ǫ)
acc	-a	-ar	–(ǫ)
dat	-um	-um	-um
gen	-ra (see 2.1)	-ra (see 2.1)	-ra (see 2.1)

The similarities of case forms noted in the list below can be seen in the chart above:

(a) nom. sing. fem. = nom. pl. neut. = acc. pl. neut.
(b) nom. sing. neut. = acc. sing. neut.
(c) acc. sing. fem. = acc. pl. masc.
(d) dat. sing. masc. = dat. pl. (all)
(e) gen. sing. masc. = gen. sing. neut.
(f) nom. pl. fem. = acc. pl. fem.

The same identities are present in the declension of the art. (8.2) and for the most part also in the declension of the dem. pronouns (12.1, with the exception of identity (a), where the nom. sing. fem. *sú* is different).

13.3. The Adjective *annarr* '(an)other, second'.

The adj. *annarr* means 'other, another, one of two'. It is also an ordinal number meaning 'second'. We have encountered several forms already: *annat* (R.S. 2), *annan* (R.S. 5), *annarr* (R.S. 7, 12(1)), and *ǫðrum* (R.S. 13(3)). The full declension is as follows:

	Masc	Fem	Neut
Sg *nom*	annarr	ǫnnur	annat
acc	annan	aðra	annat
dat	ǫðrum	annarri	ǫðru
gen	annars	annarrar	annars
Pl *nom*	aðrir	aðrar	ǫnnur
acc	aðra	aðrar	ǫnnur
dat	ǫðrum	ǫðrum	ǫðrum
gen	annarra	annarra	annarra

Annarr is always declined strong. The declension looks complicated, but most of the differences in the paradigm are the result of three regular sound changes:

- *u*-umlaut (11.2.2): *ǫnnur, ǫðrum, ǫðru*;
- loss of the vowel of the second syllable upon addition of an ending that begins with a vowel (3.5): *aðra, aðrir, ǫðrum*, etc.;
- the change of *-nn-* to *-ð-* when followed directly by *-r*: *aðra, aðrir, ǫðrum*, etc. This change also takes place in the nom. sing. of the noun *maðr* (stem *mann-*; see 2.6).

In the nom./acc. sing. neut., **annart* was simplified to *annat*. In the acc. sing. masc., **annaran* became *annan*.

13.4. Weak Adjectives: Plural.

The following passages contain examples of weak adjectives.

(1) Ór *Egils sǫgu Skalla-Grímssonar* (25. kap.)
(From the *Saga of Egil Skalla-Grimsson*, Chap. 25)

twelve   for   strongest   many
Tólf váru þeir til fararinnar, ok allir inir **sterkustu** menn ok margir
   shapeshifters
hamrammir.

(2) Ór *Ynglinga sǫgu* (29. kap.)
(From the *Saga of the Ynglings*, Chap. 29)

                 fond   of good (riding) horses
Aðils konungr var mjǫk kærr at góðhestum; hann átti ina **beztu**
hesta í þann tíma.

(3) Ór *Egils sǫgu Skalla-Grímssonar* (36. Kap.)
(From the *Saga of Egil Skalla-Grimsson*, Chap. 36)

                 friendly terms
Þórir var þá í inum **mestum** kærleikum við konung.

(4) Ór *Egils sǫgu Skalla-Grímssonar* (77. kap.)
(From the *Saga of Egil Skalla-Grimsson*, Chap. 77)

         west   the wood
Er þeir koma vestr af skóginum ok segja þessi tíðendi Nóregskonungi,
              expectation   harsh treatment
þá eigu vér[26] af honum   ván   inna **mestu** afarkosta.

---

[26] Recall from 8.4.3 that the *-m* of the 1 pl. ending may be dropped when the pron. follows; *eigu vér* (= *eigum vér*) is an example.

The accompanying chart gives the pl. endings of weak adjectives. They are the same for all genders (masc., fem., and neut.).

- Nom. and acc. pl. end in -*u*: *inir sterkustu menn, ina beztu hesta.*

- Dat. pl. ends in -*um*: *inum meistum kærleikum.*

- Gen. pl. ends in -*u*: *inna mestu afarkosta.*

Sg nom	-u
acc	-u
dat	-um
gen	-u

All the examples from the above readings are superlatives. Superlative adjectives are frequently preceded by the article and are declined weak in such instances. In the pl., they are far more frequent than other weak adjectives.

13.5. *u*-Umlaut: *a~u* Alternation.

Section 11.2.2 explained that *u*-umlaut changes the vowel -*a*- to -*ǫ*- in stressed syllables (the first syllable). This is called *a~ǫ* alternation. In unstressed syllables, the regular alternation is *a~u*. For example, *sterkastr* becomes *sterkustu* in the weak plural (*inir sterkustu menn*).

Both alternations (*a~ǫ* and *a~u*) can occur in the same word: f.ex., *vaskastr* bravest' becomes *vǫskustu* in the weak pl.: *allir inir vǫskustu menn.*

These two alternations are characteristic of weak verbs with vocalic link -*a*- when a personal ending in -*u*- is added. For example:

> *kalla* (-*að*-) – pres. *vér kǫllum,* past *vér kǫlluðum, þér kǫlluðuð, þeir kǫlluðu.*
>
> *elska* (-*að*-) – past *vér elskuðum, þér elskuðuð, þeir elskuðu.*

13.6. Review Paradigms: Complete Endings of Weak Adjectives and Nouns (See 9.2, 12.4, 13.4).

Weak nouns and adjectives have the same endings in the singular. There are differences between the weak and strong endings in the plural.

	Weak Adjectives			Weak Nouns		
	Masc	Fem	Neut	Masc	Fem	Neut
Sg nom	-i	-a	-a	-i	-a	-a
acc	-a	-u	-a	-a	-u	-a
dat	-a	-u	-a	-a	-u	-a
gen	-a	-u	-a	-a	-u	-a
Pl nom	-u	-u	-u	-ar	-ur	-u
acc	-u	-u	-u	-a	-ur	-u
dat	-um	-um	-um	-um	-um	-um
gen	-u	-u	-u	-a	-na	-na

13.7. Adjectives: Examples of Complete Declensions.

Section 6.7 introduced a list of common adjectives found in the sagas and gave the declensions in the singular. Here are full declensions in the singular and plural.

Using *stórr* 'big' as the model:

		Strong				Weak		
		Masc	Fem	Neut		Masc	Fem	Neut
Sg	nom	stór-r	stór	stór-t		stór-i	stór-a	stór-a
	acc	stór-an	stór-a	stór-t		stór-a	stór-u	stór-a
	dat	stór-um	stór-ri	stór-u		stór-a	stór-u	stór-a
	gen	stór-s	stór-rar	stór-s		stór-a	stór-u	stór-a
Pl	nom	stór-ir	stór-ar	stór		stór-u	stór-u	stór-u
	acc	stór-a	stór-ar	stór		stór-u	stór-u	stór-u
	dat	stór-um	stór-um	stór-um		stór-um	stór-um	stór-um
	gen	stór-ra	stór-ra	stór-ra		stór-u	stór-u	stór-u

Using *heill* 'healthy' as the model:

		Strong				Weak		
		Masc	Fem	Neut		Masc	Fem	Neut
Sg	nom	heil-l	heil	heil-t		heil-i	heil-a	heil-a
	acc	heil-an	heil-a	heil-t		heil-a	heil-u	heil-a
	dat	heil-um	heil-li	heil-u		heil-a	heil-u	heil-a
	gen	heil-s	heil-lar	heil-s		heil-a	heil-u	heil-a
Pl	nom	heil-ir	heil-ar	heil		heil-u	heil-u	heil-u
	acc	heil-a	heil-ar	heil		heil-u	heil-u	heil-u
	dat	heil-um	heil-um	heil-um		heil-um	heil-um	heil-um
	gen	heil-la	heil-la	heil-la		heil-u	heil-u	heil-u

Using *lítill* as the model:

		Strong				Weak		
		Masc	Fem	Neut		Masc	Fem	Neut
Sg	nom	lítil-l	lítil	líti-t		litl-i	litl-a	litl-a
	acc	litl-an	litl-a	líti-t		litl-a	litl-u	litl-a
	dat	litl-um	lítil-li	litl-u		litl-a	litl-u	litl-a
	gen	lítil-s	lítil-lar	lítil-s		litl-a	litl-u	litl-a
Pl	nom	litl-ir	litl-ar	lítil		litl-u	litl-u	litl-u
	acc	litl-a	litl-ar	lítil		litl-u	litl-u	litl-u
	dat	litl-um	litl-um	litl-um		litl-um	litl-um	litl-um
	gen	lítil-la	lítil-la	lítil-la		litl-u	litl-u	litl-u

EXERCISES

1. Fill in the appropriate endings and missing vowels.

   a. __ll b__rn Egils váru f__gr ok v__sk.

   b. Spjót___ (def.) váru sk__rp ok l__ng. (*spjót* neut. 'spear')

c. Hross___ (def.) váru sv__rt ok f__gr. (*hross* neut. 'horse')

d. Rewrite the previous sentence in the singular.

_____

2. Fill in the appropriate endings and missing vowels.

Skalla-Grím__ valð__ sér marg__ vask__ menn til ferð_____ (def.).
Þeir tók__ með sér m__rg__ góð__ hesta ok m__rg góð skip.
All___ vár__ þeir sterk___ ok stór___ ok __ll váru skip___ (def.) in
bezt__. Á __ll skip_____ (def.) váru m__rg spjót ok sverð. Þá fór__
þeir til m__rg__ land__.

3. Change from singular to plural or vice versa.

inn stóri maðr _____

ins vaska manns _____

inum góða manni _____

inir beztu menn _____

inum vǫskustum mǫnnum _____

ina sterku menn _____

it bezta spjót _____

inu góða hrossi _____

in fǫgru skip _____

inum góðum hestum _____

stórum hrossum _____

góðan mann _____

vǫskum manni _____

stórum hestum _____

fǫgr skip _____

langt sverð _____

góðs hests _____

4. Write the strong forms of the adjectives *stórr* and *langr* in the following cases:

	stórr	langr
a. nom. sing. fem. = nom./acc. pl. neut.:	_____	_____
b. nom./acc. sing. neut.:	_____	_____
c. acc. sing. fem. = acc. pl. masc.:	_____	_____
d. dat. sing. masc. = dat. pl. (all):	_____	_____
e. gen. sing. masc./neut.:	_____	_____
f. nom./acc. pl. fem.:	_____	_____

5. Write the adj. *annarr* in the following case forms:

    a. nom. sing. fem. = nom./acc. pl. neut.:   _____

    b. nom./acc. sing. neut.:   _____

    c. acc. sing. fem. = acc. pl. masc.:   _____

    d. dat. sing. masc. = dat. pl. (all):   _____

    e. gen. sing. masc./neut.:   _____

    f. nom./acc. pl. fem.:   _____

6. Conjugate the following weak verbs with vocalic link -*a*-.

	kalla	**svara**	**tala**
Pres *1sg*	ek _____	ek _____	ek _____
2sg	þú _____	þú _____	þú _____
3sg	hon _____	þat _____	hann _____
1pl	vér _____	vér _____	vér _____
2pl	þér _____	þér _____	þér _____
3pl	þær _____	þau _____	þeir _____
Past *1sg*	ek _____	ek _____	ek _____
2sg	þú _____	þú _____	þú _____
3sg	hon _____	þat _____	hann _____
1pl	vér _____	vér _____	vér _____
2pl	þér _____	þér _____	þér _____
3pl	þær _____	þau _____	þeir _____

7. Translate the Reading Selections.

    a. Skalla-Grímr bjósk til ferðar þeirar, er fyrr var frá sagt; hann valði sér menn af heimamǫnnum sínum ok nábúum þá er váru sterkastir at afli ok hraustastir þeira, er til váru.... Tólf váru þeir til fararinnar, ok allir inir sterkustu menn ok margir hamrammir.

_____

_____

_____

_____

_____

_____

b. Snemma um várit bjuggu þeir Kveld-Úlfr skip sín; þeir hǫfðu mikinn skipakost ok góðan, bjuggu tvá knǫrru mikla ok hǫfðu á hvárum þrjá tigu manna, þeira er liðfœrir váru, ok um fram konur ok ungmenni.... En er þeir váru búnir, þá sigldu þeir í brott; þeir sigldu í eyjar þær, er Sólundir heita; þat eru margar eyjar ok stórar ok svá mjǫk vágskornar, at þat er mælt, at þar munu fáir menn vita allar hafnir.

_____

_____

_____

_____

_____

_____

_____

_____

_____

_____

c. Þá snerisk Egill aptr ok mælti hátt: "Þat skírskota ek undir þik, Arinbjǫrn, ok þik, Þórðr, ok þá menn alla er nú heyra mál mitt, lenda menn ok lǫgmenn ok alla alþýðu, at ek banna jarðir þær allar er átt hefr Bjǫrn Brynjólfsson, at byggja ok vinna ok allra gagna af at neyta. Banna ek þér, Berg-Ǫnundr, ok ǫllum ǫðrum mǫnnum, útlenzkum ok innlenzkum, tignum ok ótignum, en hverjum er þat gjǫrir legg ek við lagabrot landsréttar, goðagremi ok griðarof."

_____

_____

_____

_____

_____

_____

_____

_____

_____

_____

d. Qll váru bǫrn Egils mannvæn ok vel viti borin; Þorgerðr var ellzt barna Egils.

_____

_____

_____

e. Aðils konungr var mjǫk kærr at góðhestum; hann átti ina beztu hesta í þann tíma.

_____

_____

_____

f. Þórir var þá í inum mestum kærleikum við konung.

_____

_____

g. Er þeir koma vestr af skóginum ok segja þessi tíðendi Nóregskonungi, þá eigu vér af honum ván inna mestu afarkosta.

_____

_____

_____

VOCABULARY

Aðils *m* Adils (*personal name*)
af *adv* from; off
afarkostir *m pl* harsh terms or treatment
afl *n* strength
allr (*pl n* ǫll, *dat* ǫllum) *adj* all
alþýða *f* the common people, the public
annarr (*pl dat* ǫðrum) *adj* other
aptr *adv* back
Arinbjǫrn *m* Arinbjorn (*personal name*)
átt (*inf* eiga) *ppart* owned (*sg*)
banna (-að-) *vb* forbid, prohibit
barn *n* child
bera (berr; bar, báru; borinn) *vb* carry, bear
berg *n* rock, boulder
brott *adv* í brott away (*motion*)
búa (býr; bjó, bjuggu; búinn) *vb* dwell, prepare; *refl* búask prepare (oneself)
búinn (*inf* búa) *ppart* prepared (*nom*

pl masc)
byggja (bygð-) *vb* inhabit, dwell; rent, let out
eiga (á, eigu; átti; áttr) *vb* own; have
ellztr *superl adj* oldest
ey (*pl* -jar) *f* island
fár *adj* few
ferð *f* trip, journey
fram *adv* forward
fyrr *adv* before
gagn *n* advantage, benefit, produce, revenue
gjǫrir *var of* gerir (*inf* gera) *vb* does
goðagremi *f* wrath of the gods
góðhestr *m* good (riding) horse
griðarof *n pl* breach of the peace, trucebreaking
hamrammr *adj* fierce, furious in battle (*lit.* 'shape-mighty'; used of warriors who 'changed shape', i.e., went berserk)
heimamaðr *m* servant
heyra (-ð-) *vb* hear

hraustr *adj* bold
hvárr *indef pron* each (of two)
hǫfn (*pl* hafnir) *f* harbor
innlenzkr *adj* native
knǫrr (*pl acc* knǫrru) *m* ship; merchant vessel
kærleikr *m* friendly terms
kærr *adj* dear
lagabrot *n* lawbreaking
landsréttr *m* law of the land
leggja (lagð-, lag(i)ðr/laginn) *vb* lay, place; set, fix, arrange
liðfœrr *adj* able-bodied
lǫgmaðr *m* lawman, lawyer
mannvænn *adj* promising
margr *adj* many
mál *n* (legal) case, matter
mikinn *acc sg masc of* **mikill**
munu (mun, munu; mundi) *vb* will, be likely
nábúi *m* neighbor
neyta (-tt-) *vb* [*w gen*] make use of
ótiginn *adj* not noble (of family), of common descent
sigla (-d-) *vb* sail
skipakostr *m* naval force
skírskota (-að-) *vb* refer to, appeal to

skógr *m* forest, woods
snemma *adv* early, soon
snerisk (*inf* **snúask**) *refl vb* turned (himself) (*sg*)
snúa (snýr; snøri/sneri; snúinn) *vb* turn; *refl* **snúask** turn oneself
Sólundir *pl* Solundir, islands off the west coast of Norway (*place name*)
stórskip *n* large ship
tiginn *adj* noble (of family)
tólf *num* twelve
ungmenni *n* young people, children
útlenzkr *adj* foreign
ván *f* expectation, prospect
velja (valð-) *vb* choose, select
vestr *adv* west, westwards
vinna (vinnr; vann, unnu; unninn) *vb* work; till, cultivate (land)
Ynglingar *m pl* line of early Swedish kings
þrír *num* three; **þrír tigir** *num* [*w gen*] thirty
þrjá *num* three (*masc acc of* **þrír**)
ǫðrum *dat pl of* **annarr**
ǫll *nom/acc pl neut of* **allr**
ǫllum *dat pl of* **allr**
Ǫnundr *m* Onund (*personal name*)

PHRASES

átt hefr = **hefr átt** has owned
banna jarðir at byggja ok vinna forbid lands to be rented and worked
búask til prepare (oneself) for
kærr at fond of
lagabrot landsréttar breaking the law of the land

leggja við accuse of, charge with, declare guilty of or subject to
sterkr at afli strong
um fram in addition
vera til exist, be at hand
skírskota ek undir þik I call you to witness

Notes

_____

_____

_____

_____

_____

_____

_____

LESSON 14

Ór *Ynglinga sǫgu* (3. Kap. 'Frá brœðrum Óðins')
(From the *Saga of the Ynglings*, Chap. 3 'About Odin's Brothers')

brothers   the one   the other   brothers

Óðinn átti tvá brœðr. Hét annarr Vé, en annarr Vílir. Þeir brœðr hans

ruled the realm   away

stýrðu ríkinu, þá er hann var í brottu. Þat var eitt sinn, þá er Óðinn

had traveled far   long stayed   to [the] gods [it] seemed

var farinn langt í brott ok hafði lengi dvalzk, at Ásum þótti

improbable his [returning] home   began brothers   divide

ørvænt hans heim. Þá tóku brœðr hans at skipta arfi hans, en

a little later

konu hans, Frigg, gengu þeir báðir at eiga. En litlu síðar kom Óðinn
heim. Tók hann þá við konu sinni.

14.1. Numerals.

The first four numerals are declined in Icelandic. Several examples of *einn* 'one', *tvá* 'two', and *þrír* 'three' have already occurred: acc. sing. masc. *einn* (R.S. 3.9, 4), nom. sing. neut. *eitt* (R.S. 7), acc. sing. neut. *eitt* (R.S. 14), dat. sing. neut. *einu* (R.S. 9); acc. pl. masc. *tvá* (R.S. 10, 13(2), 14); acc. pl. masc. *þrjá* (R.S. 13(2)).

Numerals decline similarly to strong adjectives:

	einn 'one'				**tveir 'two'**		
	Masc	**Fem**	**Neut**		**Masc**	**Fem**	**Neut**
nom	einn	ein	eitt		tveir	tvær	tvau
acc	einn	eina	eitt		tvá	tvær	tvau
dat	einum	einni	einu		tveim(r)	tveim(r)	tveim(r)
gen	eins	einnar	eins		tveggja	tveggja	tveggja

	þrír 'three'				**fjórir 'four'**		
	Masc	**Fem**	**Neut**		**Masc**	**Fem**	**Neut**
nom	þrír	þrjár	þrjú		fjórir	fjórar	fjǫgur
acc	þrjá	þrjár	þrjú		fjóra	fjórar	fjǫgur
dat	þrim(r)	þrim(r)	þrim(r)		fjórum	fjórum	fjórum
gen	þriggja	þriggja	þriggja		fjǫgurra	fjǫgurra	fjǫgurra

Einn is also used as an indef. pron. It means 'a, an, a certain one' in the singular and 'some' in the plural. The endings follow Special Stem Rule 2.1.1 (nom. sing. masc. *einn*, dat. sing. fem. *einni*, gen. sing. fem. *einnar*, gen. pl. *einna*).

	Masc	Fem	Neut
Pl *nom*	einir	einar	ein
acc	eina	einar	ein
dat	einum	einum	einum
gen	einna	einna	einna

The numerals above four are indeclinable. The numbers five through twenty are as follows.

5	fimm	9	níu	13	þrettán	17	sjautján
6	sex	10	tíu	14	fjórtán	18	átján
7	sjau	11	ellifu	15	fimmtán	19	nítján
8	átta	12	tólf	16	sextán	20	tuttugu

14.2. Verbs: Weak Verbs with Vowel Alternation.

It was noted in 5.6 that certain weak verbs have different vowels in the pres. and past stems. These verbs have a root consisting of a short vowel followed by a single consonant, and their infinitve has stem-final *-j-*: *kveðja, segja, velja, hyggja,*[27] *spyrja.*

The past stem of these verbs preserves the basic vowel, whereas the pres. stem and inf. show the effect of *i*-umlaut caused by the stem-final *-j-*.[28] This *-j-* no longer appears in the singular forms, but its effect continues in the umlauted stem vowel: *hann kveðr, hann velr; hann hyggr, hann spyrr.* The verb *segja* is exceptional in that *-i-* (from the original *-j-*) remains in the pres. forms (*ek segi, þú/hann segir*).

As explained (5.6), the most common vowel alternations between pres. and past are *-e-* ~ *-a-* and *-y-* ~ *-u-*:

Examples of *-e-* ~ *-a-* and *-y-* ~ *-u-* Vowel Alternations:

Pres	Past	Inf	3sg Pres	3sg Past
e	– a	at kveðja	hann kveðr	hann kvaddi
		at segja	hann segir	hann sagði
		at velja	hann velr	hann valði
y	– u	at hyggja	hann hyggr	hann hugði
		at spyrja	hann spyrr	hann spurði

14.3. Reflexive Possessive Adjective.

The poss. Pronouns 'his', 'her(s)', 'its', and 'their(s)' can be ambiguous in English, because these pronouns do not clarify whether the possessor

---

[27] The double *-gg-* of *hyggja* is a later development. The past tense *hugði* shows the basic stem *hug-* with a single *-g-*.

[28] This process is *j*-umlaut, which is parallel to *i*-umlaut (11.2.1). The sound **j** (like the **y** in the English words 'yes' and 'you') is similar to the sound **i**, but is pronounced more rapidly and functions as a consonant. It involves the same tongue position in the mouth as **i** (high and front), exerting the same umlauting influence on the stem vowel in the preceding syllable. It is common to consider *i*-umlaut and *j*-umlaut as the same process, "*i/j*-umlaut" or "front mutation".

is the same person as the subject of the sentence or is someone else. For example, in 'Thorolf greeted Eirik beside **his ship**', it is not possible to determine who owns the ship. Is it Thorolf's ship or is it Eirik's (or someone else's) ship?

Old Norse avoids this confusion by employing two ways to express possession in the 3rd person. On the one hand, if the possessive 'his', 'her', 'its', or 'their' refers back to the subject of the sentence or clause, then *sinn*, a special refl. poss. adj.[29] is used. One often translates *sinn* as 'his own', 'her own', 'its own', or 'their own'. On the other hand, when the possessive refers to persons or things other than the subject of the sentence, then the gen. pron. *hans*, *hennar*, *þess*, or *þeira* is used.

In the example of Thorolf greeting Eirik 'beside **his** ship', it would be *hjá skipi* **sínu** if it were Thorolf's own ship, but *hjá skipi* **hans** if it were someone else's (f.ex., Eirik's) ship.

This difference is also illustrated in this lesson's R.S. When Odin's brothers took his (Odin's) wife:

> *þeir gengu báðir at eiga konu* **hans**.

But when Odin took back his own wife:

> *Tók hann þá við konu* **sinni**.

The refl. poss. adj. *sinn* declines like the numeral *einn* (14.1):

	Masc	Fem	Neut
Sg *nom*	sinn	sín	sitt
acc	sinn	sína	sitt
dat	sínum	sinni	sínu
gen	síns	sinnar	síns
Pl *nom*	sínir	sínar	sín
acc	sína	sínar	sín
dat	sínum	sínum	sínum
gen	sinna	sinna	sinna

- Note that all vowels followed by only one *n* are long (accented).
- Several of these forms have been encountered in earlier reading selections: acc. sing. masc. *tók þá skjǫld* **sinn** (R.S. 10; NB: do not confuse this form with the neut. noun *sinn* 'time' which also appears in R.S. 10 and in R.S. 14); acc. sing. neut. *Bjǫrn hóf upp bónorð* **sitt** (R.S. 9); acc. pl. masc. *stórlyndr við* **sína** *menn* (R.S. 6), acc. pl. neut. *bjuggu þeir Kveld-Úlfr skip* **sín** (R.S. 13(2)); and dat. pl. masc. *grimmr* **sínum** *óvinum* (R.S. 6); *hann valði sér menn af heimamǫnnum* **sínum** (R.S. 13(1)).

---

[29] English has poss. pronouns, while Old Norse distinguishes the declinable poss. adj. *sinn* from the indeclinable gen. pronouns *hans*, *hennar*, etc.

The following passage has additional examples of the refl. poss. adj.

Ór *Egils sǫgu Skalla-Grímssonar* (59. Kap.)
(From the *Saga of Egil Skalla-Grimsson*, Chap. 59)

              sons   his   power   began
Haraldr inn hárfagri setti sonu **sína** til ríkis í Nóregi, þá er hann tók

 grow old   made   supreme king of sons   his
at eldask, gerði Eirík konung yfirkonung sona **sinna** allra, ok er

                 seventy (of) winters   delivered   hands
Haraldr hafði verit sjau tigu   vetra konungr, þá seldi hann í hendr

     son   his   kingdom
Eiríki syni **sínum**   ríki.

14.4. Declension of *sonr* in the Singular and Plural.

The declension of the masc. noun *sonr* is somewhat irregular (see R.S. 3, 6.6, 9, 14.3, 15). The chart below gives the singular and plural of *sonr*.

	Sing	**Pl**
nom	sonr	synir
acc	son	sonu (syni)
dat	syni	sonum
gen	sonar	sona

14.5. Suffixed article: Plural.

When suffixed to pl. forms in -*ar*, -*ir*, and -*r* (masc. and fem., nom. and acc.), the article loses its initial *i-*, in the same way that it does after forms ending in a vowel: *hestar* + *inir* = *hestarnir*, likewise *hlutirnir*, *hendrnir*.

When the dat. pl. art. *inum* is attached to a noun (ending in -*um*), the resultant ending -*uminum* is contracted to -*unum*: *skipunum*.

Since the detached article in the masc. dat. sing. is also *inum*, the sing. and pl. forms of masc. dat. nouns can be confused unless attention is paid to two points:

- the weak adj. and the noun forms are different:

  sing.: *af inum sterka hesti*
     pl.: *af inum sterkum hestum*

- the forms of the suffixed art. are different:

  sing.: *af hestinum*
     pl: *af hestunum*

14.6. Review Paradigms: Suffixed Art. in the Sing. and Pl.

The tables below summarize the suffixed article in all cases of the singular and plural. The strong nouns *hestr, staðr, fǫr, jǫrð, á,* and *skip,* and the weak nouns *goði, saga,* and *hjarta* have been used examples.

Strong Nouns:

	Masc		Fem			Neut
	'horse'	'place'	'journey'	'earth'	'river'	'ship'
Sg nom	hestr-inn	staðr-inn	fǫr-in	jǫrð-in	á-in	skip-it
acc	hest-inn	stað-inn	fǫr-ina	jǫrð-ina	á-na	skip-it
dat	hesti-num	stað-inum	fǫr-inni	jǫrðu-nni	á-nni	skipi-nu
gen	hests-ins	staðar-ins	farar-innar	jarðar-innar	ár-innar	skips-ins
Pl nom	hestar-nir	staðir-nir	farar-nar	jarðir-nar	ár-nar	skip-in
acc	hesta-na	staði-na	farar-nar	jarðir-nar	ár-nar	skip-in
dat	hestu-num	stǫðu-num	fǫru-num	jǫrðu-num	á-num	skipu-num
gen	hesta-nna	staða-nna	fara-nna	jarða-nna	á-nna	skipa-nna

Weak Nouns:

	Masc	Fem	Neut
	'chieftain'	'story'	'heart'
Sg nom	goði-nn	saga-n	hjarta-t
acc	goða-nn	sǫgu-na	hjarta-t
dat	goða-num	sǫgu-nni	hjarta-nu
gen	goða-ns	sǫgu-nnar	hjarta-ns
Pl nom	goðar-nir	sǫgur-nar	hjǫrtu-n
acc	goða-na	sǫgur-nar	hjǫrtu-n
dat	goðu-num	sǫgu-num	hjǫrtu-num
gen	goða-nna	sagna-nna	hjartna-nna

14.7. Suffixed Article: Contraction with Monosyllabic Strong Nouns Ending in a Vowel.

As mentioned earlier (4.8, 14.5), the article regularly contracts when suffixed to a noun ending in a vowel. The following reading selection contains an exception to that rule. The exception occurs when both the art. and the noun are monosyllabic, that is, both have just one syllable: f.ex., *á + -in = áin* ('the river'). When either the noun or the art. has more than one syllable (is polysyllabic), the normal rule comes into play and the art. loses its initial *i-*: acc. *á + ina = ána*; dat. *á + inni = ánni*; gen. *á + innar = ánnar.*

Ór *Njáls sǫgu* (146. Kap.)

(From *Njal's Saga*, Chap. 146)

rode   east   Arnarstakk's Heath
Riðu þeir Þorgeirr austr á Arnarstakksheiði.[30] Er nú ekki at segja frá

        before   came   Old Woman's Valley River
ferð þeira, fyrr en þeir kómu til Kerlingardalsár;[31] **áin** var mikil.

rode   along   horses   saddles   rode
Riðu þeir upp með **ánni**, því at þeir sá þar hross með sǫðlum. Riðu þeir

                    were sleeping dale   stood spears
þangat til ok sá, at menn   sváfu   í dœl nǫkkurri, ok stóðu spjót

        below   took the spears   carried [them]
þeira ofan frá þeim; þeir tóku spjótin ok báru   út á **ána**.

14.8. Kinship Terms in the Plural.

The small class of nouns consisting of family members (9.5) follows a distinct pattern in the pl. These nouns end in *-r* in the nom. and acc. pl. and have a stem-final *-r-* before the dat. pl. ending *-um* and the gen. pl. ending *-a*. The stem vowel shows *i*-umlaut throughout the plural.

The chart below gives both the singular and the plural.

	Masc		Fem		
	faðir	bróðir	móðir	systir	dóttir
Sg nom	faðir	bróðir	móðir	systir	dóttir
acc	fǫður	bróður	móður	systur	dóttur
dat	fǫður	bróður	móður	systur	dóttur
gen	fǫður	bróður	móður	systur	dóttur
Pl nom	feðr	brœðr	mœðr	systr	dœtr
acc	feðr	brœðr	mœðr	systr	dœtr
dat	feðrum	brœðrum	mœðrum	systrum	dœtrum
gen	feðra	brœðra	mœðra	systra	dœtra

EXERCISES

1. Fill in the appropriate endings.

   a. Hross___ gengu upp með á___ ok kona___ gekk hjá þeim. (all def.)

   b. Hross___ horfði á á___ ok gekk þá til á_____. (all def.)

---

[30] *Arnarstakksheiðr* is the heath beside a mountain in the south of Iceland. The mountain is named *Arnarstakkr* ('Eagle's Haystack') because it is shaped like a haystack. *Arnarstakkr* is a compound of *ǫrn* (masc.) 'eagle', gen. *arnar* + *stakkr* (masc.) 'haystack'.

[31] *Kerlingardalsár* (*Kerling-ar* + *dal-s* + *ár*) literally means 'Old woman's valley's river' (that is, 'River of the Old Woman's Valley'). It is in the gen. case because it follows the prep. *til*. The last element of this compound is *ár* (= *á* + *-ar*) 'of a river', showing the contraction (loss of *-a-*) in the gen. sing. fem. ending *-ar* (see the last bullet point under 9.3).

   c. Á___ (def.) var fegrst um vár___.

   d. Spjót___ stóðu hjá búð____ (sg.) ok skip___ var í á___. (all def.)

   e. Repeat sentence **d**, making the subject of the first clause singular and the subject of the second clause plural.

---

2. Supply a poss. pron. (*hans*) or refl. poss. adj. (*sinn*) in the appropriate case.

   a. Egill fór til Englands með mǫnnum _____. Hann fór aptr til Nóregs með fǫður _____.

   b. Bjǫrn náði fundi Þóris. Hann hóf upp bónorð _____ ok bað systur _____.

   c. Þórir vildi ekki gefa honum systur _____.

   d. Óðinn stýrði ríki _____, þá er hann var heima, en brœðr _____ stýrðu ríki _____, þá er hann var i brottu.

3. Write the infinitive of the weak verbs with vowel shift of which the 3 sing. past forms are:

Ex: barði 'struck' _*berja*___   muldi 'crushed' ___*mylja*___

   dvalði 'delayed' _____   smurði 'anointed' _____

   flutti 'conveyed' _____   tamdi 'tamed'   _____

   hulði 'hid'   _____   vakti 'wakened'   _____

   hvatti 'whetted' _____   valði 'chose'   _____

   lamdi 'beat'   _____   þusti 'rushed'   _____

4. Change the nouns in **bold type** from singular to plural, and make any other necessary changes.

   a. **Sonr** konungs stýrði ríkinu eptir hann.

---

   b. Hann heyrði tíðendi um dauða **bróður** síns. (*dauði* masc. 'death')

---

   c. Nǫrvi átti **dóttur**, svǫrt ok døkk.

---

   d. Þá var Bjarni heima með **systur** sinni.

---

5. Translate the Reading Selections.

   a. Óðinn átti tvá brœðr. Hét annarr Vé, en annarr Vílir. Þeir brœðr hans stýrðu ríkinu, þá er hann var í brottu. Þat var eitt sinn, þá er Óðinn var farinn langt í brott ok hafði lengi dvalzk, at Ásum þótti ørvænt hans heim. Þá tóku brœðr hans at skipta arfi hans, en konu hans, Frigg, gengu þeir báðir at eiga. En litlu síðar kom Óðinn heim. Tók hann þá við konu sinni.

_____

_____

_____

_____

_____

_____

_____

_____

_____

_____

b. Haraldr inn hárfagri setti sonu sína til ríkis í Nóregi, þá er hann tók at eldask, gerði Eirík konung yfirkonung sona sinna allra, ok er Haraldr hafði verit sjau tigu vetra konungr, þá seldi hann í hendr Eiríki syni sínum ríki.

_____

_____

_____

_____

_____

_____

c. Riðu þeir Þorgeirr austr á Arnarstakksheiði. Er nú ekki at segja frá ferð þeira, fyrr en þeir kómu til Kerlingardalsár; áin var mikil. Riðu þeir upp með ánni, því at þeir sá þar hross með sǫðlum. Riðu þeir þangat til ok sá, at menn sváfu í dœl nǫkkurri, ok stóðu spjót þeira ofan frá þeim; þeir tóku spjótin ok báru út á ána.

_____

_____

_____

_____

_____

_____

_____

_____

_____

VOCABULARY

Arnarstakkr *m* 'Eagle's Haystack', a mountain in the south of Iceland (*place name*)
Arnarstakksheiðr *f* Heath of Arnarstakkr (*place name*)
austr *adv* east
átján *num* eighteen
átta *num* eight
brottu *adv* **í brottu** away (*location*)
dvelja (dvalð-) *vb* delay, defer; *refl* **dveljask** stay
dœl *f* dale, hollow
ellifu *num* eleven
fimm *num* five
fimmtán *num* fifteen
fjórtán *num* fourteen
Frigg *f* Frigg, wife of Odin (*mythological name*)
heiðr *f* heath
hross *n* horse
hvetja (hvatt-) *vb* whet, sharpen
hylja (hulð-) *vb* hide, cover
Kerlingardalsá *f* 'River of the Old Woman's Valley' (*place name*)
langt *adv* far
lemja (lamd-) *vb* beat, thrash
lengi *adv* long, a long time
litlu *adv* a little
nítján *num* nineteen
níu *num* nine
ríða (ríðr; reið, riðu; riðinn) *vb* ride

ríki (-j-) *n* realm, kingdom; power
selja (-d-) *vb* deliver, hand over
sex *num* six
sextán *num* sixteen
síð *adv* late
síðar *comp adv* (*see* **síð**) later
sjau *num* seven; **sjau tigir** *num* [*w gen*] seventy
sjautján *num* seventeen
smyrja (smurð-) *vb* anoint, 'smear'
sofa (sefr; svaf, sváfu; sofinn) *vb* sleep
spjót *n* spear
stakkr *m* haystack
stýra (-ð-) *vb* [*w dat*] rule, govern
sváfu (*inf* **sofa**) *vb* were sleeping
sǫðull *m* saddle
taka (tekr; tók, tóku; tekinn) *vb* take; [*w inf*] begin to do
temja (tamd-) *vb* tame
tíu *num* ten
tuttugu *num* twenty
Vé *m* Ve, brother of Odin (*mythological name*)
Vílir *m* Vili, brother of Odin (*mythological name*)
yfirkonungr *m* supreme king
þrettán *num* thirteen
þykkja (þótt-) *vb* seem
þysja (þust-) *vb* rush
ǫrn (*gen* arnar) *m* eagle

PHRASES

annarr ... annarr ... the one ... the other ...
fyrr en before
litlu síðar a little later
ofan frá below

setja til ríkis put in power
selja í hendr turn over (to)
sjau tigu for seventy years (lit. winters)
upp með up along

Notes

_____

_____

_____

_____

_____

LESSON 15

Ór *Egils sǫgu Skalla-Grímssonar* (81. kap.)
(From the *Saga of Egil Skalla-Grimsson*, Chap. 81)

then   (whether)   Seer here
Síðan stóð Egill upp ok mælti hátt: "Hvárt er Ǫnundr sjóni hér í

the assembly slope
þingbrekkunni?"

        am   glad
Ǫnundr kvazk þar vera, – "ek em feginn orðinn, Egill, er þú ert

                                            ('stands between')
        everything improve concerning   here   impedes
kominn; mun þat allt bœta til um þat, er hér stendr milli

máls manna."

                                           ('seeks with suits')
(whether) are you responsible for this that   your   prosecutes
"Hvárt ræðr þú því, er Steinarr, sonr þinn, sœkir sǫkum

                    drawn   crowd
Þorstein, son minn, ok hefir dregit saman fjǫlmenni, til þess at gera at

       outlaw
Þorstein urðarmanni?"

                                ('unreconciled')
    cause   that   at odds   have
"Því veld ek eigi," segir Ǫnundr, "er þeir eru ósáttir, hefi ek þar

('laid to')
said   words   asked   be reconciled
lagt til mǫrg orð ok beðit Steinar sættask við Þorstein...."

quickly   clear   whether
"Brátt mun þat," segir Egill, "ljóst verða, hvárt þú mælir þetta af

                            ('that')
earnestness   insincerity   think the latter less   remember
alvǫru eða hégóma, þótt ek ætla þat síðr vera munu. Man ek

                      ('would seem')
those   to each (of the two) of us   would have seemed unlikely   we (two)
þá daga, at hvárumtveggja okkrum mundi þykkja ólíkligt, at vit

would   prosecute each other   restrain   our
myndim sǫkum sœkjask eða stilla eigi sonu okkra, at þeir

('travel not with')
   not commit   folly   such   hear   here is in prospect   seems to me
fari eigi með fíflsku slíkri, sem ek heyri, at hér horfisk til. Sýnisk mér

   counsel   while   we (two)   are   alive   near situated   dispute
þat ráð, meðan vit erum á lífi ok svá nær staddir deilu þeira, at

('under us')   ('set down')
we (two)   take   in our hands   settle [it]   let
vit   takim mál þetta undir okkr ok setim niðr, en látim eigi þá

('incite')
drive   sons   our   pack-horses
Tungu-Odd ok Einar   etja   saman sonum okkrum sem kapalhestum."

15.1. Preterite-Present Verbs: Present Tense.

As mentioned earlier (3.7), modial auxiliary verbs are helping verbs ('can', 'may', 'shall', 'will', etc.) that are used with an infinitive to express characteristics such as ability, possibility, necessity, intention, etc. Most modal auxiliaries (with the major exceptions of *hafa*, *vera*, and *vilja*) belong to a small but important class of verbs known as **preterite presents**.

Preterite presents are so called because their present tense is formed like the preterite (past tense)[32] of strong verbs. Pret.-pres. endings are identical to the past-tense endings of strong verbs (shown at right; see also 6.2, 8.4, 9.9). Also like strong verbs, pret.-pres. verbs often have different stem vowels in sing. and pl. pres. (6.4): *þat má, þeir megu; þat skal, þeir skulu*, etc.

1sg	–
2sg	-t
3sg	–
1pl	-um
2pl	-uð
3pl	-u

Below are the three most common pret.-pres. auxiliaries, conjugated in the pres. tense: *mega* ('be able to, may'), *munu* ('will, shall [*futurity*]; be likely'), and *skulu* ('shall [*necessity*], must'):

Pres. Tense of Pret.-Pres. Verbs (Modal Auxiliaries)

	mega	munu	skulu
1sg	má	mun	skal
2sg	mátt	munt	skalt
3sg	má	mun	skal
1pl	megum	munum	skulum
2pl	meguð	munuð	skuluð
3pl	megu	munu	skulu

- Several examples have appeared in the readings:
  - *þú mátt* (R.S. 7), *þat má* (R.S. 11), both from *mega*;
  - *muntu* (R.S. 11) (= *munt þú*, 10.1.1), *þat mun* (R.S. 10, 15), *fáir menn munu* (R.S. 13(2)), all from *munu*.

- *Munu* and *skulu* are unique in that their infinitives end in -*u* instead of -*a*. In these pret.-pres. verbs, the 3 pl. pres. is the same as the inf.: *at munu* (R.S. 15) – *þeir munu* (R.S. 13(2)); *at skulu* – *þeir skulu*.

---

[32] Preterite is from the Latin word *præteritum* meaning 'past'. It is used grammatically to decribe a simple past tense such as *tók* ('took') as distinct from a perf. tense such as *hefir tekit* ('has taken') and *hafði tekit* ('had taken').

- In most other pret.-pres. verbs (with the exception of *muna*, see 15.3), the 3 pl. pres. is different from the inf.: *at kunna* (R.S. 11) – *þeir kunnu*; *at mega* – *þeir megu* (R.S. 16 below).
- When the 2 sing. ending -*t* is added to a stem ending in a vowel, it is doubled: *mátt*.

In addition to the modal auxiliaries, there are a few other pret.-pres. verbs. We have already seen *muna* 'remember': *ek man* (R.S. 15); and *vita* 'know': *ek veit* (R.S. 11). Other common examples are *eiga* 'own, be married to', *kunna* 'know; be able', and *þurfa* 'need'. These verbs are conjugated as follows:

Pres. Tense of Pret.-Pres. Verbs

	eiga	kunna	muna	vita	þurfa
1sg	á	kann	man	veit	þarf
2sg	átt	kannt	mant	veizt	þarft
3sg	á	kann	man	veit	þarf
1pl	eigum	kunnum	munum	vitum	þurfum
2pl	eiguð	kunnuð	munið	vituð	þurfuð
3pl	eigu	kunnu	muna	vitu	þurfu

15.2. *Munu* 'will, shall, be likely' vs. *muna* 'remember'.

The modal auxiliary verb *munu* 'will, shall, be likely (expressing futurity or probability)' can be confused with the verb *muna* 'to remember' (f.ex., *ek man* R.S. 15). In addition to having different infinitives, these two verbs are distinguishable in several other ways:

- *Munu* has the root vowel -*u*- in the pres. sing. (*ek mun* 'I will'), while *muna* has the vowel -*a*- (*ek man* 'I remember').
- *Munu* has past endings in the pres. pl. (*munum, munuð, munu*), whereas *muna* has normal pres. endings (*munum, munið, muna*). Only the 1 pl. *munum* is the same in both verbs.
- Because *munu* is a modal auxiliary, it is regularly accompanied by an infinitive: *fáir menn munu **vita*** 'few men are likely **to know**' (R.S. 13(2)), *brátt mun þat ljóst **verða*** 'that will quickly **become** clear' (R.S. 15).

15.3. Preterite-Present Verbs: Past Tense.

Preterite-present verbs in the past tense have the same endings as weak verbs in the past tense (shown at right; see also 5.5, 9.9): 3 sing. *átti* (R.S. 3.9, 6, 6.6, 8.1(1), 9.6(2), 13.4(2), 14), *mátti* (R.S 12(1)) *mundi* (R.S. 15); 3 pl. *máttu* (R.S 12(1)). In addition, the past stem usually has a dental suffix like weak verbs (see 5.3.2): *átt-*, *mátt-*, *mund-*.

1sg	-a
2sg	-ir
3sg	-i
1pl	-um
2pl	-uð
3pl	-u

Here is the past tense of the seven most common pret.-pres. verbs (see 15.1 for the pres.):

Past Tense of Pret.-Pres. Verbs

	mega	munu	skulu
1sg	mátta	munda	skylda
2sg	máttir	mundir	skyldir
3sg	mátti	mundi	skyldi
1pl	máttum	mundum	skyldum
2pl	máttuð	munduð	skylduð
3pl	máttu	mundu	skyldu

	eiga	kunna	muna	vita	þurfa
1sg	átta	kunna	munda	vissa	þurfta
2sg	áttir	kunnir	mundir	vissir	þurftir
3sg	átti	kunni	mundi	vissi	þurfti
1pl	áttum	kunnum	mundum	vissum	þurftum
2pl	áttuð	kunnuð	mundið	vissuð	þurftuð
3pl	áttu	kunnu	munda	vissu	þurftu

- *Kunna* 'know; be able' and *vita* 'know' have distinctive past-tense stems: *kunn-* and *viss-*. The expected dental suffix has assimilated to the final consonant of the stem.

- *Kunna* has the same forms in the pres. pl. and past pl.

- *Munu* and *muna* are identical in the past sing. and 1 pl., but differ in the 2 pl. and 3 pl. forms.

- Two other pret.-pres. verbs are *kná* 'know how, be able', which follows the conjugation of *mega*, and *unna* 'love', which follows the congjuagtion of *kunna*.

15.4. Verbs: More on *vera*.

In the pres. tense, *vera* conjugates as a pret.-pres. verb. The strong past endings are added to the stem *er-*, except in the 1st person where *em* is used.

	Pres	Past
1sg	em	var
2sg	er-**t**	var-**t**
3sg	er	var
1pl	er-**um**	vár-**um**
2pl	er-**uð**	vár-**uð**
3pl	er-**u**	vár-**u**

In the past tense, *vera* conjugates as a strong verb, with regular strong past endings added to the stems *var-* (sing.) and *vár-* (pl.). Because of this, the sing. and pl. of *vera* employ the same endings but the stems are different.

15.5. Verbs: Present Subjunctive (See Also 8.5, 8.6).

The pres. subjunct. is characterized by the presence of *-i-* in all endings except the 1 sing. (which ends in *-a*). This *-i-* in the ending does not cause *i*-umlaut (11.2.1).

1sg	-a
2sg	-ir
3sg	-i
1pl	-im
2pl	-ið
3pl	-i

With *fara* and *taka* as examples, we have seen: *hann fari* (R.S. 8), *þeir fari*, *vit takim* (both in R.S. 15). Note that the 3 sing. and 3 pl. forms are identical (*hann fari*, *þeir fari*).

Pres. Subjunct. of *fara* and *taka*

	fara	taka
1sg	fara	taka
2sg	farir	takir
3sg	fari	taki
1pl	farim	takim
2pl	farið	takið
3pl	fari	taki

Other examples are: *hann siti* (R.S. 8), *vit látim* (R.S. 15), *þú eigir*, *vér etim*, *vér gerim*, *þér ráðið*, *þér gerið* (all in R.S. 16 below).

15.6. Verbs: Impersonal Constructions Expressing Opinion or Belief.

Icelandic employs several impersonal constructions to express opinion or belief. These constructions consist of a verb in the 3 sing. plus a dat. pron., and are equivalent to the English expressions 'it appears to me' and 'it seems to me'.

Often the verb is reflexive: *virðisk mér* 'it seems to me' (R.S. 11), from *virðask*; *sýnisk mér* 'it appears to me' (R.S. 15), from *sýnask*. The non-refl. verb *þykkja* is also common: *Ásum þótti* 'it seemed to the Æsir' (R.S. 14), *hvárumtveggja okkrum mundi þykkja* 'it would have seemed to each of us' (R.S. 15). Old English possessed a parallel construction which survived into Shakespearean times as 'methinks, methought'.

These expressions do not mean 'I think, I thought', but 'to me it seems, to me it seemed' (pres. and past). Because they are impersonal expressions ('[it] seems', '[it] appears'), the verb is in the 3 sing. and the pronoun is usually omitted; f.ex.:

> *Ásum þótti* '[it] seemed to the Æsir' (R.S. 14).

Sometimes the neut. pron. *þat* 'it' accompanies the verb; f.ex.:

> *óráðligt sýnisk mér* **þat** '**it** seems inadvisable to me' (from *Fóstbrœðra saga*, ch. 1).

In this example, the presence of *þat* implies a certain sense of emphasis, and one could also translate using 'that'.

In Old Icelandic, verbs in dependent clauses that follow these impersonal constructions are in the subjunctive; f.ex.:

> **Sýnisk mér** *þat ráð … at vit* **takim** *mál þetta undir okkr ok* **setim** *niðr, en* **látim** *eigi þá Tungu-Odd ok Einar etja saman sonum okkrum sem kapalhestum* (R.S. 15).

EXERCISES

1. Conjugate the following pret.-pres. verbs in the pres. and past tenses.

	eiga	mega	skulu	vita
Pres 1sg	_____	_____	_____	_____
2sg	_____	_____	_____	_____
3sg	_____	_____	_____	_____
1pl	_____	_____	_____	_____
2pl	_____	_____	_____	_____
3pl	_____	_____	_____	_____
Past 1sg	_____	_____	_____	_____
2sg	_____	_____	_____	_____
3sg	_____	_____	_____	_____
1pl	_____	_____	_____	_____
2pl	_____	_____	_____	_____
3pl	_____	_____	_____	_____

2. Identify whether the following phrases contain the verb *munu* 'will, shall, be likely' or *muna* 'remember'.

Ex.: þér munið __*muna*__

    a. ek mun _____   **c.** þeir muna _____

    b. þú mant _____   **d.** þér munduð _____

e. þau mundu _____   **f.** þær munda _____

g. Engi maðr mundi þá fyrri daga. _____

h. Engi maðr mundi þurfa at berjask. _____

i. Translate sentences **g** and **h**.

g. _____

h. _____

3. Supply the correct form of the pronoun, noun, or name in parentheses.

a. (þú) _____ sýnisk   **e.** (hann) _____ þótti

b. (konungr) _____ þótti   **f.** (vér) _____ mundi þykkja

c. sýndisk (Bjǫrn) _____   **g.** (menn) _____ þykkir

d. (Gísli) _____ virðisk   **h.** virðisk (þeir) _____

4. Give the pres. subjunct. form of the verb in parentheses.

Ex.: Sýnisk Þórólfi at Eiríkr (hyggja) _**hyggi**_ vandliga at skipinu.

a. Mér sýnisk, konungsson, at þú (hyggja) _____ vandliga at skipinu.

b. Svá virðisk yðr sem ek (vilja) _____ vera yfirmaðr yðarr?

c. Ásum þykkir ørvænt at Óðinn _____ heim koma.

d. Agli þykkir at Steinarr (fara) _____ með fíflsku. (NB: *Agli*, dat. of *Egill*)

e. Agli þykkir at Steinarr ok Þorsteinn (fara) _____ með fíflsku.

5. Translate the Reading Selection.

Síðan stóð Egill upp ok mælti hátt: "Hvárt er Ǫnundr sjóni hér í þingbrekkunni?"

Ǫnundr kvazk þar vera, – "ek em feginn orðinn, Egill, er þú ert kominn; mun þat allt bœta til um þat, er hér stendr milli máls manna."

"Hvárt ræðr þú því, er Steinarr, sonr þinn, sœkir sǫkum Þorstein, son minn, ok hefir dregit saman fjǫlmenni, til þess at gera at Þorstein urðarmanni?"

"Því veld ek eigi," segir Ǫnundr, "er þeir eru ósáttir, hefi ek þar lagt til mǫrg orð ok beðit Steinar sættask við Þorstein...."

_____

_____

_____

_____

_____

_____

_____

"Brátt mun þat," segir Egill, "ljóst verða, hvárt þú mælir þetta af alvǫru eða hégóma, þótt ek ætla þat síðr vera munu. Man ek þá daga, at hvárumtveggja okkrum mundi þykkja ólíkligt, at vit myndim sǫkum sœkjask eða stilla eigi sonu okkra, at þeir fari eigi með fíflsku slikri, sem ek heyri, at hér horfisk til. Sýnisk mér þat ráð, meðan vit erum á lífi ok svá nær staddir deilu þeira, at vit takim mál þetta undir okkr ok setim niðr, en látim eigi þá Tungu-Odd ok Einar etja saman sonum okkrum sem kapalhestum."

Vocabulary

alvara *f* earnestness
beðit *ppart of* **biðja**
biðja (biðr; bað, báðu; beðinn) *vb* ask
brátt *adv* quickly
bœta (-tt-) *vb* better, improve
brekka *f* slope
deila *f* dispute
draga (dregr; dró, drógu; dreginn) *vb* pull, draw
etja (att-) *vb* [*w dat*] incite, egg on; make (horses) fight

feginn *adj* happy, glad, pleased
fíflska *f* folly, foolishness
fjǫlmenni *n* crowd
hégómi *m* insincerity
hér *adv* here
horfa (-ð-) *vb* look
hvárrtveggja *indef pron* each (of two)
hvárt *conj* whether (often used to introduce a yes/no question)
kapalhestr *m* packhorse
leggja (lagð-) *vb* lay

láta (lætr; lét, létu; látinn) *vb* let, allow

líf *n* life

ljóss *adj* clear

meðan *conj* while

milli *prep* [*w gen*] between

muna (man, muna; mundi; munaðr) *vb* remember

munu (mun, munu; mundi) *vb* will, shall (*futurity*), be likely

myndim (*inf* **munu**) *vb* (we) would, should (*1pl past subjunct*)

nær *adv* near, nearly

okkarr *poss adj* our (two)

okkr *pron* us (two) (*acc of* vit)

orð *n* word

ólíkligr *adj* unlikely

ósáttr *adj* unreconciled, at odds

ráð *n* counsel, advice

ráða (ræðr; réð, réðu; ráðinn) *vb* [*w dat*] counsel, advise; plan, arrange

síðan *adv* then, afterwards

síðr *comp adv* less

sjóni *m* 'The Seer' (*nickname*)

skulu (skal, skulu; skyldi) *vb* shall (necessity)

slíkr *adj* such

staddr *adj* placed, situated

Steinarr *m* Steinar (*personal name*)

stilla (-lt-) *vb* restrain, calm, still

sýnask (-d-) *refl vb* [*w dat*] appear, seem (*impers*)

sættask (-tt-) *refl vb* become reconciled

sœkja (sótt-) *vb* seek

sǫk *f* lawsuit

Tungu-Oddr *m* Tungu-Odd (*personal name*)

urðarmaðr *m* outlaw

valda (veldr; olli, ollu; valdit) *vb* [*w dat*] cause

vit *pron* we (two)

þingbrekka *f* slope on which assembly meetings were held

ætla (-að-) *vb* think

PHRASES

á lifi alive

fara með fíflsku commit folly

horfask til be in prospect

hvárrtveggja okkarr each of (the two of) us

hvárt ræðr þú því are you responsible for this

leggja til orð say

setja niðr settle (a dispute)

standa milli separate, set at odds

sýnisk mér it seems to me

sættask við be reconciled with

sœkja sǫkum prosecute

taka undir sik take charge of

þótt ek ætla þat síðr mun vera although I think that is less likely

Notes

_____

_____

_____

_____

_____

_____

_____

_____

_____

LESSON 16

Ór *Njáls sǫgu* (58. kap.)
(From *Njal's Saga*, Chap. 58)

Ríða þeir brœðr nú til Hlíðarenda. Gunnarr var heima ok gekk út;

welcome
Kolskeggr gekk út með honum ok Hjǫrtr, bróðir þeira, ok fagna þeim

intended
vel ok spurðu, hvert þeir ætlaði at fara.

farther — *(to) us* — *own*
"Eigi lengra," segja þeir; "oss er sagt, at þú eigir hest góðan, ok vilju

we offer — *horse-fight*
vér bjóða þér hestaat."

('go, spread')
small — *can* — *be told*
Gunnarr svarar: "Litlar sǫgur megu ganga frá hesti mínum; hann

unproved in all respects
er ungr ok óreyndr at ǫllu."

opportunity — *grant* — *Hildigunn supposed this*
"Kost munt þú láta at etja," segja þeir, "ok gat þess til Hildigunnr

surmised this — *would [be] proud of*
"Hildigunnr gat þess til," segja þeir, "at þú myndir góðr af hestinum."

why spoke you
"Hví tǫluðuð þér um þat?" segir Gunnarr.

no one would dare
"Þeir menn váru," segja þeir, "er mæltu, at engi myndi þora at etja

our
við várn hest."

dare — *maliciously*
"Þora mun ek at etja," segir Gunnarr, "en gráliga þykki mér þetta
mælt."

('intend')
we — *agree*
"Skulu vér til þess ætla þá?" segja þeir.

(to) you — *your* — *prevail in*
"Þá mun yðr fǫr yður þykkja bezt," segir Gunnarr, "ef þér ráðið

this — *ask (of) you* — *we*
þessu, en þó vil ek þess biðja yðr, at vér etim svá hestunum, at vér

('make to others pleasure')
entertain others — *(to) us no trouble* — *you* — *no*
gerim ǫðrum gaman, en oss engi vandræði ok þér gerið mér enga

('[it] is not to be helped but I')

shame   you   me   I will be forced to

skǫmm. En ef þér gerið til mín sem til annarra, þá er eigi ráðit, nema ek

('bend   it   to you')

  deal with you   you   hard   bear up

sveigja þat at yðr, at yðr mun þykkja hart undir at búa. Mun ek þar

                    ('before')
                    first

eptir gera, sem þér gerið fyrir."

                    ('how to them [it] had gone')
                    how they had fared

  Ríða þeir þá heim. Spurði Starkaðr at, hversu þeim hefði farizk.

   said   promised

Þeir sǫgðu, at Gunnarr gerði góða ferð þeira; – "hann   hét   at etja

             we determined when   horse-fight should   it appeared

hesti sínum, ok kváðu vér á, nær þat hestavíg skyldi vera. Fannsk þat á

in all   to be inferior to us   he was evasive

í ǫllu, at honum þótti sik   skorta   við oss, ok bazk hann undan."

        often   appear   slow to stir up

  "Þat mun opt á finnask," segir Hildigunnr, "at Gunnarr er seinþreyttr

     trouble   hard to handle   can not   escape

til vandræða, en harðdrœgr, ef hann má eigi undan komask."

16.1. Verbs: Past Subjunctive.

The past subjunct. endings are identical to the pres. subjunct. endings (15.5), but the stems are different. For example, earlier reading selections have shown the following past subjunctives:

1sg	-a
2sg	-ir
3sg	-i
1pl	-im
2pl	-ið
3pl	-i

> *hann væri* (R.S. 3.9, 8, 10, 12(1))
> þeir ætlaði, þat hefði (R.S. 16)
> *hann myndi* (R.S. 11, 16), *þú myndir* (R.S. 16), *vit myndim* (R.S. 15)

Formation of the Past Subjunctive Stem.

Inf		Past indic		Past subjunct
kalla	–	kallað-	–	hann/þeir kallaði
hafa	–	hafð-	–	hann/þeir hefði
vera	–	þeir váru	–	hann/þeir væri

The past subjunct. is characterized by *i*-umlaut of the stem vowel in all verbs except weak verbs with vocalic link -*a*- (5.3.1).

- In these weak verbs with vocalic link -*a*-, the past subjunct. stem is the same as the past indic.: f.ex., *kallað*-.

- In the remaining weak verbs, the past subjunct. employs the stem of the past indicative with *i*-umlaut where applicable (11.2.1): f.ex., past indic. *hafð-* → past subjunct. *hefð-*.

- In strong verbs, the past subjunct. stem is based on the 3 pl. past indic. stem with *i*-umlaut where applicable: f.ex., 3 pl. past *vár-u* → past subjunct. *vær-*.

The same stem vowel occurs throughout the entire past subjunct.: *hann væri, þeir væri* (vs. *hann var, þeir váru*). In addition to the vowels listed in the table in 11.1, the stem vowels *-ó-* and *-u-* also undergo alternations in the past subjunctive.

Past indic		Past subjunct	Examples
ó	–	œ	koma – þeir kómu – hann/þeir kœmi
u	–	y	munu – þeir mundu – hann/þeir myndi

16.2. The Verb *vera*: Present and Past Subjunctive.

The pres. subjunct. of *vera* is irregular. The special stem *sé-* is employed, and the vowels of the regular subjunct. endings are dropped.

	Sing		Pl	
1	ek	sé	vér	sém
2	þú	sér	þú	séð
3	hann hon þat	sé	þeir þær þau	sé

The past subjunct. of *vera* is regular, based on the stem *vær-*:

	Sing		Pl	
1	ek	væra	vér	værim
2	þú	værir	þú	værið
3	hann hon þat	væri	þeir þær þau	væri

16.3. Personal Pronouns: 1st and 2nd Person Dual.

In addition to sing. *ek* 'I', *þú* 'you' and pl. *vér* 'we', *þér* 'you' (3.6), Old Norse also employs **dual** pronouns, *vit* 'we two' and *þit* 'you two'. *Vit* and *þit* refer to only two people, while *vér* and *þér* refer to three or more people.

Dual Pronouns

	1st		2nd	
Dual nom	vit	'we'	þit/it	'you'
acc	okkr	'us'	ykkr	'you'
dat	okkr	'(to) us'	ykkr	'(to) you'
gen	okkar	'of us'	ykkar	'of you'

Dual pronouns use the regular plural form of the verb. For example:

Vit erum 'we [the two of us] are' (R.S. 15)
Vér erum 'we [more than two] are'
Vit sǫgðum 'we [the two of us] said'
Vér sǫgðum 'we [more than two] said'

Þit eruð 'you [the two of you] are'
Þér eruð 'you [more than two] are'
Þit sǫgðuð 'you [the two of you] said'
Þér sǫgðuð 'you [more than two] said'

The presence of the *-u-* in the ending causes *a~ǫ* alternation (11.2.2) in the verb stem: *vit tǫkum, þit tǫkuð* (from *taka*), *vit sǫgðum, þit sǫgðuð* (from *segja*), etc.

16.4. Adjectives: Possessive Adjectives.

Declinable poss. adjectives exist in the 1st and 2nd persons. These poss. adjectives are all based on the gen. form of the corresponding pers. pron. (see 3.6).

Pers. pron.	Gen.	Poss. adj.
ek 'I'	*mín* 'of me'	*minn* 'my'
þú 'you (sing.)'	*þín* 'of you (sing.)'	*þinn* 'your (sing.)'
—	*sín* 'of oneself'	*sinn* 'one's own'
vit 'we two'	*okkar* 'of us two'	*okkarr* 'our (dual)'
þit 'you two'	*ykkar* 'of you two'	*ykkarr* 'your (dual)'
vér 'we'	*vár* 'of us'	*várr* 'our (pl.)'
þér 'you (pl.)'	*yðar* 'of you (pl.)'	*yðarr* 'your (pl.)'

The poss. adjectives *minn* 'my' and *þinn* 'your (sing.)' are declined like *sinn* (14.3).

Poss. Adjectives *minn* and *þinn*

		minn 'my'			þinn 'your (sing.)'	
	Masc	Fem	Neut	Masc	Fem	Neut
Sg nom	minn	mín	mitt	þinn	þín	þitt
acc	minn	mína	mitt	þinn	þína	þitt
dat	mínum	minni	mínu	þínum	þinni	þínu
gen	míns	minnar	míns	þíns	þinnar	þíns
Pl nom	mínir	mínar	mín	þínir	þínar	þín
acc	mína	mínar	mín	þína	þínar	þín
dat	mínum	mínum	mínum	þínum	þínum	þínum
gen	minna	minna	minna	þinna	þinna	þinna

Dual and Pl. Poss. Adjectives *okkarr, ykkarr, várr,* and *yðarr*

The other poss. adjectives, *okkarr* 'our (dual)', *ykkarr* 'your (dual)', *várr* 'our (pl.)', *yð(v)arr* 'your (pl.)' are declined like regular strong adjectives: f.ex., acc. pl. masc. *sonu okkra*, dat. *sonum okkrum, hvárum-tveggja okkrum* (all in R.S. 15).

okkarr 'our (dual)'			ykkarr 'your (dual)'		
Masc	**Fem**	**Neut**	**Masc**	**Fem**	**Neut**
Sg nom	okkarr	okkur	okkart	ykkarr	ykkur	ykkart
acc	okkarn	okkra	okkart	ykkarn	ykkra	ykkart
dat	okkrum	okkarri	okkru	ykkrum	ykkarri	ykkru
gen	okkars	okkarrar	okkars	ykkars	ykkarrar	ykkars
Pl nom	okkrir	okkrar	okkur	ykkrir	ykkrar	ykkur
acc	okkra	okkrar	okkur	ykkra	ykkrar	ykkur
dat	okkrum	okkrum	okkrum	ykkrum	ykkrum	ykkrum
gen	okkarra	okkarra	okkarra	ykkarra	ykkarra	ykkarra

várr 'our (pl.)'			yð(v)arr 'your (pl.)'		
Masc	**Fem**	**Neut**	**Masc**	**Fem**	**Neut**
Sg nom	várr	vár	várt	yð(v)arr	yður	yð(v)art
acc	várn	vára	várt	yð(v)arn	yðra	yð(v)art
dat	várum	várri	váru	yðrum	yð(v)arri	yðru
gen	várs	várrar	várs	yð(v)ars	yð(v)arrar	yð(v)ars
Pl nom	várir	várar	vár	yðrir	yðrar	yður
acc	vára	várar	vár	yðra	yðrar	yður
dat	várum	várum	várum	yðrum	yðrum	yðrum
gen	várra	várra	várra	yð(v)arra	yð(v)arra	yð(v)arra

There are no poss. adjectives in the 3rd person. Instead, the gen. pronouns *hans, hennar, þess,* and *þeira* are used as indeclinable poss. pronouns: *sonr* **hans** (R.S. 3), *spenum* **hennar** (R.S. 5), *yfirmaðr* **þeira** (R.S. 2), etc.

16.5. The Indefinite Pronoun *hvárrtveggja*.

The indef. pron. *hvárrtveggja* 'each of two, both' is composed of *hvárr* 'each' + *tveggja*, gen. pl. of the numeral *tveir* 'two' (14.1). Only *hvárr-* is declined in this compound pronoun: *til hvárstveggja* 'to each of two' (gen. sing. masc.), *í hvárutveggja liði* 'in each army' (dat. sing. neut.), *hvárirtveggja* 'both (men)' (nom. pl. masc.), etc. In the 1st and 2nd persons, this pronoun is regularly followed by a poss. adj. instead of a gen. pron.: *hvárumtveggja* **okkrum** 'each of the two of us' (R.S. 15). In the 3rd person it is a regular gen. pronoun: *hvárrtveggja þeira,* 'each of the two of them.'

EXERCISES

1. Indicative to Subjunctive, Present and Past. Write the 3 sing. and 3 pl. pres. and past subjunct. forms of the following verbs.

a. Weak Verbs　　　　　　　**Pres**　　　　　　**Past**

Ex: hafa (*past stem* hafð-):　　hann _hafi_　　　hann _hefði_

　　　　　　　　　　　　　　þeir _hafi_　　　þeir _hefði_

dvelja (*past stem* dvalð-): hon _____ hon _____

                         þær _____ þær _____

fagna (*past stem* fagnað-): hann _____ hann _____

                         þeir _____ þeir _____

gera (*past stem* gerð-): þat _____ þat _____

                         þau _____ þau _____

spyrja (*past stem* spurð-): hon _____ hon _____

                         þær _____ þær _____

b. Strong Verbs **Pres** **Past**

Ex: halda (*3 pl. past* heldu): hon *haldi* hon *heldi*

                         þær *haldi* þær *heldi*

bjóða (*3 pl. past* buðu): hann _____ hann _____

                         þeir _____ þeir _____

bera (*3 pl. past* báru): þat _____ þat _____

                         þau _____ þau _____

hlaupa (*3 pl. past* hljópu): hann _____ hann _____

                         þeir _____ þeir _____

taka (*3 pl. past* tóku): hon _____ hon _____

                         þær _____ þær _____

2. Past Subjunctive to Indicative. Provide the requested forms of the following verbs on the basis of the 3 sing. past subjunct.

a. Weak Verbs. The 3 sing. past subjunct. of each verb is given. Supply the (1) past-tense indic. stem, (2) 3 sing. past indic., and (3) inf. forms of the verb.

Ex: þat berði: (1) past indic. stem: *barð-*

                   (2) þat *barði* (3) at *berja*

hon legði: (1) past indic. stem: _____

                   (2) hon _____ (3) at _____

hon skipti: (1) past indic. stem: _____

                   (2) hon _____ (3) at _____

hann velði: (1) past indic. stem: _____

                   (2) hann _____ (3) at _____

þat ætlaði: (1) past indic. stem: _____

                   (2) þat _____ (3) at _____

b. Strong Verbs. The 3 sing. past subjunct. of each verb is given. Supply the (1) 3 pl. past indic., (2) 3 sing. past indic., and (3) inf. forms of the verb.

Ex: hann bæri: (1) þeir _báru_____

                (2) hann _bar_____   (3) at _bera_____

hon gengi: (1) þær _____

                (2) hon _____   (3) at _____

hon gæti: (1) þær _____

                (2) hon _____   (3) at _____

þat kœmi: (1) þau _____

                (2) þat _____   (3) at _____

hann stœði: (1) þeir _____

                (2) hann _____   (3) at _____

3. Complete the paradigm of *vera* in the indicative and subjunctive.

		Indicative	Subjunctive
Pres.:	ek	em	_____
	þú	_____	sér
	hann	_____	_____
	vér	_____	sém
	þér	eruð	_____
	þeir	_____	_____

		Indicative	Subjunctive
Past:	ek	_____	væra
	þú	vart	_____
	hann	_____	_____
	vér	várum	_____
	þér	_____	værið
	þeir	_____	_____

4. Supply a gen. pron. (*mín, þín, vár, yðar*) or a poss. adj. (*minn, þinn, várr, yðarr*) in the appropriate case.

a. Farðu leið þ____ og kom þá aptr til m___. (*leið* fem. 'way, road')

b. Þórólfr gekk ofan til skips m____.

c. Steinarr, sonr þ____, sœkir sǫkum Þorstein, son m____.

d. Góð þykki mér fǫr m___.

e. Litlar sǫgur megu ganga frá hesti þ_____.

f. Þér skuluð ekki láta vánda menn komask í milli yð___ og v___.

g. Þat skaltu segja konungi yð____, at Haraldr Svíakonungr fór þessa leið. (*Svíakonungr* 'king of the Swedes')

h. Engi mun þora at etja við yð___ hesta.

i. Bróðir þ_____ bað systur m_____, en faðir m_____ vildi ekki gefa honum dóttur sína.

5. Translate the Reading Selection.

Ríða þeir brœðr nú til Hlíðarenda. Gunnarr var heima ok gekk út; Kolskeggr gekk út með honum ok Hjǫrtr, bróðir þeira, ok fagna þeim vel ok spurðu, hvert þeir ætlaði at fara.

"Eigi lengra," segja þeir; "oss er sagt, at þú eigir hest góðan, ok vilju vér bjóða þér hestaat."

Gunnarr svarar: "Litlar sǫgur megu ganga frá hesti mínum; hann er ungr ok óreyndr at ǫllu."

"Kost munt þú láta at etja," segja þeir, "ok gat þess til Hildigunnr at þú myndir góðr af hestinum."

_____

_____

_____

_____

_____

_____

_____

_____

_____

_____

_____

_____

"Hví tǫluðuð þér um þat?" segir Gunnarr.

"Þeir menn váru," segja þeir, "er mæltu, at engi myndi þora at etja við várn hest."

"Þora mun ek at etja," segir Gunnarr, "en gráliga þykki mér þetta mælt."

"Skulu vér til þess ætla þá?" segja þeir.

"Þá mun yðr fǫr yður þykkja bezt," segir Gunnarr, "ef þér ráðið þessu, en þó vil ek þess biðja yðr, at vér etim svá hestunum, at vér gerim ǫðrum gaman, en oss engi vandræði ok þér gerið mér enga skǫmm. En ef þér gerið til mín sem til annarra, þá er eigi ráðit, nema ek sveigja þat at yðr, at yðr mun þykkja hart undir at búa. Mun ek þar eptir gera, sem þér gerið fyrir."

_____

_____

_____

_____

_____

_____

_____

_____

_____

_____

_____

_____

_____

_____

_____

Ríða þeir þá heim. Spurði Starkaðr at, hversu þeim hefði farizk. Þeir sǫgðu, at Gunnarr gerði góða ferð þeira; – "hann hét at etja hesti sínum, ok kváðu vér á, nær þat hestavíg skyldi vera. Fannsk þat á í ǫllu, at honum þótti sik skorta við oss, ok bazk hann undan."

"Þat mun opt á finnask," segir Hildigunnr, "at Gunnarr er seinþreyttr til vandræða, en harðdrœgr, ef hann má eigi undan komask."

_____

_____

_____

_____

_____

_____

_____

_____

_____

VOCABULARY

af *prep* [*w dat*] of
bjóða (býðr; bauð, buðu; boðinn) *vb* offer
eiga (á, eigu; átti; áttr) *vb* own
fagna (-að-) *vb* [*w dat*] welcome
geta (getr; gat, gátu; getinn) *vb* [*w gen*] guess
Gunnarr *m* Gunnar (*personal name*)
harðdrœgr *adj* hard to handle
harðr *adj* hard
heita (heitir; hét, hétu; heitinn) *vb* promise
Hildigunnr *f* Hildigunn (*personal name*)
Hjǫrtr *m* Hjort ('Deer') (*personal name*)
Hlíðarendi *m* Hlidarendi, a farm in southern Iceland (*place name*)
hví *adv* why
Kolskeggr *m* Kolskegg (*personal name*)
kostr *m* opportunity
leið *f* way, road
lengra *adv* farther

mega (má, megu; mátti; mátt) *vb* be able
nema *conj* but (that), except
nær *conj* when
opt *adv* often
oss *pron* us (*pl*) (*acc/dat of* **vér**)
óreyndr *adj* unproved
seinþreyttr *adj* slow to stir up; **seinþreyttr til vandræða** slow to be drawn into a quarrel
skǫmm *f* shame, disgrace
Starkaðr *m* Starkad (*personal name*)
undan *adv* away
Svíakonungr *m* king of the Swedes
vandræði *n pl* trouble
várr *poss adj* our (*pl*)
vér *pron* we (*pl*)
yðarr *poss adj* your (*pl*)
yðr *pron* you (*acc/dat of* **þér**)
þér *pron* you (*pl*)
þora (-ð-) *vb* dare
þó *adv* yet, nevertheless
ætla (-að-) *vb* think, intend; agree

PHRASES

at ǫllu in all respects
biðjask undan be evasive
etja hestum incite horses (to fight)
finnask á appear
gera gaman entertain

geta til suppose, surmise
hversu þeim hefði farizk how they had made out
komask undan escape
kveða á fix, determine

Notes

_____

_____

_____

_____

_____

_____

_____

_____

_____

LESSON 17

Ór *Snorra Eddu* (15., 17. kap.)
(From *Snorri's Edda*, Chaps. 15, 17)

the ash   Urd's Well   Norns   chief places   of the gods
Frá askinum, Urðarbrunni, nǫrnum ok hǫfuðstǫðum goðanna.

the chief place   the holy place
Þá mælti Gangleri: "Hvar er hǫfuðstaðrinn eða helgistaðrinn goðanna?"

Hárr svarar: "Þat er at aski Yggdrasils....

hall   the well
"Þar stendr salr einn fagr undir askinum við brunninn, ok ór þeim

hall   three maidens   'Fate' 'Becoming' 'Debt'   these
sal koma þrjár meyjar, þær er svá heita: Urðr, Verðandi, Skuld. Þessar

shape   life them   Norns yet   more
meyjar skapa mǫnnum aldr. Þær kǫllum vér nornir. Enn eru fleiri

each   shape life
nornir, þær er koma til hvers barns, er borit er, at skapa aldr, ok eru

god-kinned   others of elves   the third of dwarves
þessar goðkunnigar, en aðrar álfa ættar, en inar þriðju dverga

ættar...."

can   (the) heaven
Þá mælti Gangleri: "Mikil tíðendi kannt þú at segja af himninum?

more of chief places   Urd's Well
Hvat er þar fleiri hǫfuðstaða en at Urðarbrunni?"

places   magnificent   place
Hárr segir: "Margir staðir eru þar gǫfugligir. Sá er einn staðr þar, er

Elf-Land   people   Light-Elves
kallaðr er Álfheimr. Þar byggvir fólk þat, er Ljósálfar heita, en

Dark-Elves   down   unlike   much more unlike
Døkkálfar búa niðri í jǫrðu, ok eru þeir ólíkir sýnum ok miklu ólíkari

('fairer')
in reality Light-Elves   more beautiful   sun   Dark-Elves
reyndum. Ljósálfar eru fegri en sól sýnum, en Døkkalfar eru

blacker   pitch   yet   place   none
svartari en bik. Þar er enn sá staðr, er Breiðablik er kallaðr, ok engi er

('fairer')
more beautiful   walls
þar fegri staðr. Þar er ok sá, er Glitnir heitir, ok eru veggir hans

pillars   posts   red   gold   roof   silver   yet
ok steðr allar ok stólpar af rauðu gulli, en þak hans af silfri. Þar er enn

end   at   bridgehead
sá staðr, er Himinbjǫrg heita. Sá stendr á himins enda við brúarsporð,

heaven
þar er Bifrǫst kemr til himins. Þar er enn mikill staðr, er Valaskjálf

owns   the gods   thatched with pure silver
heitir. Þann stað á Óðinn. Þann gerðu goðin ok þǫkðu skíru silfri,

('high-seat')
hall   throne
ok þar er Hliðskjálfin í þessum sal, þat hásæti, er svá heitir, ok þá

('all regions')
sees   over the whole world   southern
er Alfǫðr sitr í því sæti, þá sér hann of   alla heima. Á sunnanverðum

('fairer')
heaven's end   hall   most beautiful   brighter   the sun
himins enda er sá salr, er allra er   fegrstr   ok bjartari en sólin, er

has   perished
Gimlé heitir. Hann skal standa, þá er bæði himinn ok jǫrð hefir farizk,

inhabit   place   just   for all   ages
ok byggja þann stað góðir menn ok réttlátir of allar aldir."

17.1. Adjectives: Declension of Comparative Adjectives.

Reading Selection 16 has several comp. adjectives:

fleiri – referring to *nornir* (nom. pl. fem.)

fegri – referring to *staðr* (nom. sing. masc.) and *Ljósálfar* (nom. pl. masc.)

svartari – referring to *Døkkálfar* (nom. pl. masc.)

bjartari – referring to *salr* (nom. sing. masc.)

Comparative adjectives have a special declension:

	Masc	Fem	Neut
Sg *nom*	-i	-i	-a
acc	-a	-i	-a
dat	-a	-i	-a
gen	-a	-i	-a
Pl *nom*	-i	-i	-i
acc	-i	-i	-i
dat	-um	-um	-um
gen	-i	-i	-i

Compare this with the weak adj. declension (13.6). Even when used in weak adj. position, comp. adjectives take comp. adj. endings: *inna fyrri konunga* (R.S. 7.2).

17.2. Adjectives: Formation of Comparatives.

The comp., like the superl. (7.5), is formed with either of two suffixes. The comp. suffixws are *-ar-* and *-r-*.

Comparative adverbs add no further endings: *meir* (R.S. 2), *fyrr* (R.S. 13(1), 14.7), *síðar* (R.S. 14).

Comparative adjectives add the appropriate comp. ending (17.1) after *-ar-* or *-r-*: *svartar-i* and *fegr-i* in the R.S. above.

When the comp. suffix is *-r-*, the stem vowel often undergoes *i*-umlaut (11.2.1): *fagr – fegri, smár* 'small' *– smæri*. The relationship of the stem vowel in the positive and comp. forms is:

Positive form	Comp with -r	Examples
a	e	fagr – fegri
á	æ	smár – smæri
ǫ	ø	þrǫngr 'narrow' – þrøngri
ó	œ	stórr – stœrri
u	y	ungr – yngri
(j)ú	ý	djúpr 'deep' – dýpri

See 7.5 for a similar change in the formation of the superl. with *-st-*, *fagr – fegri – fegrstr*; so also *smár – smæri – smæstr, stórr – stœrri – stœrstr, ungr – yngri – yngstr*, etc. When the adj. stem has a front vowel to begin with, *i*-umlaut has no effect and the vowel remains unchanged in the comp. and superl.: *vænn – vænni – vænstr*.

Using *stœrri* 'bigger' as an example, comp. adjectives decline as follows.

	Masc	Fem	Neut
Sg *nom*	stœrri	stœrri	stœrra
acc	stœrra	stœrri	stœrra
dat	stœrra	stœrri	stœrra
gen	stœrra	stœrri	stœrra
Pl *nom*	stœrri	stœrri	stœrri
acc	stœrri	stœrri	stœrri
dat	stœrrum	stœrrum	stœrrum
gen	stœrri	stœrri	stœrri

17.3. Adjectives and Adverbs: Irregular Comparatives and Superlatives.

A few Icelandic comparatives and superlatives are formed from stems that are different from the simple (positive) adjective. These irregular forms are sometimes called **suppletive** paradigms, because parts of the paradigm were "supplied" from different words. Several of these irregular forms correspond to English, where for example 'good' employs 'better' and 'best' for the comp. and superl., while 'bad' employs 'worse' and 'worst'. Below are the most common of these adjectives.

adj.: *góðr – betri – beztr*	(be) 'good' – 'better' – 'best'
adv.: *vel – betr – bezt*	(do) 'well' – 'better' – 'best'
adj.: *illr – verri – verstr*	(be) 'bad' – 'worse' – 'worst'
adv.: *illa – verr – verst*	(do) 'badly' – 'worse' – 'worst'
adj.: *lítill – minni – minnstr*	(be) 'little' – 'littler' – 'littlest'
adv.: *lítt – minnr – minnst*	(do) 'little' – 'less' – 'least'
adj.: *mikill – meiri – mestr*	'big' – 'bigger' – 'biggest'
adv.: *mjǫk – meir(r) – mest*	'much, very' – 'more' – 'most'
adj.: *margr – fleiri – flestr* (no corresponding adv.)	'many' – 'more' – 'most'
adj.: *gamall – ellri – ellstr* (no corresponding adv.)]	'old' – 'older' – 'oldest'
adj. *fyrri – fyrstr*	'former' – 'first, foremost'
adv. *fyrr – fyrst*	'before, earlier' – 'first, earliest'
(no corresponding positive forms)	

17.4. Verbs: Present Participles.

As mentioned earlier (8.7), participles are verbal adjectives, and Old Norse has two types of participles: pres. and past. Pres. participles employ the suffix *-and-* (corresponding to English '-ing') and are easily recognized. For example, the pres. part. *Verðandi* 'Becoming', from the verb *verða* 'become', appears in the R.S. as the name of one of the Norns.

Pres. participles have the same special declension as comp. adjectives (17.1). Using *verðandi* as an example:

	Masc	Fem	Neut
Sg nom	verðandi	verðandi	verðanda
acc	verðanda	verðandi	verðanda
dat	verðanda	verðandi	verðanda
gen	verðanda	verðandi	verðanda
Pl nom	verðandi	verðandi	verðandi
acc	verðandi	verðandi	verðandi
dat	verðǫndum	verðǫndum	verðǫndum
gen	verðandi	verðandi	verðandi

- Note that the fem. sing. ends in *-i*. This explains the ending *-i* of the name of the Norn *Verðandi*.

17.5. Verbs: Preterite Infinitive.

The preterite infinitive is a special form of the infinitive that appears chiefly in three verbs: *munu*; *skulu*; and *vilja*. The pret. inf. is formed by adding the ending *-u* to the weak past-tense stem of the verb.

    munu 'will, shall' (futurity) – pret. inf. *mundu*

skulu 'shall, must' (necessity) – pret. inf. *skyldu*
vilja 'want, wish' – pret. inf. *vildu*

- The pret. inf. is identical in form with the 3 pl. past.

The pret. inf. only occurs in one type of construction, called the **accusative with infinitive**, because the main verb is followed by an object in the acc. case followed by an infinitive. When the main verb is in the pres. tense, a normal inf. (f.ex., *munu*) follows; but when the main verb is in the past, a pret. inf. (f.ex., *mundu*) follows. Note that in both examples below, the object *hana* is in the acc.

> Pres. tense: *Ek **hygg** hana **munu** heim koma* 'I **think** she (lit. 'her') **will** come home'.
>
> Past tense: *Ek **hugða** hana **mundu** heim koma* 'I **thought** she (lit. 'her') **would** come home'.

This type of construction is frequent with reflexive verbs (10.5.1):

> Pres.: *Hann **kvezk munu** fara* 'he **says** he (lit. 'says himself') **will** go'.
>
> Past: *Hann **kvazk mundu** fara* 'he **said** he (lit. 'said himself') **would** go'.

Ór Þorsteins þætti stangarhǫggs (3. Kap.)
(From the *Tale of Thorstein Staff-Struck*, Chap. 3)

Ok er þeir kómu þar, þá spurði hann, hvert þeir ætluðu, en þeir

	('should')	
	search for	had to
sǫgðusk hrossa	leita	**skyldu.**

17.6. Nouns: Plural of Strong Nouns with *a~ǫ~e* alternation.

Nouns showing *a~ǫ~e* (or *ja~jǫ~i*) alternation in the sing. (see 11.5 and 11.6) also show this alternation in the plural. Masculine *vǫllr, ǫrn, skjǫldr*, and fem. *hǫnd* illustrate the patterns:

	Masc			**Fem**
	'field'	**'eagle'**	**'shield'**	**'hand'**
Sg nom	vǫllr	ǫrn	skjǫldr	hǫnd
acc	vǫll	ǫrn	skjǫld	hǫnd
dat	velli	erni	skildi	hendi
gen	vallar	arnar	skjaldar	handar
Pl nom	vellir	ernir	skildir	hendr
acc	vǫllu	ǫrnu	skjǫldu	hendr
dat	vǫllum	ǫrnum	skjǫldum	hǫndum
gen	valla	arna	skjalda	handa

EXERCISES

1. Fill in the appropriate endings and missing vowels.

   a. Marg___ hǫfuðstað___ eru á himn__ ok all__ eru þeir fegr__ ok
      bjartar__ en hǫfuðstað_____ (def.) á jǫrð_____ (def.). Óðin__
      átt__ hǫfuðstað sem Valaskjálf hét__, en in__ vitr___ nornir átt__
      fagr__ hǫfuðstað undir ask_____ (def.).

   b. Egil__ valð__ sér góð__ menn ok sterk__ ok fór með þeim til
      Himinbj__rg__ (pl.).

   c. Supply exercise **b** with a plural subject and make other necessary
      changes.

   _____

   _____

   d. Ljósálfar er__ ljós___ álf___ sem bú__ í þeim stað, er Álfheim__
      heit___.

   e. Urðr ok Skuld er__ vitr___ norn___, er skap__ m__rg___
      mǫnn___ aldr.

2. Supply the missing comparatives and superlatives (see 17.3.). The
forms listed have appeared in the Reading Selections.

Positive form	Comparative	Superlative
Ex.: góðr 'good'	*betri*	beztr (R.S. 7)
bjartr 'bright'	bjartari (R.S. 17)	_____
gamall 'old'	_____	ellztr (R.S. 13)
gørviligr 'accomplished'	_____	gørviligstr (R.S. 9)
hraustr 'bold'	_____	hraustastr (R.S. 13)
hvítr 'white'	_____	hvítastr (R.S. 7)
margr 'many'	fleiri (R.S. 17)	_____
mikill 'big'	_____	mestr (R.S. 8(2))
mjǫk 'much' (adv.)	meir (R.S. 2)	_____
sið 'late' (adv.)	síðar (R.S. 14)	_____
sterkr 'strong'	_____	sterkastr (R.S. 13)
vaskr 'brave'	_____	vaskastr (R.S. 8)
vitr 'wise'	_____	vitrastr (R.S. 7)

3. Change the adjectives in the following phrases to their corresponding
comparatives.

   a. vitr hǫfðingi: _____

   b. inn gamli bróðir: _____

c. góðan hest: _____

d. inn unga svein: _____

e. ina góðu hesta: _____

f. inum vaska bogmanni: _____

g. inum sterkum nábúum: _____

h. stórt haf: _____

i. stór hǫf: _____

j. inu smá skipi: _____

k. ins hvíta grass: _____

l. djúp á: _____

m. in djúpa á: _____

n. fagra mey: _____

o. með mikilli vináttu: _____

p. svartrar nætr: _____ (NB: *nætr*, gen. of *nótt*)

q. margar eyjar ok stórar: _____

r. inna bjartra sala: _____

4. Translate the Reading Selections.

    a. Frá askinum, Urðarbrunni, nǫrnum ok hǫfuðstǫðum goðanna.

    Þá mælti Gangleri: "Hvar er hǫfuðstaðrinn eða helgistaðrinn goðanna?"

        Hárr svarar: "Þat er at aski Yggdrasils....

    "Þar stendr salr einn fagr undir askinum við brunninn, ok ór þeim sal koma þrjár meyjar, þær er svá heita: Urðr, Verðandi, Skuld. Þessar meyjar skapa mǫnnum aldr. Þær kǫllum vér nornir. Enn eru fleiri nornir, þær er koma til hvers barns, er borit er, at skapa aldr, ok eru þessar goðkunnigar, en aðrar álfa ættar, en inar þriðju dverga ættar...."

_____

_____

_____

_____

_____

_____

_____

_____

_____

_____

Þá mælti Gangleri: "Mikil tíðendi kannt þú at segja af himninum? Hvat er þar fleiri hǫfuðstaða en at Urðarbrunni?"

Hárr segir: "Margir staðir eru þar gǫfugligir. Sá er einn staðr þar, er kallaðr er Álfheimr. Þar byggvir fólk þat, er Ljósálfar heita, en Døkkálfar búa niðri í jǫrðu, ok eru þeir ólíkir sýnum ok miklu ólíkari reyndum. Ljósálfar eru fegri en sól sýnum, en Døkkalfar eru svartari en bik. Þar er enn sá staðr, er Breiðablik er kallaðr, ok engi er þar fegri staðr. Þar er ok sá, er Glitnir heitir, ok eru veggir hans ok steðr allar ok stólpar af rauðu gulli, en þak hans af silfri.

Þar er enn sá staðr, er Himinbjǫrg heita. Sá stendr á himins enda við brúarsporð, þar er Bifrǫst kemr til himins. Þar er enn mikill staðr, er Valaskjálf heitir. Þann stað á Óðinn. Þann gerðu goðin ok þǫkðu skíru silfri, ok þar er Hliðskjálfin í þessum sal, þat hásæti, er svá heitir, ok þá er Alfǫðr sitr í því sæti, þá sér hann of alla heima. Á sunnanverðum himins enda er sá salr, er allra er fegrstr ok bjartari en sólin, er Gimlé heitir. Hann skal standa, þá er bæði himinn ok jǫrð hefir farizk, ok byggja þann stað góðir menn ok réttlátir of allar aldir."

---

b. Ok er þeir kómu þar, þá spurði hann, hvert þeir ætluðu, en þeir sǫgðusk hrossa leita skyldu.

Vocabulary

Alfǫðr *m* 'All-Father', a name of Odin
askr *m* ash tree
Álfheimr *m* 'Land of the Elves' (*place name*)
álfr *m* elf
Bifrǫst *f* the rainbow bridge to heaven
bik *n* pitch
bjartr *adj* bright, radiant
brunnr *m* well
djúpr *adj* deep
dvergr *m* dwarf
endi *m* end
engi *indef pron* none, no one
enn *adv* yet
farask (fersk; fórsk, fórusk; farizk) *refl vb* perish
fleiri *adj* more
fólk *n* people
Gimlé *n* Gimle (*place name*)
Glitnir *m* Glitnir (*place name*)
goð *n* god
gull *n* gold
gǫfugligr *adj* magnificent
hásæti *n* throne
Himinbjǫrg *n pl* 'Heaven Mountains' (*place name*)
Hliðskjálf *f* Hlidskjalf, name of Odin's throne
hverr *indef pron* each
hǫfuðstaðr *m* capital, chief place
leita (-að-) *vb* [*w gen*] seek, search for
meyjar *pl of* **mær**
miklu *adv* [*w comp*] much
mær *f* girl, maiden
niðri *adv* down (in)
norn *f* Norn
of *prep* [*w acc/dat*] over (*distance*);

for, during (*time*)
ólíkr *adj* unlike, different
réttlátr *adj* just
réttr *adj* straight; right, just
salr (*dat* sal) *m* hall
silfr *n* silver
sjá (sér; sá, sá(u); séð) *vb* see
skapa (-að-) *vb* shape, form
skírr *adj* pure
Skuld *f* Skuld ('Debt'), one of the Norns
smár *adj* small
sól *f* sun
staðr *m* place
stoð (*pl* steðr) *f* pillar
stólpi *m* post
sunnanverðr *adj* southern

svartr *adj* black
Urðarbrunnr *m* 'Urd's Well' (*place name*)
Urðr *f* Urd ('Fate'), one of the Norns
Valaskjálf *f* 'Vali's Seat' (*place name*)
veggr *m* wall
Verðandi *f* Verdandi ('Becoming', *pres part of* **verða**), one of the Norns
við *prep* [*w acc*] at
Yggdrasill *m* the tree of life
þekja (þakð-) *vb* thatch
þessar *dem pron* these (*fem pl nom/acc*)
þrǫngr *adj* narrow
þær *pron* they (*fem pl nom/acc*)

PHRASES

fegri sýnum more beautiful (in appearance)
of alla heima over all regions, over the whole world
ólíkr sýnum different in appearance

Notes

_____

_____

_____

_____

_____

_____

_____

_____

_____

_____

_____

_____

_____

_____

_____

_____

Appendices

Hundreds of Medieval Icelandic Manuscripts have survived, preserving a range of Old Norse texts including sagas, laws, histories, church documents, and European literature, such as French romances, translated into Old Icelandic. The manuscripts come in a variety of sizes and states of preservation. The covers of some were made of wood while others were encased in calfskin. Some have only written text while others are illustrated. Many today are remnants; that is, pages or sections of what were once full books. (Photo Courtesy of Árni Magnússon Manuscript Institute, Reykjavík.)

Appendix 1
Pronunciation Guide to Old Icelandic
(With a Discussion of Modern Icelandic Pronunciation)

Reconstruction of Old Icelandic sounds is by nature approximate. In most instances we infer the pronunciation from spellings in manuscripts and rhymes in poetry. There was no standard spelling. Writers and poets often employed their personal or regional pronunciation, and sounds sometimes changed over decades and centuries.

Stress in Old Norse and Old and Modern Icelandic typically falls on the first syllable of the word. For example, *kona, gerði,* and *konungr* are pronounced **ko**-na, **ger**-ði, and **kon**-ungr. Compounds have secondary stress on the first syllable of the second element. For example, the syllable -*móð*- in **kon**unga**móð**ir ('mother of kings') has secondary stress.

Old Icelandic Vowels

Vowels are sounds made by the unobstructed passage of air through the mouth. Old Norse vowels are classified as long or short. For most vowels, length is indicated by an acute accent, *á, é, í, ó, ú, ý*. The vowels *æ* and *œ* (sometimes spelled *ǿ*) are always long.

Long vowels in Old Icelandic were longer versions of the corresponding short vowels. For example, *a* and *á* were articulated alike, but *á* was originally longer in duration. Below is a chart showing the pronunciation of Old Icelandic vowels around the beginning of the 13th century. By this time, *á* had acquired rounding and merged into a long, low, round back vowel like the **au** in c**au**ght.

The vowels *au, ei,* and *ey* are diphthongs, with the tongue gliding from the first vowel to the position of the second. For example, *ei* begins with *e* and glides towards *i*.

Vowel	Old Icelandic Pronunciation	Examples
a	as **a** in father, but shorter	*faðir*
á	as **au** in c**au**ght, with rounded lips and longer than *ǫ*	*láta*
e	as **e** in bet	*bekkr*
é	as **e** in bet, but longer	*þér*
i	**i** in sin	*sinn*
í	as **ee** in seen	*líta*
o	as **o** in sole, but shorter	*kona*
ó	as **o** in boat	*bjóða*
u	as **oo** in took	*sumar*
ú	as **oo** in moon	*búa*

y	as **ee** in s**ee**n, but pronounced with rounded lips; as in German *für*	*systir*
ý	as **ee** in s**ee**n, but pronounced with rounded lips; as in German *für*, but longer	*býðr*
æ	as **a** in n**a**p, but longer	*lætr*
œ	as **e** in b**e**t, but longer and pronounced with rounded lips; as in German *können*	*dœl*
ø	as **e** in b**e**t, but pronounced with rounded lips; as in German *können*. By early thirteenth century *ø* merged with *ǫ*.	*søkkva*
ǫ	as **au** in c**au**ght, pronounced with rounded lips and shorter than *á*	*kǫttr*
au	as **ou** in h**ou**se	*nauð*
ei	as **ei** in v**ei**n	*heita*
ey	Old Icelandic *e* + *y*	*heyra*

Old Icelandic Consonants

Consonants are sounds made by a narrowing or closure of the vocal tract, which results in obstruction of the free flow of air. The Old Icelandic consonants *b, d, h, k, l, m, n, s,* and *t* were probably similar to the corresponding sounds in modern English.

Old Icelandic distinguished the pronunciation of single and double consonants. Double letters form long consonants; for instance, the -*mm*- in *stemma* is pronounced twice as long as the -*m*- in *heima*. In words that employ stop consonants (*p, t, k, b, d, g*) like *staddr* and *liggja*, the lengthening results in a pause before the release of air forming the consonant. We can hear a similar distinction in English between the single **k** in 'bee keeper' vs. the double **kk** in 'boo**kk**eeper', or the single **d** in 'red eye' vs. the double **dd** in 'red **d**ye'.

In Old Icelandic *f* and *v* were likely pronounced using both the lower and upper lips.

Below is a pronunciation chart for the Old Icelandic consonants that differ from English.

Consonant	Old Icelandic Pronunciation	Examples
f	1) at the beginning of a word: as *f* in **f**ather 2) in the middle or at the end of a word: as **v** in ha**v**e	*faðir* *hafa*
g	1) at the beginning of word or after *n*: as **g** in **g**ood 2) preceding *s* or *t*: as **ch** in Scots English lo**ch**	*góðr, langr* *lagt*
j	as **y** in **y**es	*jarl*
p	as **p** in **p**in preceding *s* or *t*: as *f* in a**f**ter	*penningr* *eptir*
r	trilled as Scots English **r**	*rauðr*

s	as **s** in **s**it, not as English **z**	*sitja*
v	as **w** in **w**est or **v** in **v**est	*vestr*
þ	as **th** in **th**ing	*þing*
ð	as **th** in **th**is, bro**th**er	*bróðir*
x	as **chs** in Scots English lo**chs**	*øx*
z	as **ts** in prin**ts**	*brauzk*

Modern Icelandic Pronunciation

A trend in teaching Old Norse-Icelandic is to read the texts with Modern Icelandic pronunciation. For those interested in reading the texts with the modern pronunciation, the following two charts provide guidance. Much of the grammar and basic vocabulary of Old Icelandic come into Modern Icelandic with few changes, and employing modern pronunciation is a good start to learning Modern Icelandic.

Modern Icelandic Vowels

In the 14th century, Icelandic long vowels began to mutate into diphthongs (a sequence of two vowel sounds pronounced together). As a result, many of the long vowels in Modern Icelandic differ from the corresponding short vowels in quality as well as length. In Modern Icelandic, the short vowels *a*, *e*, and *o* are still pronounced much as they were in Old Icelandic. However, the long vowels have changed. In most instances, Modern Icelandic long *á* resembles the diphthong **ou** in English 'h**ou**se'. Long *é* is pronounce like **ye** in English '**ye**s', and long *ó* is like the long **o** in English 'g**o**' or the **ow** of 'sn**ow**', with a glide toward **w** at the end.

Modern *y* and *ý* have lost their lip rounding and merged with *i* and *í*. The diphthong *ey* has also merged with *ei*. On the other hand, modern *au* has acquired lip rounding.

Soon after the beginning of the 13th century, *ø* merged with *ǫ*, represented by *ö*. The merged vowel is pronounced as a mid (i.e., half-low) front rounded vowel, like *ö* in German *schön*. In addition, *œ* merged with *æ*, both now represented by *æ*, and this merged vowel is pronounced like Modern English long **i** as in mile.

Vowel	Modern Icelandic Pronunciation	Examples
a	as **a** in f**a**ther	*faðir*
	before *ng* and *nk*: as **ou** in h**ou**se	*langr*
á	as **ou** in h**ou**se	*láta*
e	as **e** in b**e**t	*bekkr*
é	as **ye** in **ye**s	*þér*
i	**i** in s**i**n	*sinn*
í	as **ee** in s**ee**n	*líta*
o	as **o** in s**o**le	*kona*
ó	as **o** in g**o**	*bjóða*
ö	as **u** in c**u**t, but with rounded lips	*köttr*

u	as **u** in p**u**t	*sumar*
ú	as **oo** in m**oo**n	*búa*
y	as **i** in s**i**n	*systir*
ý	as **ee** in s**ee**n	*býðr*
æ	as **i** in m**i**le	*lætr, dæl*
au	as **ay** in h**ay**, but with rounded lips	*nauð*
ei, ey	as **ei** in v**ei**n	*heita, heyra*

Modern Icelandic Consonants

The consonants *h, k, l, m, n* are pronounced much as in Modern English.

As in English, the consonants *p, t, k* are pronounced voiceless (with no vibration of the vocal cords). Unlike English, the consonants *b, d, g* are also pronounced voiceless.

The two consonant series *p, t, k* and *b, d, g* are distinguished from each other by the presence of aspiration (a puff of air) following *p, t, k*, while *b, d* and *g* are not aspirated.

In Modern Icelandic (and English), the letters *f* and *v* are pronounced with the lower lip in contact with the upper teeth.

Consonant	Modern Icelandic Pronunciation	Examples
f	1) at the beginning of a word: as **f** in **f**ather	*faðir*
	2) before *n* or *l*: as Modern Icelandic **p**	*nafn, kafli*
	3) elsewhere: as **v** in ha**v**e	*hafa*
g	1) at the beginning of word or after *n*: as **g** in **g**ood, but voiceless	*góðr, langr*
	2) preceding *s* or *t*: as **ch** in Scots English lo**ch**	*lagt*
	3) after vowels and before *a, u, ð, r*: as **ch** in Scots English lo**ch**, but voiced	*fluga*
	4) between a vowel and a following *i* or *j*: as **y** in **y**es	*eigi, segja*
	5) between *ó, á, ú*, and a following *a, u*: silent	*fljúga*
	6) in sequences -*angt* and -*angs*: silent	*langt, langs*
j	as **y** in **y**es	*jarl*
p	as **p** in **p**in	*penningr*
	preceding *s* or *t*: as **f** in a**f**ter	*eptir*
r	trilled as Scots English **r**	*rauðr*
s	as **s** in **s**it, not as English **z**	*sitja*
v	as **v** in **v**est	*vestr*
þ	as **th** in **th**ing	*þing*
ð	as **th** in bro**th**er	*bróðir*
x	as **chs** in Scots English lo**chs**	*øx*
z	as **ts** in prin**ts**	*brauzk*
hv	most commonly pronounced as **kv**	*hvítr*

A few double consonants in Modern Icelandic have special pronunciations.

- *pp*, *tt*, and *kk* are pronounced with a preceding pause resembling a weakly pronounced *h*. For example, *upp*, *dóttir*, and *ekki* are pronounced [uʰpp], [dóʰttir], and [eʰkki]. This is called **pre-aspiration**.
  pp is pronounced as *f* in *father* when it precedes *t*: *keppti* [kefti].

- *nn* sounds like [tn] when it follows a vowel with an accent mark or diphthong at the end of a word: *einn* [eitn].

- *ll* sounds like [tl] when preceding a vowel, *r*, or *n*: *kalla* [katla], *allr* [atlr]. It also has this pronunciation at the end of words: *mikill* [mikitl]. Before *t*, *d*, and *s*, double *ll* is pronounced like a single *l*: *alls* [als], *allt* [alt]. In loan words and nicknames *ll* is pronounced as long *l*: *mylla* 'mill' [milla] and *Kalli* [kalli].

- The sequences *rn* and *rl* usually are pronounced [rtn] and [rtl]: *Bjarni* [bjartni], or *karlar* [kartlar].

Sequences of three consonants are often simplified at the end of a syllable. For example, the *b* in *kumbl* is silent and the word is pronounced [kuml], similar to the English pronunciation of 'twelfth' as [twelth] in quick speech. When the sequence occurs over a syllable break, all three consonants are pronounced, f.ex., *landnám* (the syllable breaks between *land-* and *-nám*).

Appendix 2
Reference Grammar
of Old Norse – Old Icelandic

ARTICLE

	Masc	Fem	Neut
Sg *nom*	inn	in	it
acc	inn	ina	it
dat	inum	inni	inu
gen	ins	innar	ins
Pl *nom*	inir	inar	in
acc	ina	inar	in
dat	→	inum	←
gen	→	inna	←

NOUNS: Strong

Masc

				Endings
Sg *nom*	hest-r	stað-r	bekk-r	-r*
acc	hest	stað	bekk	–
dat	hest-i	stað-i	bekk	-i, –
gen	hest-s	stað-ar	bekkj-ar	-s, -ar
Pl *nom*	hest-ar	stað-ir	bekk-ir	-ar, -ir
acc	hest-a	stað-i	bekk-i	-a, -i
dat	hest-um	stǫð-um	bekkj-um	-um
gen	hest-a	stað-a	bekkj-a	-a

Fem

							Endings
Sg *nom*	fǫr	jǫrð	Bjǫrg	á	heið-r	bók	(ǫ)–, -r
acc	fǫr	jǫrð	Bjǫrg-u	á	heið-i	bók	(ǫ)–, (-u), -i
dat	fǫr	jǫrð-u	Bjǫrg-u	á	heið-i	bók	(ǫ)–, -u, -i
gen	far-ar	jarð-ar	Bjarg-ar	á-r	heið-ar	bók-ar	-ar
Pl *nom*	far-ar	jarð-ir		á-r	heið-ar	bœk-r	-ar, -ir, -⁽ⁱ⁾r
acc	far-ar	jarð-ir		á-r	heið-ar	bœk-r	-ar, -ir, -⁽ⁱ⁾r
dat	fǫr-um	jǫrð-um		á-m	heið-um	bók-um	-um
gen	far-a	jarð-a		á	heið-a	bók-a	-a

Fem Pl endings: -ar, -ir, -(i)r.

Neut

				Endings
Sg *nom*	skip	barn	líki	–
acc	skip	barn	líki	–
dat	skip-i	barn-i	lík-i	-i
gen	skip-s	barn-s	líki-s	-s
Pl *nom*	skip	bǫrn	líki	(ǫ)–
acc	skip	bǫrn	líki	(ǫ)–
dat	skip-um	bǫrn-um	lík-um	-um
gen	skip-a	barn-a	lík-a	-a

Kinship Terms

				Endings
Sg *nom*	fað-ir	móð-ir	syst-ir	-ir
acc	fǫð-ur	móð-ur	syst-ur	-ur
dat	fǫð-ur	móð-ur	syst-ur	-ur
gen	fǫð-ur	móð-ur	syst-ur	-ur
Pl *nom*	feð-r	mœð-r	syst-r	-⁽ⁱ⁾r
acc	feð-r	mœð-r	syst-r	-⁽ⁱ⁾r
dat	feð-rum	mœð-rum	syst-rum	-⁽ⁱ⁾rum
gen	feð-ra	mœð-ra	syst-ra	-⁽ⁱ⁾ra

Kinship endings: -ir, -ur, -(i)r, -(i)rum, -(i)ra.

a~ǫ~e Alternation

	Masc			Fem
Sg *nom*	vǫll-r	ǫrn	skjǫld-r	hǫnd
acc	vǫll	ǫrn	skjǫld	hǫnd
dat	vell-i	ern-i	skild-i	hend-i
gen	vall-ar	arn-ar	skjald-ar	hand-ar
Pl *nom*	vell-ir	ern-ir	skild-ir	hend-r
acc	vǫll-u	ǫrn-u	skjǫld-u	hend-r
dat	vǫll-um	ǫrn-um	skjǫld-um	hǫnd-um
gen	vall-a	arn-a	skjald-a	hand-a

---

* With modifications, see Section 2.1.

Strong Nouns with Suffixed Article

	Masc		Fem			Neut
Sg nom	hestr-**inn**	staðr-**inn**	fǫr-**in**	jǫrð-**in**	á-**in**	skip-**it**
acc	hest-**inn**	stað-**inn**	fǫr-**ina**	jǫrð-**ina**	á-**na**	skip-**it**
dat	hesti-**num**	stað-**inum**	fǫr-**inni**	jǫrðu-**nni**	á-**nni**	skipi-**nu**
gen	hests-**ins**	staðar-**ins**	farar-**innar**	jarðar-**innar**	ár-**innar**	skips-**ins**
Pl nom	hestar-**nir**	staðir-**nir**	farar-**nar**	jarðir-**nar**	ár-**nar**	skip-**in**
acc	hesta-**na**	staði-**na**	farar-**nar**	jarðir-**nar**	ár-**nar**	skip-**in**
dat	hestu-**num**	stǫðu-**num**	fǫru-**num**	jǫrðu-**num**	á-**num**	skipu-**num**
gen	hesta-**nna**	staða-**nna**	fara-**nna**	jarða-**nna**	á-**nna**	skipa-**nna**

NOUNS: Weak

	Masc	Fem			Neut		Endings		
Sg nom	bog-**i**	tung-**a**	sag-**a**	ell-**i**	aug-**a**	hjart-**a**	-i	-a, -i	-a
acc	bog-**a**	tung-**u**	sǫg-**u**	ell-**i**	aug-**a**	hjart-**a**	-a	-u, -i	-a
dat	bog-**a**	tung-**u**	sǫg-**u**	ell-**i**	aug-**a**	hjart-**a**	-a	-u, -i	-a
gen	bog-**a**	tung-**u**	sǫg-**u**	ell-**i**	aug-**a**	hjart-**a**	-a	-u, -i	-a
Pl nom	bog-**ar**	tung-**ur**	sǫg-**ur**	/////	aug-**u**	hjǫrt-**u**	-ar	-ur	-u
acc	bog-**a**	tung-**ur**	sǫg-**ur**	/////	aug-**u**	hjǫrt-**u**	-a	-ur	-u
dat	bog-**um**	tung-**um**	sǫg-**um**	/////	aug-**um**	hjǫrt-**um**	→	-um	←
gen	bog-**a**	tung-**na**	sag-**na**	/////	aug-**na**	hjart-**na**	-a	-na	←

Weak Nouns with Suffixed Article

	Masc	Fem			Neut	
Sg nom	bogi-**nn**	tunga-**n**	saga-**n**	elli-**n**	auga-**t**	hjarta-**t**
acc	boga-**nn**	tungu-**na**	sǫgu-**na**	elli-**na**	auga-**t**	hjarta-**t**
dat	boga-**num**	tungu-**nni**	sǫgu-**nni**	elli-**nni**	auga-**nu**	hjarta-**nu**
gen	boga-**ns**	tungu-**nnar**	sǫgu-**nnar**	elli-**nnar**	auga-**ns**	hjarta-**ns**
Pl nom	bogar-**nir**	tungur-**nar**	sǫgur-**nar**	/////	augu-**n**	hjǫrtu-**n**
acc	boga-**na**	tungur-**nar**	sǫgur-**nar**	/////	augu-**n**	hjǫrtu-**n**
dat	bogu-**num**	tungu-**num**	sǫgu-**num**	/////	augu-**num**	hjǫrtu-**num**
gen	boga-**nna**	tunga-**nna**	sagna-**nna**	/////	augna-**nna**	hjartna-**nna**

ADJECTIVES: Strong

	Masc					Endings
Sg nom	stór-**r**	lang-**r**	vitr	heil-**l**	lítil-**l**	-r*
acc	stór-**an**	lang-**an**	vitr-**an**	heil-**an**	litl-**an**	-an
dat	stór-**um**	lǫng-**um**	vitr-**um**	heil-**um**	litl-**um**	-um
gen	stór-**s**	lang-**s**	vitr-**s**	heil-**s**	lítil-**s**	-s
Pl nom	stór-**ir**	lang-**ir**	vitr-**ir**	heil-**ir**	litl-**ir**	-ir
acc	stór-**a**	lang-**a**	vitr-**a**	heil-**a**	litl-**a**	-a
dat	stór-**um**	lǫng-**um**	vitr-**um**	heil-**um**	litl-**um**	-um
gen	stór-**ra**	lang-**ra**	vitr-**a**	heil-**la**	lítil-**la**	-ra*

---

* With modifications, see Section 2.1.

ADJECTIVES: **Strong** (cont.)

	Fem					Endings
Sg nom	stór	lǫng	vitr	heil	lítil	(ǫ)–
acc	stór-a	lang-a	vitr-a	heil-a	litl-a	-a
dat	stór-ri	lang-ri	vitr-i	heil-li	lítil-li	-ri*
gen	stór-rar	lang-rar	vitr-ar	heil-lar	lítil-lar	-rar*
Pl nom	stór-ar	lang-ar	vitr-ar	heil-ar	litl-ar	-ar
acc	stór-ar	lang-ar	vitr-ar	heil-ar	litl-ar	-ar
dat	stór-um	lǫng-um	vitr-um	heil-um	litl-um	-um
gen	stór-ra	lang-ra	vitr-a	heil-la	lítil-la	-a

	Neut					Endings
Sg nom	stór-t	lang-t	vitr-t	heil-t	líti-t	-t
acc	stór-t	lang-t	vitr-t	heil-t	líti-t	-t
dat	stór-u	lǫng-u	vitr-u	heil-u	litl-u	-u
gen	stór-s	lang-s	vitr-s	heil-s	lítil-s	-s
Pl nom	stór	lǫng	vitr	heil	lítil	(ǫ)–
acc	stór	lǫng	vitr	heil	lítil	(ǫ)–
dat	stór-um	lǫng-um	vitr-um	heil-um	litl-um	-um
gen	stór-ra	lang-ra	vitr-a	heil-la	lítil-la	-a

Possessive Adjectives

Singular	**minn**			**þinn**			**sinn**		
	Masc	Fem	Neut	Masc	Fem	Neut	Masc	Fem	Neut
Sg nom	minn	mín	mitt	þinn	þín	þitt	sinn	sín	sitt
acc	minn	mína	mitt	þinn	þína	þitt	sinn	sína	sitt
dat	mínum	minni	mínu	þínum	þinni	þínu	sínum	sinni	sínu
gen	míns	minnar	míns	þíns	þinnar	þíns	síns	sinnar	síns
Pl nom	mínir	mínar	mín	þínir	þínar	þín	sínir	sínar	sín
acc	mína	mínar	mín	þína	þínar	þín	sína	sínar	sín
dat	→	mínum	←	→	þínum	←	→	sínum	←
gen	→	minna	←	→	þinna	←	→	sinna	←

Dual	**okkarr**			**ykkarr**		
	Masc	Fem	Neut	Masc	Fem	Neut
Sg nom	okkarr	okkur	okkart	ykkarr	ykkur	ykkart
acc	okkarn	okkra	okkart	ykkarn	ykkra	ykkart
dat	okkrum	okkarri	okkru	ykkrum	ykkarri	ykkru
gen	okkars	okkarrar	okkars	ykkars	ykkarrar	ykkars
Pl nom	okkrir	okkrar	okkur	ykkrir	ykkrar	ykkur
acc	okkra	okkrar	okkur	ykkra	ykkrar	ykkur
dat	→	okkrum	←	→	ykkrum	←
gen	→	okkarra	←	→	ykkarra	←

---

* With modifications, see Section 2.1.

Plural	**várr**			**yð(v)arr**		
	Masc	**Fem**	**Neut**	**Masc**	**Fem**	**Neut**
Sg nom	várr	vár	várt	yð(v)arr	yður	yð(v)art
acc	várn	vára	várt	yð(v)arn	yðra	yð(v)art
dat	várum	várri	váru	yðrum	yð(v)arri	yðru
gen	várs	várrar	várs	yð(v)ars	yð(v)arrar	yð(v)ars
Pl nom	várir	várar	vár	yðrir	yðrar	yður
acc	vára	várar	vár	yðra	yðrar	yður
dat	→	várum	←	→	yðrum	←
gen	→	várra	←	→	yð(v)arra	←

ADJECTIVES: Weak

	Masc		**Fem**		**Neut**		Endings		
Sg nom	stór-i	lang-i	stór-a	lang-a	stór-a	lang-a	-i	-a	-a
acc	stór-a	lang-a	stór-u	long-u	stór-a	lang-a	-a	-u	-a
dat	stór-a	lang-a	stór-u	long-u	stór-a	lang-a	-a	-u	-a
gen	stór-a	lang-a	stór-u	long-u	stór-a	lang-a	-a	-u	-a
Pl nom	stór-u	long-u	stór-u	long-u	stór-u	long-u	→	-u	←
acc	stór-u	long-u	stór-u	long-u	stór-u	long-u	→	-u	←
dat	stór-um	long-um	stór-um	long-um	stór-um	long-um	→	-um	←
gen	stór-u	long-u	stór-u	long-u	stór-u	long-u	→	-u	←

ADJECTIVES: Comparative

	Masc	**Fem**	**Neut**	**Masc**	**Fem**	**Neut**	Endings		
Sg nom	arm-ar-i	arm-ar-i	arm-ar-a	yng-r-i	yng-r-i	yng-r-a	-i	-i	-a
acc	arm-ar-a	arm-ar-i	arm-ar-a	yng-r-a	yng-r-i	yng-r-a	-a	-i	-a
dat	arm-ar-a	arm-ar-i	arm-ar-a	yng-r-a	yng-r-i	yng-r-a	-a	-i	-a
gen	arm-ar-a	arm-ar-i	arm-ar-a	yng-r-a	yng-r-i	yng-r-a	-a	-i	-a
Pl nom	→	arm-ar-i	←	→	yng-r-i	←	→	-i	←
acc	→	arm-ar-i	←	→	yng-r-i	←	→	-i	←
dat	→	orm-ur-um	←	→	yng-r-um	←	→	-um	←
gen	→	arm-ar-i	←	→	yng-r-i	←	→	-i	←

ADJECTIVES: Superlative

Strong (Regular strong endings)

	Masc	**Fem**	**Neut**	**Masc**	**Fem**	**Neut**
Sg nom	arm-ast-r	orm-ust	arm-ast	yng-st-r	yng-st	yng-st
acc	arm-ast-an	arm-ast-a	arm-ast	yng-st-an	yng-st-a	yng-st
dat	orm-ust-um	arm-ast-ri	orm-ust-u	yng-st-um	yng-st-ri	yng-st-u
gen	arm-ast-s	arm-ast-rar	arm-ast-s	yng-st-s	yng-st-rar	yng-st-s
Pl nom	arm-ast-ir	arm-ast-ar	orm-ust	yng-st-ir	yng-r-i	yng-st
acc	arm-ast-a	arm-ast-ar	orm-ust	yng-st-a	yng-r-i	yng-st
dat	→	orm-ust-um	←	→	yng-st-um	←
gen	→	arm-ast-ra	←	→	yng-st-ra	←

ADJECTIVES: **Superlative** (cont.)

Weak   (Regular weak endings)

	Masc	Fem	Neut	Masc	Fem	Neut
Sg nom	arm-**ast-i**	arm-**ast-a**	arm-**ast-a**	yng-**st-i**	yng-**st-a**	yng-**st-a**
acc	arm-**ast-a**	ǫrm-**ust-u**	arm-**ast-a**	yng-**st-a**	yng-**st-u**	yng-**st-a**
dat	arm-**ast-a**	ǫrm-**ust-u**	arm-**ast-a**	yng-**st-a**	yng-**st-u**	yng-**st-a**
gen	arm-**ast-a**	ǫrm-**ust-u**	arm-**ast-a**	yng-**st-a**	yng-**st-u**	yng-**st-a**
Pl nom	→	ǫrm-**ust-u**	←	→	yng-**st-u**	←
acc	→	ǫrm-**ust-u**	←	→	yng-**st-u**	←
dat	→	ǫrm-**ust-um**	←	→	yng-**st-um**	←
gen	→	ǫrm-**ust-u**	←	→	yng-**st-u**	←

PRONOUNS: **Personal**

	1st	2nd	3rd Masc	Fem	Neut	Refl
Sg nom	ek	þú	han-**n**	hon	þat	░
acc	mik	þik	han-**n**	han-**a**	þat	sik
dat	mér	þér	hon-**um**	hen-**ni**	því	sér
gen	mín	þín	han-**s**	hen-**nar**	þess	sín
Du nom	vit	(þ)it				░
acc	okkr	ykkr				sik
dat	okkr	ykkr				sér
gen	okkar	ykkar				sín
Pl nom	vér	(þ)ér	þei-**r**	þæ-**r**	þau	░
acc	oss	yðr	þá	þæ-**r**	þau	sik
dat	oss	yðr	→	þei-**m**	←	sér
gen	vár	yð(v)ar	→	þei(r)-**ra**	←	sín

PRONOUNS: **Demonstrative**

	Masc	Fem	Neut	Masc	Fem	Neut
Sg nom	sá	sú	þat	þessi/sjá	þessi/sjá	þetta
acc	þan-**n**	þá	þat	þenna	þessa	þetta
dat	þei-**m**	þei(r)-**ri**	því	þess-**um**	þessa-**ri**	þessu
gen	þess	þei(r)-**rar**	þess	þessa	þessa-**rar**	þessa
Pl nom	þei-**r**	þæ-**r**	þau	þess-**ir**	þess-**ar**	þessi
acc	þá	þæ-**r**	þau	þess-**a**	þess-**ar**	þessi
dat	→	þei-**m**	←	→	þess-**um**	←
gen	→	þei(r)-**ra**	←	→	þessa-**ra**	←

PRONOUNS: Interrogative, Indefinite, etc.

Interrogative

(Regular strong adj. endings)

	Masc	Fem	Neut		Masc	Fem	Neut
Sg *nom*	hver-**r**	hver	hver-**t**/hvat		hvár-**r**	hvár	hvár-**t**
acc	hver-**n**	hverj-**a**	hver-**t**/hvat		hvár-**n**	hvár-**a**	hvár-**t**
dat	hverj-**um**	hver-**ri**	hverj-**u**		hvár-**um**	hvár-**ri**	hvár-**u**
gen	hver-**s**	hver-**rar**	hver-**s**		hvár-**s**	hvár-**rar**	hvár-**s**
Pl *nom*	hver-**ir**	hverj-**ar**	hver		hvár-**ir**	hvár-**ar**	hvár
acc	hverj-**a**	hverj-**ar**	hver		hvár-**a**	hvár-**ar**	hvár
dat	→	hverj-**um**	←		→	hvár-**um**	←
gen	→	hver-**ra**	←		→	hvár-**ra**	←

Indefinite

(Regular strong adj. endings)

	Masc	Fem	Neut		Masc	Fem	Neut
Sg *nom*	nǫkkur-**r**	nǫkkur	nǫkku-**t**		ein-**n**	ein	ei-**tt**
acc	nǫkkur-**n**	nǫkkur-**a**	nǫkku-**t**		ein-**n**	ein-**a**	ei-**tt**
dat	nǫkkur-**um**	nǫkkur-**ri**	nǫkkur-**u**		ein-**um**	ein-**ni**	ein-**u**
gen	nǫkkur-**s**	nǫkkur-**rar**	nǫkkur-**s**		ein-**s**	ein-**nar**	ein-**s**
Pl *nom*	nǫkkur-**ir**	nǫkkur-**ar**	nǫkkur		ein-**ir**	ein-**ar**	ein
acc	nǫkkur-**a**	nǫkkur-**ar**	nǫkkur		ein-**a**	ein-**ar**	ein
dat	→	nǫkkur-**um**	←		→	ein-**um**	←
gen	→	nǫkkur-**ra**	←		→	ein-**na**	←

	Masc	Fem	Neut
Pl *nom*	báð-**ir**	báð-**ar**	bæð-**i**
acc	báð-**a**	báð-**ar**	bæð-**i**
dat	→	báð-**um**	←
gen	→	be-**ggja**	←

Negative

	Masc	Fem	Neut
Sg *nom*	engi	engi	ekki
acc	eng-**an**	eng-**a**	ekki
dat	eng-**um**	eng-**ri**	eng-**u**
gen	engi-**s**/enski-**s**	eng-**ra**	engi-**s**/enski-**s**
Pl *nom*	eng-**ir**	eng-**ar**	engi
acc	eng-**ir**	eng-**ar**	engi
dat	→	eng-**um**	←
gen	→	eng-**um**	←

NUMERALS

(For *einn* 'one', see Indefinite Pronouns)

	Masc	Fem	Neut		Masc	Fem	Neut		Masc	Fem	Neut
nom	tvei-**r**	tvæ-**r**	tvau		þrí-**r**	þrj-**ár**	þrj-**ú**		fjór-**ir**	fjór-**ar**	fjǫg-**ur**
acc	tvá	tvæ-**r**	tvau		þrj-**á**	þrj-**ár**	þrj-**ú**		fjór-**a**	fjór-**ar**	fjǫg-**ur**
dat	→	tvei-**m(r)**	←		→	þri-**m(r)**	←		→	fjór-**um**	←
gen	→	tve-**ggja**	←		→	þri-**ggja**	←		→	fjǫgur-**ra**	←

VERBS: Weak

Indicative

Pres	lofa	tala	lifa	flytja	kveðja	Endings
1sg	lof-a	tal-a	lif-i	flyt	kveð	(-a/i)–
2sg	lof-a-r	tal-a-r	lif-i-r	flyt-r	kveð-r	(-a/i)-r*
3sg	lof-a-r	tal-a-r	lif-i-r	flyt-r	kveð-r	(-a/i)-r*
1pl	lof-um	tǫl-um	lif-um	flytj-um	kveðj-um	-um
2pl	lof-ið	tal-ið	lif-ið	flyt-ið	kveð-ið	-ið
3pl	lof-a	tal-a	lif-a	flytj-a	kveðj-a	-a
Past	(-að-)	(-að-)	(-ð-)	(flutt-)	(kvadd-)	
1sg	lof-að-a	tal-að-a	lif-ð-a	flut-t-a	kvad-d-a	-að/ð†-a
2sg	lof-að-ir	tal-að-ir	lif-ð-ir	flut-t-ir	kvad-d-ir	-að/ð†-ir
3sg	lof-að-i	tal-að-i	lif-ð-i	flut-t-i	kvad-d-i	-að/ð†-i
1pl	lof-uð-um	tǫl-uð-um	lif-ð-um	flut-t-um	kvǫd-d-um	-að/ð†-um
2pl	lof-uð-uð	tǫl-uð-uð	lif-ð-uð	flut-t-uð	kvǫd-d-uð	-að/ð†-uð
3pl	lof-uð-u	tǫl-uð-u	lif-ð-u	flut-t-u	kvǫd-d-u	-að/ð†-u

Subjunctive

Pres						
1sg	lof-a	tal-a	lif-a	flytj-a	kveðj-a	-a
2sg	lof-ir	tal-ir	lif-ir	flyt-ir	kveð-ir	-ir
3sg	lof-i	tal-i	lif-i	flyt-i	kveð-i	-i
1pl	lof-im	tal-im	lif-im	flyt-im	kveð-im	-im
2pl	lof-ið	tal-ið	lif-ið	flyt-ið	kveð-ið	-ið
3pl	lof-i	tal-i	lif-i	flyt-i	kveð-i	-i
Past	(-að-)	(-að-)	(-ð-)	(flutt-)	(kvadd-)	
1sg	lof-að-a	tal-að-a	lif-ð-a	flyt-t-a	kved-d-a	-að/(i)ð†-a
2sg	lof-að-ir	tal-að-ir	lif-ð-ir	flyt-t-ir	kved-d-ir	-að/(i)ð†-ir
3sg	lof-að-i	tal-að-i	lif-ð-i	flyt-t-i	kved-d-i	-að/(i)ð†-i
1pl	lof-að-im	tal-að-im	lif-ð-im	flyt-t-im	kved-d-im	-að/(i)ð†-im
2pl	lof-að-ið	tal-að-ið	lif-ð-ið	flyt-t-ið	kved-d-ið	-að/(i)ð†-ið
3pl	lof-að-i	tal-að-i	lif-ð-i	flyt-t-i	kved-d-i	-að/(i)ð†-i

Imperative

	lof-a	tal-a	lif	flyt	kveð	-a/–

Participles

Pres	lof-andi	tal-andi	lif-andi	flytj-andi	kveðj-andi	(See below)
Past	(-að-)	(-að-)	(-ð-)	(flutt-)	(kvadd-)	
m	lof-að-r	tal-að-r	lif-ð-r	flut-t-r	kvad-d-r	-að/ð†
f	lof-uð	tǫl-uð	lif-ð	flut-t	kvǫd-d	(+ Adj.
n	lof-a-t	tal-a-t	lif-t	flut-t	kvat-t	Endings)

---

* With modifications, see Section 7.8.

† With modifications, see Section 5.4.

VERBS: Weak (cont.)

Indicative

Pres	duga	vaka	Endings
1sg	dug-i	vak-i	-i
2sg	dug-i-r	vak-i-r	-i-r
3sg	dug-i-r	vak-i-r	-i-r
1pl	dug-um	vǫk-um	-um
2pl	dug-ið	vak-ið	-ið
3pl	dug-a	vak-a	-a
Past	(-ð-)	(-t-)	
1sg	dug-ð-a	vak-t-a	-ð*-a
2sg	dug-ð-ir	vak-t-ir	-ð*-ir
3sg	dug-ð-i	vak-t-i	-ð*-i
1pl	dug-ð-um	vǫk-t-um	-ð*-um
2pl	dug-ð-uð	vǫk-t-uð	-ð*-uð
3pl	dug-ð-u	vǫk-t-u	-ð*-u

Subjunctive

Pres

	duga	vaka	
1sg	dug-a	vak-a	-a
2sg	dug-ir	vak-ir	-ir
3sg	dug-i	vak-i	-i
1pl	dug-im	vak-im	-im
2pl	dug-ið	vak-ið	-ið
3pl	dug-i	vak-i	-i
Past	(-ð-)	(-t-)	
1sg	dyg-ð-a	vek-t-a	(i)-ð*-a
2sg	dyg-ð-ir	vek-t-ir	(i)-ð*-ir
3sg	dyg-ð-i	vek-t-i	(i)-ð*-i
1pl	dyg-ð-im	vek-t-im	(i)-ð*-im
2pl	dyg-ð-ið	vek-t-ið	(i)-ð*-ið
3pl	dyg-ð-i	vek-t-i	(i)-ð*-i

Imperative

	dug(-i)	vak(-i)	(-i)

Participles

Pres	dug-andi	vak-andi	(See below)
Past			
m	[þol-ð-r]	vak-t-r	(-a)ð*-
f	[þol-ð]	vǫk-t	(+ Adj.
n	dug-a-t	vak-a-t	Endings)

VERBS: Strong

Indicative

Pres	renna	rísa
1sg	renn	rís
2sg	renn-r	rís-s
3sg	renn-r	rís-s
1pl	renn-um	rís-um
2pl	renn-ið	rís-ið
3pl	renn-a	rís-a
Past	(rann, runnu)	(reis, risu)
1sg	rann	reis
2sg	rann-t	reis-t
3sg	rann	reis
1pl	runn-um	ris-um
2pl	runn-uð	ris-uð
3pl	runn-u	ris-u

Subjunctive

Pres

	renna	rísa
1sg	renn-a	rís-a
2sg	renn-ir	rís-ir
3sg	renn-i	rís-i
1pl	renn-im	rís-im
2pl	renn-ið	rís-ið
3pl	renn-i	rís-i
Past	(runnu)	(risu)
1sg	rynn-a	ris-a
2sg	rynn-ir	ris-ir
3sg	rynn-i	ris-i
1pl	rynn-i	ris-im
2pl	rynn-ið	ris-ið
3pl	rynn-i	ris-i

Imperative

	renn	rís

Participles

Pres	renn-andi	rís-andi
Past	(runninn)	(risinn)
m	runn-inn	ris-inn
f	runn-in	ris-in
n	runn-it	ris-it

---

* With modifications, see Section 5.4.

bjóða	fara	gefa	bera	láta	hlaupa	Endings
býð	fer	gef	ber	læt	hleyp	–
býð-r	fer-r	gef-r	ber-r	læt-r	hleyp-r	-r*
býð-r	fer-r	gef-r	ber-r	læt-r	hleyp-r	-r*
bjóð-um	fǫr-um	gef-um	ber-um	lát-um	hlaup-um	-um
bjóð-ið	far-ið	gef-ið	ber-ið	lát-ið	hlaup-ið	-ið
bjóð-a	far-a	gef-a	ber-a	lát-a	hlaup-a	-a
(bauð, buðu)	(fór, fóru)	(gaf, gáfu)	(bar, báru)	(lét, létu)	(hljóp, hljópu)	
bauð	fór	gaf	bar	lét	hljóp	–
baut-t	fór-t	gaf-t	bar-t	léz-t	hljóp-t	-t
bauð	fór	gaf	bar	lét	hljóp	–
buð-um	fór-um	gáf-um	bár-um	lét-um	hljóp-um	-um
buð-uð	fór-uð	gáf-uð	bár-uð	lét-uð	hljóp-uð	-uð
buð-u	fór-u	gáf-u	bár-u	lét-u	hljóp-u	-u
bjóð-a	far-a	gef-a	ber-a	lát-a	hlaup-a	-a
bjóð-ir	far-ir	gef-ir	ber-ir	lát-ir	hlaup-ir	-ir
bjóð-i	far-i	gef-i	ber-i	lát-i	hlaup-i	-i
bjóð-im	far-im	gef-im	ber-im	lát-im	hlaup-im	-im
bjóð-ið	far-ið	gef-ið	ber-ið	lát-ið	hlaup-ið	-ið
bjóð-i	far-i	gef-i	ber-i	lát-i	hlaup-i	-i
(buðu)	(fóru)	(gáfu)	(báru)	(létu)	(hljópu)	
byð-a	fœr-a	gæf-a	bær-a	lét-a	hlyp-a	(i)-a
byð-ir	fœr-ir	gæf-ir	bær-ir	lét-ir	hlyp-ir	(i)-ir
byð-i	fœr-i	gæf-i	bær-i	lét-i	hlyp-i	(i)-i
byð-im	fœr-im	gæf-im	bær-im	lét-im	hlyp-im	(i)-im
byð-ið	fœr-ið	gæf-ið	bær-ið	lét-ið	hlyp-ið	(i)-ið
byð-i	fœr-i	gæf-i	bær-i	lét-i	hlyp-i	(i)-i
bjóð	far	gef	ber	lát	hlaup	–
bjóð-andi	far-andi	gef-andi	ber-andi	lát-andi	hlaup-andi	(See below)
(boðinn)	(farinn)	(gefinn)	(borinn)	(látinn)	(hlaupinn)	
boð-inn	far-inn	gef-inn	bor-inn	lát-inn	hlaup-inn	(Like Article)
boð-in	far-in	gef-in	bor-in	lát-in	hlaup-in	
boð-it	far-it	gef-it	bor-it	lát-it	hlaup-it	

---

* With modifications, see Section 7.8.

VERBS: Preterite-Present

Indicative

Pres	mega	munu	skulu	eiga	kná
1sg	má	mun	skal	á	kná
2sg	má-tt	mun-t	skal-t	á-tt	kná-tt
3sg	má	mun	skal	á	kná
1pl	meg-um	mun-um	skul-um	eig-um	kneg-um
2pl	meg-uð	mun-uð	skul-uð	eig-uð	kneg-uð
3pl	meg-u	mun-u	skul-u	eig-u	kneg-u
Past	(mátt-)	(mund-)	(skyld-)	(átt-)	(knátt-)
1sg	má-tt-a	mun-d-a	skyl-d-a	á-tt-a	kná-tt-a
2sg	má-tt-ir	mun-d-ir	skyl-d-ir	á-tt-ir	kná-tt-ir
3sg	má-tt-i	mun-d-i	skyl-d-i	á-tt-i	kná-tt-i
1pl	má-tt-um	mun-d-um	skyl-d-um	á-tt-um	kná-tt-um
2pl	má-tt-uð	mun-d-uð	skyl-d-uð	á-tt-uð	kná-tt-uð
3pl	má-tt-u	mun-d-u	skyl-d-u	á-tt-u	kná-tt-u

Subjunctive

Pres					
1sg	meg-a	mun-a/myn-a	skyl-a	eig-a	kneg-a
2sg	meg-ir	mun-ir/myn-ir	skyl-ir	eig-ir	kneg-ir
3sg	meg-i	mun-i/myn-i	skyl-i	eig-i	kneg-i
1pl	meg-im	mun-im/myn-im	skyl-im	eig-im	kneg-im
2pl	meg-ið	mun-ið/myn-ið	skyl-ið	eig-ið	kneg-ið
3pl	meg-i	mun-i/myn-i	skyl-i	eig-i	kneg-i
Past	(mátt-)	(mund-)	(skyld-)	(átt-)	(knátt-)
1sg	mæ-tt-a	myn-d-a	skyl-d-a	æ-tt-a	knæ-tt-a
2sg	mæ-tt-ir	myn-d-ir	skyl-d-ir	æ-tt-ir	knæ-tt-ir
3sg	mæ-tt-i	myn-d-i	skyl-d-i	æ-tt-i	knæ-tt-i
1pl	mæ-tt-im	myn-d-im	skyl-d-im	æ-tt-im	knæ-tt-im
2pl	mæ-tt-ið	myn-d-ið	skyl-d-ið	æ-tt-ið	knæ-tt-ið
3pl	mæ-tt-i	myn-d-i	skyl-d-i	æ-tt-i	knæ-tt-i

Imperative

				eig	

Participles

Pres	meg-andi			eig-andi	
Past	má-tt			á-tt	

Pret. Infinitive

		mun-d-u	skyl-d-u		kná-tt-u

kunna	muna	unna	vita	þurfa	Endings
kann	man	ann	veit	þarf	–
kann-t	man-t	ann-t	veiz-t	þarf-t	-t
kann	man	ann	veit	þarf	–
kunn-um	mun-um	unn-um	vit-um	þurf um	-um
kunn-uð	mun-ið	unn-uð	vit-uð	þurf-uð	-uð
kunn-u	mun-a	unn-u	vit-u	þurf-u	-u
(kunn-)	(mund-)	(unn-)	(viss-)	(þurft-)	
kunn-a	mun-d-a	unn-a	vis-s-a	þurf-t-a	-ð*-a
kunn-ir	mun-d-ir	unn-ir	vis-s-ir	þurf-t-ir	-ð*-ir
kunn-i	mun-d-i	unn-i	vis-s-i	þurf-t-i	-ð*-i
kunn-um	mun-d-um	unn-um	vis-s-um	þurf-t-um	-ð*-um
kunn-uð	mun-d-ið	unn-uð	vis-s-uð	þurf-t-uð	-ð*-uð
kunn-u	mun-d-a	unn-u	vis-s-u	þurf-t-u	-ð*-u
kunn-a	mun-a	unn-a	vit-a	þurf-a	-a
kunn-ir	mun-ir	unn-ir	vit-ir	þurf-ir	-ir
kunn-i	mun-i	unn-i	vit-i	þurf-i	-i
kunn-im	mun-im	unn-im	vit-im	þurf-im	-im
kunn-ið	mun-ið	unn-ið	vit-ið	þurf-ið	-ið
kunn-i	mun-i	unn-i	vit-i	þurf-i	-i
(kunn-)	(mund-)	(unn-)	(viss-)	(þurft-)	
kynn-a	myn-d-a	ynn-a	vis-s-a	þyrf-t-a	(i)-ð*-a
kynn-ir	myn-d-ir	ynn-ir	vis-s-ir	þyrf-t-ir	(i)-ð*-ir
kynn-i	myn-d-i	ynn-i	vis-s-i	þyrf-t-i	(i)-ð*-i
kynn-im	myn-d-im	ynn-im	vis-s-im	þyrf-t-im	(i)-ð*-im
kynn-ið	myn-d-ið	ynn-ið	vis-s-ið	þyrf-t-ið	(i)-ð*-ið
kynn-i	myn-d-i	ynn-i	vis-s-i	þyrf-t-i	(i)-ð*-i
kunn	mun	unn	vit		–
kunn-andi	mun-andi	unn-andi	vit-andi	þurf-andi	(See below)
kunn-a-t	mun-a-t	unn(-a)-t	vit-a-t	þurf-t	(-a)-t
					-ð*-u

---

* With modifications, see Sections 5.4, 15.3.

VERBS: Reflexive

Indicative

	Weak			Strong	Endings
Pres	**kallask**	**sýnask**	**gleðjask**	**farask**	wk | str
1sg	kǫll-**umk**	sýn-**umk**	gleðj-**umk**	fer-**umk**	-umk
2sg	kall-**a-sk**	sýn-**i-sk**	gle-**zk**	fer-**sk**	-sk*
3sg	kall-**a-sk**	sýn-**i-sk**	gle-**zk**	fer-**sk**	-sk*
1pl	kǫll-**um(s)k**	sýn-**um(s)k**	gleðj-**um(s)k**	fǫr-**um(s)k**	-um(s)k
2pl	kall-**izk**	sýn-**izk**	gleð-**izk**	far-**izk**	-izk
3pl	kall-**ask**	sýn-**ask**	gleðj-**ask**	far-**ask**	-ask
Past	(-að-)	(-d-)	(gladd-)		
1sg	kǫll-**uð-umk**	sýn-**d-umk**	glǫd-**d-umk**	fór-**umk**	-umk
2sg	kall-**að-isk**	sýn-**d-isk**	glad-**d-isk**	fór-**zk**	-isk | -zk
3sg	kall-**að-isk**	sýn-**d-isk**	glad-**d-isk**	fór-**sk**	-isk | -sk*
1pl	kǫll-**uð-um(s)k**	sýn-**d-um(s)k**	glǫd-**d-um(s)k**	fór-**um(s)k**	-um(s)k
2pl	kǫll-**uð-uzk**	sýn-**d-uzk**	glǫd-**d-uzk**	fór-**uzk**	-uzk
3pl	kǫll-**uð-usk**	sýn-**d-usk**	glǫd-**d-usk**	fór-**usk**	-usk

Subjunctive

Pres

1sg	kǫll-**umk**	sýn-**umk**	gleðj-**umk**	fǫr-**umk**	-umk
2sg	kall-**isk**	sýn-**isk**	gleð-**isk**	far-**isk**	-isk
3sg	kall-**isk**	sýn-**isk**	gleð-**isk**	far-**isk**	-isk
1pl	kall-**im(s)k**	sýn-**im(s)k**	gleð-**im(s)k**	far-**im(s)k**	-im(s)k
2pl	kall-**izk**	sýn-**izk**	gleð-**izk**	far-**izk**	-izk
3pl	kall-**isk**	sýn-**isk**	gleð-**isk**	far-**isk**	-isk
Past	(-að-)	(-d-)	(gladd-)		
1sg	kǫll-**uð-umk**	sýn-**d-umk**	gled-**d-umk**	fœr-**umk**	(i)-umk
2sg	kall-**að-isk**	sýn-**d-isk**	gled-**d-isk**	fœr-**isk**	(i)-isk
3sg	kall-**að-isk**	sýn-**d-isk**	gled-**d-isk**	fœr-**isk**	(i)-isk
1pl	kall-**að-im(s)k**	sýn-**d-im(s)k**	gled-**d-im(s)k**	fœr-**im(s)k**	(i)-im(s)k
2pl	kall-**að-izk**	sýn-**d-izk**	gled-**d-izk**	fœr-**izk**	(i)-izk
3pl	kall-**að-isk**	sýn-**d-isk**	gled-**d-isk**	fœr-**isk**	(i)-isk

Imperative

	kall-**a-sk**	sýn-**sk**	gle-**zk**	far-**sk**	-sk*

Participles

Pres	kall-**andi-sk**	sýn-**andi-sk**	gleðj-**andi-sk**	far-**andi-sk**	-sk
	(-að-)	(-d-)	(gladd-)		
Past	kall-**a-zk**	sýn-**zk**	gla-**zk**	far-**izk**	-zk | -izk

---

* Dental consonant + -*sk* = -*zk*, see Section 10.5.

VERBS: Irregular

vera 'be'

	Indicative	Subjunctive
Pres		
1sg	em	sé
2sg	er-**t**	sé-**r**
3sg	er	sé
1pl	er-**um**	sé-**m**
2pl	er-**uð**	sé-**ð**
3pl	er-**u**	sé
Past		
1sg	var	vær-**a**
2sg	var-**t**	vær-**ir**
3sg	var	vær-**i**
1pl	vár-**um**	vær-**im**
2pl	vár-**uð**	vær-**ið**
3pl	vár-**u**	vær **i**

Imperative

Sg	ver
Pl	ver-**ið**

Participles

Past	ver-**it**

hafa 'have'

	Indicative	Subjunctive
Pres		
1sg	hef-**(i)**	haf-**a**
2sg	hef-**(i)r**	haf-**ir**
3sg	hef-**(i)r**	haf-**i**
1pl	hǫf-**um**	haf-**im**
2pl	haf-**ið**	haf-**ið**
3pl	haf-**a**	haf-**i**
Past		
1sg	haf-**ð-a**	hef-**ð-a**
2sg	haf-**ð-ir**	hef-**ð-ir**
3sg	haf-**ð-i**	hef-**ð-i**
1pl	hǫf-**ð-um**	hef-**ð-im**
2pl	hǫf-**ð-uð**	hef-**ð-ið**
3pl	hǫf-**ð-u**	hef-**ð-i**

Imperative

	haf

Participles

Pres	haf-**andi**

Past	
m	haf-**ð-r**
f	hǫf-**ð**
n	haf-**t**

VERBS: Present Participle Declension

	Masc	Fem	Neut	Endings (Like Comp. Adj.)		
Sg nom	verð-**and-i**	verð-**and-i**	verð-**and-a**	-i	-i	-a
acc	verð-**and-a**	verð-**and-i**	verð-**and-a**	-a	-i	-a
dat	verð-**and-a**	verð-**and-i**	verð-**and-a**	-a	-i	-a
gen	verð-**and-a**	verð-**and-i**	verð-**and-a**	-a	-i	-a
Pl nom	→	verð-**and-i**	←	→	-i	←
acc	→	verð-**and-i**	←	→	-i	←
dat	→	verð-**ǫnd-um**	←	→	-um	←
gen	→	verð-**and-i**	←	→	-i	←

Appendix 3
Vocabulary of Words and Phrases

This vocabulary is a complete listing of words and significant phrases in the lessons, exercises, and readings. Words are alphabetized employing the following conventions.

- *ð* is listed with *d*.
- *þ, æ, œ, ǫ, ø* come at the end of the alphabet in that order.
- Short vowels and long vowels are treated as separate letters. Words beginning with a short (unaccented) vowel are alphabetized ahead of words beginning with a long (accented) vowel. The same rule applies to short and long vowels within a word. For example, *austr* comes before *á*, and *farmaðr* comes before *fá*.

a, á, b, d, ð, e, é, f, g, h, i, í, j, k, l, m, n, o, ó,
p, r, s, t, u, ú, v, x, y, ý, z, þ, æ, œ, ǫ(ö), ø

Principal parts of verbs are listed as follows:

- Weak verbs:
  infinitive (dental suffix or past-tense stem)
- Strong verbs:
  infinitive (3sg. pres.; 3sg. past, 3pl. past; ppart.)
- Preterite-present verbs:
  infinitive (3sg. pres, 3pl. pres.; 3sg past; ppart. or pret. inf.)

Where phrases and idioms are listed, the Icelandic convention of using the pronouns **einnhverr** 'somebody' [sb] and **eitthvat** 'something' [sth] has been adopted to indicate which case the object of a verb or preposition takes, and to distinguish whether the object is a person or thing.

> **[e-n]** (**einhvern**) =somebody [sb] *acc*
> **[e-t]** (**eitthvat**) =something [sth] *acc*
> **[e-m]** (**einhverjum**) =(for) [sb] *dat*
> **[e-u]** (**einhverju**) =(for) [sth] *dat*
> **[e-s]** (**einhvers**) =(of) [sb] or [sth] *gen*

Examples:

> **fala [e-t] af [e-m]** offer to buy [sth] from [sb]
> **firra [e-n] [e-u]** deprive [sb] of [sth]
> **mæla [e-t] við [e-n]** say [sth] to [sb]
> **segja [e-m] frá [e-m]** tell, inform [sb] about [sb]
> **segja [e-m] til [e-s]** tell, inform [sb] where [sth/sb] is to be found

A

Aðalból *n* Adalbol (*place name*)

Aðalsteinn *m* Athelstane (*personal name*)

Aðils *m* (*indecl*) Adils (*personal name*)

aðrar *adj, see* **annarr**

af *prep* [*w dat*] off, out of, from; of; with; in regard to, concerning; on account of, by reason of; **skjóta af** shoot with

af *adv* off, away; **verða af** come about, appear

afarkostir *m pl* hard terms

afl *n* strength; **sterkr at afli** strong

aka (ekr; ók, óku; ekinn) *vb* drive

aldar, aldir *f, see* **ǫld**

aldr *m* age, life; **á ungum aldri** young, of a young age

aldri *adv* never

aldrlag *n* fate, destiny; end of life

Alfǫðr *m* 'All-Father', a name of Odin

allmikill *adj* very great

allr (*f* ǫll, *n* allt) *adj/pron* all, entire, whole; **um alla hluti** in all respects; **alls konar** of every kind, of all kinds; **allra helzt** especially, most of all; **at ǫllu** in all respects

allvaldr *m* sovereign, king

alskipaðr *adj* fully manned

alt *adv* all the way

alvara *f* earnestness, seriousness

alþýða *f* all the people, the majority of people, the public, the common people

Andvari *m* Andvari ('Vigilance') (*personal name*), dwarf whose gold is used to pay Otr's wergild

annarr (*f* ǫnnur, *n* annat; *acc m* annan, *f* aðra, *dat m* ǫðrum, *n* ǫðru; *pl m* aðrir, etc.; *see* 13.3) *adj* other, another; second; **annarr... annarr...** *indef pron* the one... the other...; **at ǫðrum kosti** otherwise

aptr *adv* back

arfr *m* inheritance

Arinbjǫrn *m* Arinbjorn (*personal name*)

armr (*f* ǫrm, *n* armt) *adj* wretched, vile, wicked; poor, unfortunate

Arnarstakkr *m* 'Eagle's Haystack', a mountain in the south of Iceland (*place name*)

Arnarstakksheiðr *f* Heath of Arnarstakkr (*place name*)

askr *m* ash (tree)

at *prep* [*w dat*] at, to; with respect to; for, as; **auðigr at fé** wealthy; **kærr at** fond of; **sterkr at afli** strong; **vera/verða at sætt** constitute a settlement or agreement

at *adv* **berask at** happen; [e-t] **er/var at** it is/was [sth]; **gaman sé at** it is amusing

at *conj* that; so that

at *inf marker* to

auðigr *adj* wealthy; **auðigr at fé** wealthy

Auðhumla *f* Audhumla (*mythological name*, the primeval cow)

Auðr *f* Aud (*personal name*)

auga *n* eye

auka (eykr; jók, jóku; aukinn) *vb* increase

Aurland *n* Aurland (*place name*)

ausa (eyss; jós, jósu/jusu; ausinn) *vb* sprinkle, pour

austr *adv* east

austanverðr *adj* eastern

Á

á *prep* [*w acc*] on, onto, into (*motion*); with respect to; [*w dat*] on, at, in (*location*); **á dǫgum** in the days; **á einu hverju sumri** one summer; **á himni** in heaven; **á lífi** alive; **á ungum aldri** young; **fegrð á hár (líki)** beauty of hair (body); **kveða á** fix, determine

á *adv* **á brott** away; **hversu lízk þér á** how do you like

á (*gen* ár; *pl* ár, *dat* ám, *gen* á) *f* river

á *vb, see* **eiga**

áðr *adv* before, already; *conj* before

ágætr (*superl* ágætastr) *adj* excellent, outstanding

Álfheimr *m* 'Land of the Elves' (*place*

name)
álfr *m* elf
Álfr *m* Alf ('Elf') (*personal name*)
álit *n* appearance, countenance; **fagr**
  álitum beautiful (in appearance),
  handsome
ár *n* year
Ásgerðr *f* Asgerd (*personal name*)

áss (*dat* æsi/ás, *gen* áss/ásar; *pl* æsir,
  acc ásu/æsi) *m* god; **Æsir** *pl* one of
  the two major groups of gods
át *vb*, *see* **eta**
átján *num* eighteen
átt, átti, áttar *vb*, *see* **eiga**
átta *num* eight

B

bað *vb*, *see* **biðja**
bak *n* back
Baldr *m* Baldr (*mythological name*)
bani *m* death
banna (-að-) *vb* forbid, prohibit;
  banna jarðir at byggja ok vinna
  forbid lands to be rented and worked
bar *vb*, *see* **bera**
bardagi *m* battle
barðisk *vb*, *see* **berja**
barn (*pl* bǫrn) *n* child
barsk, báru *vb*, *see* **bera**
batt *vb*, *see* **binda**
bauð *vb*, *see* **bjóða**
baugr (*dat* baug(i)) *m* ring
bazk *vb*, *see* **biðja**
báðir (*f* báðar, *n* bæði, *gen* beggja)
  adj/pron dual both
báru *vb*, *see* **bera**
beðit *vb*, *see* **biðja**
beiða (-dd-) *vb* [*w gen*] ask; *refl*
  beiðask request for oneself
bein *n* bone
beinlauss *adj* boneless
bekkr (*dat* bekk, *gen* -jar; *pl* -ir) *m*
  bench
belgr (*dat* belg, *gen* -s/jar; *pl* -ir) *m*
  pelt, skin of an animal (taken off
  whole); skin-bag; bellows
bera (berr; bar, báru; borinn) *vb*
  carry, bear; **bera saman** collect,
  gather together; **bera út á** carry out
  into; **bera vápn á [e-n]** raise
  weapons against [sb]; **vel viti
  borinn** intelligent, endowed with
  good sense; *refl* **berask at** happen
berg *n* rock, boulder
berja (barð-) *vb* beat, strike, smite;
  refl **berjask** fight
betr *comp adv* better (*see* **vel**)
betri *comp adj* better (*see* **góðr**)

bezt *superl adv* best (*see* **vel**)
beztr *superl adj* best (*see* **góðr**)
biðja (biðr; bað, báðu; beðinn) *vb* ask,
  request, bid; [*w gen*] ask for, request;
  biðja konu ask for a woman in
  marriage; *refl* **biðjask undan** be
  evasive
Bifrǫst *f* the rainbow bridge to
  heaven
bik *n* pitch
bil *n* moment
binda (bindr; batt, bundu; bundinn)
  vb bind, tie, tie up
bitu *vb*, *see* **bíta**
bíta (bítr; beit, bitu; bitinn) *vb* bite
Bjarnardóttir *f* daughter of Bjorn
bjartr *adj* bright, radiant
bjó *vb*, *see* **búa**
bjóða (býðr; bauð, buðu; boðinn) *vb*
  [*w acc of person, dat of thing*] offer
bjósk *vb*, *see* **búa**
Bjǫrgyn (*dat* Bjǫrgyn) *m* Bergen,
  Norway (*place name*)
bjǫrn (*dat* birni, *gen* bjarnar; *pl* birnir,
  acc bjǫrnu; *see* 11.5, 17.6) *m* bear
Bjǫrn (*dat* Birni, *gen* Bjarnar; *see*
  11.5) *m* Bjorn ('Bear') (*personal
  name*)
blása (blæss; blés, blésu; blásinn) *vb*
  blow
blóð *n* blood
blót *n* sacrifice
blunda (-að) *vb* shut the eyes, doze
boð *n* bidding, command; message
bogi *m* bow; **kom á boga Einars
  miðjan** struck the middle of Einars
  bow
bogmaðr *m* archer
borg (*pl* -ir) *f* stronghold, fortification;
  town
Borg *f* Borg (*place name*)

Borgarfjǫrðr *m* 'Borg's Fjord', a fjord in Western Iceland (*place name*)

borinn *ppart, see* **bera**

botn (*gen* botns; *pl* botnar) *m* bottom; head of a bay, lake, dale, etc.

bók (*pl* bœkr) *f* book

ból *n* lair

bóndi (*pl* bœndr) *see* **búandi**

bónorð *n* request, petition; **hefja upp bónorð** propose marriage

bragð *n* sudden, brisk movement; moment; **af bragði**, soon

brann *vb, see* **brenna**

brast *vb, see* **bresta**

braut *var of* **brot(t)**

brá *f* eyelash

brá, brásk *vb, see* **bregða**

brátt *adv* quickly

Brávǫllr *m* Bravoll, a plain in Sweden (*place name*)

bregða (bregðr; brá, brugðu; brugðinn) *vb* [*w dat*] cause to move; thrust (a weapon); alter, change; *refl* **bregðask** change oneself into another shape

Breiðablik *n* Breidablik ('Broad Gleam') (*mythological place name*)

brekka *f* slope

brenna (brennr; brann, brunnu; brunninn) *vb* burn

bresta (brestr; brast, brustu; brostinn) *vb* break

brestr (*pl* -ir) *m* break, crash; **eigi mun svá mikill brestr orðinn** such a great break is not likely to have occurred

brjósk *n* cartilage

brjóta (brýtr; braut, brutu; brotinn) *vb* break

brot(t) *adv* **á brott** away (*motion*); **í brot(t)** away (*motion*)

brottu *adv* **í brottu** away (*location*)

bróðir (*acc/dat/gen* bróður; *pl* brœðr, *dat* brœðr, *gen* brœðra; *see* 9.5, 14.8) *m* brother

bróðurgjǫld *n pl* ransom, wergild (blood money) for a brother

brók (*pl* brœkr) *f* pants-leg; breeches

brunnr *m* well

brúarsporðr *m* bridge-head

brúðlaup *n* wedding; **gera brúðlaup til** marry

brynja *f* coat of mail

Brynjólfr *m* Brynjolf (*personal name*)

brýtr *vb, see* **brjóta**

brœðr, brœðra *m pl, see* **bróðir**

bundit *ppart, see* **binda**

Buri *m* Buri (*personal name*)

búa (býr; bjó, bjoggu; búinn) *vb* live (in a place), dwell; *refl* **búask** prepare (oneself); **búask til** prepare (oneself) for; **undir at búa** to bear up under

búandi (*also* **bóndi**) (*pl* búendr) *m* farmer; head of a household

búð (*pl* -ir) *f* tent, booth

bygð *f* home, settlement, abode

byggja (bygð-) *vb* inhabit, dwell; rent, let out

byrðr *f* burden, load

byrr (*gen* -jar; *pl* -ir) *m* fair wind; **[e-m] gefr vel byri** *impers* [sb] gets fair winds

býr, býsk *vb, see* **búa**

bǫrn *n pl, see* **barn**

bæði *adv* both

bœkr *f pl, see* **bók**

bœndr *m pl, see* **bóndi**

bœr (*dat* bœ, *gen* bœjar; *pl* bœir) *m* farm, farmstead; farmhouse

bœta (-tt-) *vb* better, improve

bǫl (-v-) *n* trouble, misfortune, 'bale'

bǫlvasmiðr *m* trouble-smith, forger of misfortune

D

dagr *m* day; **á dǫgum** in the days (of); **í dag** today; **þann dag** on that day

dalr (*dat* dal(i)) *m* valley, dale

Danmǫrk (*dat* Danmǫrku) *f* Denmark

dauðr (*n* dautt) *adj* dead

deyja (deyr; dó, dóu; dáinn) *vb* die

deila *f* dispute

djúpr *adj* deep

dóttir (*acc/dat/gen* dóttur; *pl* dœtr, *dat* dœtrum, *gen* dœtra; *see* 9.5, 14.8) *f* daughter

draga (dregr; dró, drógu; dreginn) *vb* pull, draw; **draga fyrir** draw beyond; **draga saman** assemble

drakk *vb, see* **drekka**
drap *vb, see* **drepa**
draup *vb, see* **drjúpa**
drápu *vb, see* **drepa**
dregr *vb, see* **draga**
drekka (drekkr; drakk, drukku; drukkinn) *vb* drink
drepa (drepr; drap, drápu; drepinn) *vb* kill; [*w dat*] put
drjúpa (drýpr; draup, drupu; dropit) *vb* drip
dró *vb, see* **draga**
dvelja (dvalð-) *vb* delay, defer; *refl*

dveljask stay
dvergr *m* dwarf
dýr *n* animal, beast
dældarmaðr *m* gentle, easy man
dœgr *n* a half day (twelve hours of day or night); a full day of 24 hours; **fjǫgurra (fimm) dœgra haf**, a sail of four (five) days; **sjau dœgra sigling** a sail of seven days
dœl *f* dale, hollow
dǫgum *m, see* **dagr**
Døkkálfr *m* 'Dark-Elf'
døkkr (-v-) *adj* dark

E

eða *conj* or
Edda *f* Edda (*literary work*); **Snorra Edda** 'Snorri's Edda', *The Prose Edda* written by Snorri Sturluson
ef *conj* if
efla (-d-) *vb* make, perform
egg (-j-) *f* edge
eggja (-að-) *vb* egg on, urge, incite
Egill *m* Egil (*personal name*)
eiga (á, eigu; átti; áttr) *vb* own, possess; be married to, have (relatives); **eiga eptir** leave behind; **sem hon átti ætt til** which was characteristic for her family
eigi *adv* not, no
Einarr *m* Einar (*personal name*)
einn (*f* ein, *n* eitt) *num* one; *adj* one, a certain; **einn hverr** one, a certain; **á einu hverju sumri** one summer; (*n* **eitt**) one thing, the same thing
einvaldskonungr *m* sole ruler, monarch
Eiríkr *m* Eirik (*personal name*)
eitt *num* (*n*), *see* **einn**
ek (*acc* mik, *dat* mér, *gen* mín; *see* 3.6) *pron* I
ekki *indef pron* (*n*), *see* **engi**; *as adv* not
eldask (-ld-) *refl vb* grow old
eldr *m* fire
Elfráðr *m* Alfred (*personal name*)
Ella *m* Ælla, King of Northumbria (*personal name*)
elli *f* old age
ellifu *num* eleven

ellri *comp adj* older (*see* **gamall**)
ellstr *superl adj* oldest (*see* **gamall**)
elska (-að-) *vb* love; be fond of
em *vb, see* **vera**
en *conj* but; and (on the other hand)
en *conj* than
endi *m* end
engi (*f* engi, *n* ekki; *gen m/n* enskis) *indef pron* no one, not one, no; (*pl*) none; (*after neg*) any; (*n* **ekki**) nothing
England *n* England
enn *adv* still, yet; further, moreover
enskis *indef pron, see* **engi**
eptir *prep* [*w acc*] after (*time*); [*w dat*] after, along with; according to; **þar eptir** accordingly, from this; **eiga eptir** leave behind; **spyrja eptir** ask about
eptir *adv* behind, left over
er *rel pron/adv* when; where; who, which, that; *conj* when; since; **þar er** where; **þá er** when
er, ert, erum *vb, see* **vera**
Erlingr *m* Erling (*personal name*)
es = **er**
eta (etr; át, átu; etinn) *vb* eat
etja (att-) *vb* [*w dat*] incite, egg on; **etja hestum** incite horses (to fight)
ey (*dat* ey/eyju, *gen* -jar; *pl* -jar) *f* island
eyða (-dd-) *vb* lay waste; spend up, squander; *refl* **eyðask** be squandered, come to naught
Eylimi *m* Eylimi (*personal name*);

legendary king, father of Hjordis

eyra *n* ear

Eymundr *m* Eymund (*personal name*)

Eysteinn *m* Eystein (*personal name*)

F

faðir (*acc/dat/gen* fǫður; *pl* feðr, *dat* feðrum, *gen* feðra; *see* 9.5, 14.8) *m* father

fagna (-að-) *vb* [*w dat*] welcome

fagr (*f* fǫgr, *n* fagrt; *comp* fegri, *superl* fegrstr) *adj* beautiful, fair, fine; **fagr álitum** beautiful (in appearance), handsome

falla (fellr; fell, fellu; fallinn) *vb* fall

fannsk *vb*, *see* **finna**

fara (ferr; fór, fóru; farit) *vb* go, travel; fare; **var farinn** had travelled; **fara með fíflsku** commit folly; *refl* **farask** go (of events), turn out; perish

farar *f pl*, *see* **fǫr**

farmaðr *m* traveller, sea-farer

fá (fær; fekk, fengu; fenginn) *vb* get; [*w gen*] marry; **fá sér liðs** gather a band of men, get support

Fáfnir *m* Fafnir (*personal name*); son of Hreidmar who turns himself into a dragon

fár *adj* few

feðgar *m pl* father and son(s)

feginn *adj* glad, pleased

fegrð *f* beauty; **fegrð á hár** (**líki**) beauty of hair (body)

fegri *comp adj* more beautiful (*see* **fagr**)

fegrstr *superl adj* fairest, most beautiful (*see* **fagr**); **fegrst talaðr** most eloquent

fekk *vb*, *see* **fá**

fell *n* mountain

fell, fellr *vb*, *see* **falla**

ferð (*pl* -ir) *f* trip, journey

fé (*gen* fjár; *pl gen* fjá) *n* property, wealth, money; cattle; **auðigr at fé** wealthy

fimm *num* five

fimmtán *num* fifteen

fingr *m* finger

finna (finnr; fann, fundu; fundinn) *vb* find; *refl* **finnask** appear; **finnask á** appear; **þá er honum fannsk mikit um** whom he liked very much

Finnr *m* Finn (*personal name*)

finnskr *adj* Finnish

Firðir *m pl* the Fjords (*place name*)

fiskr *m* fish

fíflska *f* folly, foolishness; **fara með fíflsku** commit folly

fjórir (*f* fjórar, *n* fjǫgur, *all gen* fjǫgurra; *see* 14.1) *num* four

fjórtán *num* fourteen

fjǫgur, fjǫgurra *num*, *see* **fjórir**

fjǫldi *m* multitude

fjǫlkunnigr *adj* skilled in magic, 'much knowing'

fjǫlmenni *n* crowd

fjǫlmennr *adj* populous, with many people, well attended

fjǫr (-v-) *n* life

fjǫrðr (*dat* firði, *gen* fjarðar; *pl* firðir, *acc* fjǫrðu, *gen* fjarða; *see* 11.5, 17.6) *m* fjord

Fjǫrðu, Fjǫrðum *m pl*, *see* **Firðir**

fjǫrlausn *f* ransom for one's life

fjǫrsegi *m* heart ('life-muscle')

flá (flær; fló, flógu; fleginn) *vb* flay, strip

fleiri *comp adj* more (*see* **margr**)

flestr *comp adj* most (*see* **margr**)

flytja (flutt-) *vb* convey, carry; deliver (an address), recite; **flytja til eyrna** [**e-m**] convey to the ears of [sb], inform [sb]

flýja (-ð-) to flee

formáli *m* 'fore-speech', foretelling

fors (*pl* -ar) *m* waterfall

forvitni *f* curiosity

fólk *n* people

fór, fóru *vb*, *see* **fara**

fóstbróðir *m* foster-brother

fóstr (*gen* -rs) *n* fostering, fosterage

fóstri *m* foster-father

fram *adv* forward, forth; **ganga vel fram** fight valiantly; **um fram** in addition

frauð *n* froth, juice (of roasted meat)

frá *prep* [*w dat*] from; about; **segja frá** relate, tell about

frá *adv* away, off; **ofan frá** below

fránn *adj* gleaming, flashing

Freyr *m* Frey (*mythological name*, one of the Vanir)

Freysgoði *m* 'Frey's Chief' (*nickname*)

frétt (*pl* -ir) *f* news

Frigg *f* Frigg, wife of Odin (*mythological name*)

fríðastr *superl adj, see* **fríðr**

fríðr (*n* frítt) *adj* beautiful, handsome, fine; **fríðr sýnum** fine in appearance

frjósa (frýss; fraus, frusu; frosinn) *vb* freeze

frægr *adj* famous

frœkn (*also* **frœkinn**) *adj* bold, daring, valiant

fugl *m* bird

fuglsrǫdd *f* bird's voice, speech of birds

fullr *adj* full

fullsteiktr *ppart* fully roasted (*from* **steikja**)

fundr (*gen* -ar; *pl* -ir) *m* meeting; audience

funi *m* flame

furða *f* wonder, marvel

fylking *f* battle array, the ranks of an army; battalion

fylla (-d-) *vb* fill

fyrir *prep* [*w acc*] before, in front of (*motion*); for, because of; instead of; [*w dat*] before, in front of (*location*); at the head of (leading); with; for, by; because of; **fyrir … sakar** on account of, because of; **fyrir sér** of oneself; **fyrir sik** for oneself, on one's own behalf; **fyrir strauminum** with the current; **fyrir útan** [*w acc*] outside; out beyond; **fyrir því, at** because; **draga fyrir** draw beyond; **ráða fyrir** rule over

fyrr *adv* before, earlier; **fyrr en** *conj* before

fyrri *comp adj* former

fyrst *superl adv* first, earliest

fyrstr *superl adj* first, foremost

fœða (-dd-) *vb* feed

fœra (-ð-) *vb* bring, convey; send, deliver, give; take

fǫður *m, see* **faðir**

fǫr (*pl* farar) *f* journey

G

gaf *vb, see* **gefa**

gagn (*pl* gǫgn) *n* advantage, benefit, produce, revenue

galtar *m, see* **gǫltr**

gamall (*acc* gamlan, *f* gǫmul, *n* gamalt; *comp* ellri, *superl* ellstr) *adj* old

gaman *n* fun, amusement, pleasure; **gera gaman** entertain; **at gaman sé at** that it is amusing

gamli (*gen* -a) *m* old one (*nickname*) (*wk m nom sg of* **gamall**)

ganga (gengr; gekk, gengu; genginn) *vb* go, walk; go out, spread; **ganga af** leave off, be finished with; **ganga at** [e-m] attack [sb]; **ganga á hǫnd** [e-m] submit to [sb], go into [sb]'s service, become [sb]'s retainer; **ganga fyrir** go before; **ganga til** approach, go up to a thing; **ganga vel fram** fight valiantly; **ganga yfir** [e-n] befall, happen to [sb]

Gangleri *m* Gangleri (*personal name*)

garðr *m* fence, wall

gefa (gefr; gaf, gáfu; gefinn) *vb* give

gegnum (*also* **í gegnum**) *prep* [*w acc*] through

geirr *m* spear

gekk, gengir, gengit, gengr *vb, see* **ganga**

gera (-ð-) *vb* make, do, build; **gera brúðlaup til** marry; **gera gaman** entertain; *refl* **gerask** become

gert *ppart, see* **gera**

geta (getr; gat, gátu; getinn) *vb* get; [*w gen*] guess; **geta at eiga** get in marriage, marry; **geta til** suppose, surmise

Gimlé *n* Gimle (*place name*)

Gísli *m* Gisli (*personal name*)

gjald *n* (*usu in pl* gjǫld) tribute; payment; reward; compensation; wergild (blood money)

glepja (glapð-) *vb* confuse, confound

Glitnir *m* Glitnir (*place name*)

Gnitaheiðr (*gen* -ar) *f* Gnitaheath (*place name*), where Fafnir, as a dragon, lies upon great wealth

gnótt *f* abundance

gnyðja (gnudd-) *vb* grunt

goð *n* god, one of the pagan gods

goðagremi *f* wrath of the gods

goði (*pl* goðar) *m* chief, chieftain

goðkunnigr *adj* related to the gods

goðorð *n* chieftainship, rank and authority of a **goði**

góðr (*n* gott; *comp* betri, *superl* beztr) *adj* good; **góðr af** proud of

góðhestr *m* good (riding) horse

grafa (grefr; gróf, grófu; grafinn) *vb* dig

Gramr *m* Gram (*mythological name*), name of Sigurd the Dragon Slayer's sword

granahár *n* whisker

grand *n* injury

Grani *m* Grani (*mythological name*), Sigurd the Dragon-Slayer's horse

gras *n* grass, plant, herb

gráliga *adv* maliciously

gráta (grætr; grét, grétu; grátinn) *vb* cry

greiða (-dd-) *vb* pay

gremi *f* wrath, anger

griðarof *n pl* breach of the peace, trucebreaking

grimmr *adj* grim, fierce, savage

gríss (*gen* -s; *pl* -ir) *m* young pig, piglet

grjót *n* stones (*collective*), rubble

Grjótgarðr *m* Grjotgard ('Stone-Fence') (*personal name*)

gróf *vb*, *see* **grafa**

Grœnland *n* Greenland

grœnn *adj* green

grǫf (*gen* grafar; *pl* grafir/grafar) *f* pit, ditch

grǫn (*gen* granar; *pl* granar) *f* lip

gull *n* gold

gullbaugr (*dat* gullbaug(i)) *m* gold ring

Gunnarr *m* Gunnar (*personal name*)

Gunnlaugr *m* Gunnlaug (*personal name*)

gǫfugligr *adj* magnificent

gǫfugr *adj* noble

gǫgnum *var of* **gegnum**

gǫltr (*dat* gelti, *gen* galtar; *pl* geltir, *acc* gǫltu, *gen* galta) *m* boar, hog

gǫrla *adv* fully, quite

gǫrr (-v-) *adj* done; **at svá gǫrvu** thus, this being the case, as things stood

gǫrr *comp adv* more fully, clearly (*see* **gǫrva**); **at gǫrr** for certain

gǫrst *superl adv* more fully, clearly (*see* **gǫrva**)

gǫrt *var of* **gert** *ppart*, *see* **gera**

gǫrva (*comp* gǫrr, *superl* gǫrst) *adv* quite, clearly

gǫrviligstr *superl adj*, *see* **gǫrviligr**

gǫrviligr *adj* accomplished, capable, enterprising

H

haf (*pl* hǫf) *n* sea; **fjǫgurra** (**fimm**) **dœgra haf** a sail of four (five) days

hafa (hef(i)r, -ð-) *vb* have; hold, keep; take; **hafa [e-m] heim með sér** bring [sb] home with oneself; **nǫkkut hafask at** undertake ('have at') something

hafnar, hafnir *f*, *see* **hǫfn**

hafsbotn (*gen* -botns; *pl* -botnar) *m* gulf; the Arctic Ocean (*place name*)

hagr *m* state, condition

halda (heldr; helt, heldu; haldinn) *vb* [*w acc/dat*] hold, hold fast; hold on to, keep, retain; direct, hold on a course; *refl* **haldask** hold true, remain valid, stand

hamrammr *adj* fierce, furious in battle (*lit.* 'shape-mighty'; used of warriors who 'changed shape', i.e., went berserk)

hana *pron*, *see* **hon**

hanga (hengr/hangir; hékk, hengu/héngu, hanginn) *vb* hang

hann (*acc* hann, *dat* honum, *gen* hans; *pl* þeir; *see* 5.1) *pron* he

hans *poss pron* his

Haraldr *m* Harald (*personal name*)

harðr (*f* hǫrð, *n* hart) *adj* hard

harðdrœgr *adj* hard to handle

harðliga *adv* forcibly, harshly, severely; hard

harðr (*f* hǫrð, *n* hart) *adj* hard

Haukadalr (*dat* Haukadal(i)) *m* 'Hawks' Dale' (*place name*)

haust *n* fall

Hákon (*gen* -ar) *m* Hakon (*personal*

name)

hálfa *f* region, part

hár *n* hair

hár *adj* tall, high; loud

Hár *m* Har ('High') (*mythological name*, pseudonym of Odin)

hárfagr *adj* fair-haired

hásæti *n* high-seat, throne

hátt *adv* loudly

Hávarðr *m* Havard (*personal name*)

hefði, hefi, hefir, hefr *vb, see* **hafa**

hefja (hefr; hóf, hófu; hafiðr/hafinn) *vb* raise; begin; **hefja upp bónorð** propose marriage

hefna (-d-) *vb* avenge

heiðr (*pl* -ar) *f* heath

heill *adj* healthy, well, 'hale'; whole

heim *adv* (to) home (*motion*)

heima *adv* at home (*location*)

heima *m, see* **heimr**

heimamaðr *m* servant, man belonging to a household

heimr *m* home, dwelling; land, region of the world; the world; **kringla heimsins** the globe, earth; **of alla heima** over the whole world

heita (heitir; hét, hétu; heitinn) *vb* be named, be called; promise

heldi, heldr, heldu *vb, see* **halda**

Helgi *m* Helgi ('Holy') (*personal name*)

helgistaðr *m* holy place

helmingr *m* half; **skipta í helminga** divide into two equal portions

helzk *vb, see* **halda**

helzt *superl adv* especially; **allra helzt** especially, most of all

hendi *f, see* **hǫnd**

hennar *poss pron* her, hers

herkonungr *m* warrior-king

herr (*gen* -jar; *pl* -jar) *m* army, host

herra *m* master, lord

hersaga *f* war-tidings (*see also* **herr, saga**)

hersir *m* local chieftain; a military leader with power from a king

hersǫgu *f, see* **hersaga**

hestaat *n* horse fight

hestavít *n* horse fight

hestr *m* horse, stallion

heyra (-ð-) *vb* hear

hégómi *m* insincerity

hér *adv* here

hét *vb, see* **heita**

Hildigunnr *f* Hildigunn (*personal name*)

Himinbjǫrg *n pl* 'Heaven Mountains' (*place name*)

himinn *m* heaven; **á himni** in heaven

hinn *art, var of* **inn**

hinn *pron* this (the other)

hitta (-tt-) *vb* meet; *refl* **hittask** meet one another

hjarta (*pl* hjǫrtu, *gen* hjartna) *n* heart

hjartablóð *n* heart's blood

hjá *prep* [*w dat*] with, by, beside

hjálmr *m* helmet

Hjálprekr *m* Hjalprek (*personal name*), a legendary king

hjó *vb, see* **hǫggva**

Hjǫrdís *f* Hjordis (*personal name*); mother of Sigurd

Hjǫrleifr *m* Hjorleif (*personal name*)

hjǫrtr (*dat* hirti, *gen* hjartar; *pl* hirtir, *acc* hjǫrtu; *see* 11.5, 17.6) *m* deer, stag, hart

Hjǫrtr (*dat* Hirti, *gen* Hjartar; *see* 11.5) *m* Hjort ('Deer') (*personal name*)

hlaup *n* leap, jump

hlaupa (hleypr; hljóp, hljópu; hlaupinn) *vb* run

Hliðskjálf *f* Hlidskjalf, name of Odin's throne

Hlíðarendi *m* Hlidarendi, a farm in southern Iceland (*place name*)

hlíf (*pl* -ar) *f* cover, protection (esp. of a shield or armor)

hluti *m* part

hlutr (*dat* hlut, *gen* -ar; *pl* -ir) *m* part; **um alla hluti** in all respects

hlýða (-dd-) [*w dat*] *vb* listen to; **hlýða til** listen to

hlæja (hlær; hló, hlógu; hleginn) *vb* laugh

hof *n* temple

Hof *n* Hof ('Temple') (*place name*)

Hofsland *n* the Hof estate

hon (*acc* hana, *dat* henni, *gen* hennar; *pl* þær; *see* 5.1) *pron* she

honum *pron, see* **hann**

horfa (-ð-) *vb* look, (turn so as to) look on; **horfa á** look at; **horfask til** be in prospect

horn *n* horn

Horn *n* Horn, farm in Southeastern Iceland, one of the first settlements in Iceland (*place name*)

hóf *vb, see* **hefja**

hófsmaðr *m* man of moderation and restraint

hógværr *adj* gentle, quiet

Hrafn *m* Hrafn ('Raven') (*personal name*)

Hrafnkell *m* Hrafnkel (*personal name*)

hraustr *adj* bold

Hreiðmarr *m* Hreidmar (*mythological name*), father of Otr, Fafnir, and Regin

hrím *n* hoar-frost, rime

hrímsteinn *m* rime-stone

hringr *m* ring

hross *n* horse, mare

Hrotti *m* Hrotti (*mythological name*), name of a sword

Hróaldr *m* Hroald (*personal name*)

Hróðgeirr *m* Hrodgeir (*personal name*)

hrósa (-að-) *vb* [*w dat*] boast (of)

hræða (-dd-) *vb* [*w acc*] frighten; *refl* **hræðask** be frightened; **hræðask [e-t]** be afraid of [sth]

hugða, hugði *vb, see* **hyggja**

hugr (*dat* hug(i), *gen* -ar; *pl* -ir) *m* mind; mood; courage; **vera í hug [e-m]** be in [sb]'s mind

hulði, huldr *vb, see* **hylja**

hundrað (*pl* hundruð) *n* hundred

hús *n* house

hvar *int adv* where

hvarf *n* disappearance

Hvarf *n* 'Disappearance', Cape Farewell in Greenland (*place name*)

hvass (*f* hvǫss, *n* hvas(s)t) *adj* sharp, keen

hvat *n int pron* what; *rel pron* what, that which (*see* **hverr**)

hvárr *int pron* who, which (of two); *indef pron* each (of two)

hvárrtveggja *indef pron* each (of two)

hvárt *conj* whether

hváta *vb* stick (in), poke, pierce

hverr (*n* hvat, *acc m* hvern; -j-) *int pron* who, what, which; **af hverju** why, for what reason; *indef pron* each, any(one), every(one); **einn hverr** one, a certain

hversu *adv* how; **hversu lízk þér á** how do you like

hvert *adv* to where

hvetja (hvatt-) *vb* whet, sharpen

hvé *adv* how, to what extent

hví *adv* why, for what reason (*n dat of* **hvat**)

hvítr *adj* white

Hvítserkr *m* Hvitserk ('White-Shirt') (*personal name*)

hyggja (hugð-) *vb* think; **hyggja at** pay attention to, consider

hylja (huld/hulð-) *vb* hide, cover

Hœnir *m* Hœnir (*mythological name*), one of the Æsir

hǫf *n pl, see* **haf**

hǫfðingi *m* leader

hǫfðu *vb, see* **hafa**

hǫfn (*gen* hafnar; *pl* hafnir) *f* harbor

hǫfuð *n* head

hǫfuðsbani *m* death, destruction

hǫfuðstaðr *m* capital, chief place

hǫgg (-v-) *n* stroke, blow

hǫggva (hǫggr; hjó, hjoggu; hǫgg(v)inn) *vb* strike, hack, hew

hǫnd (*dat* hendi, *gen* handar; *pl* hendr) *f* hand; **ganga á hǫnd [e-m]** submit to [sb], go into [sb]'s service, become [sb]'s retainer; **ór hendi þér** out of your hand; **selja í hendr** turn over; **taka hǫndum** take hold of, seize with the hands

Hǫrðakonungr *m* king of Hǫrðaland (in Western Norway)

I

igða *f* nuthatch (species of bird)

illa (*comp* verr, *superl* verst) *adv* badly, 'ill'

illr (*comp* verri, *superl* verstr) *adj* bad, evil, 'ill'

Ingi *m* Ingi (*personal name*)

Ingibjǫrg *f* Ingibjorg (*personal name*)

inn (*f* in, *n* it) *art* the

inn *adv* in (*motion*); **inn í** into

innlenzkr *adj* native

it *art* (*n*), *see* **inn**

Í

í *prep* [*w acc*] in, into (*motion*); [*w dat*] in, within; at (*location*); **í þann tíma** at that time
Írland *n* Ireland
Ísland *n* Iceland

íslenzkr *adj* Icelandic
Ívarr *m* Ivar (*personal name*)
íþrótt (*pl* -ir) *f* skill, feat, accomplishment

J

jafna (-að-) *vb* compare, liken; **jafna til** compare with, liken to
jafningi (*pl* -jar) *m* equal, match
jalda *f poet* mare
jarl *m* earl
Játvarðr *m* Edward (*personal name*)
Jórsalaland *n* 'Jerusaem's Land',

Israel (*place name*)
Jǫlduhlaup *n* 'Mare's Leap', Slyne Head in Ireland (*place name*)
jǫrð (*dat* -u) *f* earth
jǫtunn *m* giant
Jǫtunheimar *m pl* Land of Giants

K

kalla (-að-) *vb* call, name
kanna (-að-) *vb* search, explore
kannt *vb, see* **kunna**
kapalhestr *m* packhorse
kapítuli *m* chapter
kappi *m* hero, great fighter
kasta (-að-) *vb* [*w dat*] throw, cast; **kasta boganum** throw the bow
kastali *m* castle
kaupa (keypt-) *vb* buy
kemr *vb, see* **koma**
kjósa (kýss; kaus/kǫri, kusu/kuru, kosinn/kørinn) *vb* choose
Kerlingardalsá *f* 'River of the Valley of the Old Woman' (*place name*)
klauf *vb, see* **kljúfa**
kljúfa (klýfr; klauf, klufu; klofinn) *vb* split, cleave
klyf (*pl* -jar) *f* pack (for a horse)
klæði *n* cloth; garment, clothing
knǫrr (*acc* knǫrr, *dat* knerri, *gen* knarrar; *pl* knerrir, *acc* knǫrru, *dat* knǫrrum, *gen* knarra) *m* ship; merchant vessel
Kolskeggr *m* Kolskegg (*personal name*)
koma (kemr; kom, kómu; kominn) *vb* come; *refl* **komask** reach, arrive; **koma at** arrive; **koma á** strike; **koma upp** come about, happen; **komask undan** escape

komsk *vb, see* **koma**
kona (*pl gen* kvenna) *f* woman, wife; **biðja konu** ask for a woman in marriage
konar *gen sg of obs* **konr* *m* kind, sort; **alls konar** of every kind, of all kinds
konungr *m* king
konungsson *m* prince
kostr (*gen* -ar; *pl* -ir) *m* choice, alternative; opportunity; **at ǫðrum kosti** otherwise
kómu *vb, see* **koma**
krapparúm *n* bow-room (on a ship)
kringla *f* disk, circle, orb; **kringla heimsins** the globe, earth
kunna (kann, kunnu; kunni; kunnat) *vb* know, understand; be able
kunnigr *adj* known; knowing, skilled in magic
kvað *vb, see* **kveða**
kvaddi *vb, see* **kveðja**
kváðu, kváðusk *vb, see* **kveða**
kveða (kveðr; kvað, kváðu; kveðinn) *vb* say; **kveða á** fix, determine; *refl* **kveðask** say of oneself [*w inf*]
kveðja (kvadd-) *vb* greet
kveld *n* evening
Kveld-Úlfr *m* Kveld-Ulf ('Evening-Wolf') (*personal name*)
kvikvendi *n pl* living creatures,

animals, beasts
Kvígandafell *n* 'Heifer Mountain'
(*place name*)
kyrr *adj* still, quiet
kýr (*acc/dat* kú, *gen* kýr; *pl nom/acc*

kýr, *dat* kúm, *gen* kúa) *f* cow
kǫllum *vb, see* **kalla**
kærleikr *m* friendly terms
kærr *adj* dear; **kærr at** fond of
kœmi *vb, see* **koma**

L

lagabrot *n* lawbreaking; **lagabrot landsréttar** breaking the law of the land
lagði, lagðisk *vb, see* **leggja**
lagðr *m* tuft (of wool or hair)
lagt *vb, see* **leggja**
land (*pl* lǫnd) *n* land
landnám *n* settlement, 'land taking'
Landnámabók *f* Book of Settlements
landsréttr *m* law of the land; **lagabrot landsréttar** breaking the law of the land
Langanes *n* Langanes ('Long Headland'), peninsula in Northeast Iceland (*place name*)
langfeðgar *m pl* forefathers, ancestors (through the father's line)
langr *adj* long
langt *adv* far
lausn (*gen* -ar; *pl* -ir) *f* ransom
lauss *adj* free
laust *n adj, see* **lauss**
laust *vb, see* **ljósta**
lax (*gen* lax; *pl* laxar) *m* salmon
lá *vb, see* **liggja**
láta (lætr; lét, létu; látinn) *vb* let, allow; let go, lose; put, place, set; [*w inf*] have something done; **láta fram** let go, yield, hand over; **láta lífit** lose one's life; *refl* **látask** declare (of oneself)
leggja (lagð-, lag(i)ðr/laginn) *vb* lay, place; set, fix, arrange; [*w dat*] stab, thrust; **leggja [e-t] á [e-n]** impose, lay [sth] upon [sb]; **leggja [e-u] í gegnum [e-n]** thrust [sth] through [sb]; **leggja til (orð)** say; **leggja við** accuse of, declare guilty of or subject to; *refl* **leggjask** lay oneself, lie down; **leggjask at sofa** go to sleep
leggr (*gen* -jar; *pl* -ir) *m* leg, limb; hollow bone (of arm and leg)
leið (*pl* -ir) *f* way; path, road
leit *vb, see* **líta**

leita (-að-) *vb* [*w gen*] seek, search for
lemja (lamd-) *vb* beat, thrash
lendr *adj* 'landed', having lands; **lendr maðr** 'landed man' (Norw *lendmann*), a Norwegian nobleman whose lands and income were granted by the king
lengi *adv* long, a long time
lengja (-d-) *vb* lengthen
lengra *comp adv* farther
lét, lézk *vb, see* **láta**
lið *n* troop, force, band of armed supporters; aid, assistance; **fá sér liðs** gather a band of men, get support
liðfœrr *adj* able-bodied
lifa (-ð-) *vb* live; **lifa við** live on, feed on
liggja (liggr; lá, lágu, leginn) *vb* lie
litlu *adv* a little (*dat sg neut of* **lítill**); **litlu síðar** a little later
líf *n* life; **á lífi** alive
líki *n* form, shape, likeness; body
líkligr *adj* likely, probable; **sem líkligt er** as might be expected
líknsamr *adj* gracious, merciful
líta (lítr; leit, litu; litinn) *vb* look; **líta á** look at, consider; **hversu lízk þér á** how do you like
lítill (*f* lítil, *n* lítit; *acc m* litlan, *f* litla, *dat m* litlum, *n* litlu; *pl* litlir, etc.; *comp* minni, *superl* minnstr) *adj* little, small
lítt (*comp* minnr, *superl* minnst) *adv* little
Ljósálfr *m* 'Light-Elf'
ljóss *adj* light, fair; clear
ljósta (lýstr; laust, lustu; lostinn) *vb* strike, hit
loðbrók *f* 'Hairy Breeches' (*nickname*)
lofa (-að-) *vb* praise
Loki *m* Loki (*mythological name*), the trickster god, one of the Æsir
lokit *ppart, see* **lúka**

lunga *n* lung
lúka (lýkr; lauk, luku; lokinn) *vb* [*w dat*] end, finish
lýsa (-t-) *vb* shine

lætr *vb, see* **láta**
lǫg *n pl* law(s)
lǫgmaðr *m* lawman, lawyer

M

maðr (*acc* mann, *dat* manni, *gen* manns; *pl nom/acc* menn, *dat* mǫnnum, *gen* manna; *see* 2.6) *m* man; person, human being; **hvat manna** what sort of man
Magnús *m* Magnus (*personal name*)
man *vb, see* **muna**
mann, manna, manns *m, see* **maðr**
mannfólk *n* mankind, humanity
mannraun *f* trial (of courage), danger, peril; adversity
mannvænn *adj* promising
margr (*f* mǫrg, *n* mar(g)t; *comp* fleiri, *superl* flestr) *adj* [*w sg*] many a (in collective sense); [*w pl*] many; **mǫrgu sinni** many a time, on many occasions
marka (-að-) *vb* notice; infer
má *vb, see* **mega**
mál *n* speech, language; case, matter, affair
málmr *m* ore; metal
mátt, mátti *vb, see* **mega**
með *prep* [*w acc*] with (bringing, carrying along, or forcing); [*w dat*] with (accompanying or being together); along; with, by, using; between; **upp með** up along
meðan *conj* while
mega (má, megu; mátti; mátt) *vb* be able, be allowed; **vera má þat** maybe
mein *n* hurt, harm; **verða [e-m] at meini** cause [sb] harm
meir(r) *comp adv* more (*see* **mjǫk**)
meiri *comp adj* greater (*see* **mikill**)
menn *m pl, see* **maðr**
mest *superl adv* most (*see* **mjǫk**); **sem mest** as much as possible
mestr *superl adj* greatest; most (*see* **mikill**)
metnaðarmaðr *m* man of ambition
mey, meyjar *f, see* **mær**
mér *pron, see* **ek** (*see also* 3.6)
miðla (-að-) *vb* share
miðr (-j-) *adj* middle; **boga Einars**

miðjan to the middle of Einars bow
mik *pron, see* **ek** (*see also* 3.6)
mikill (*f* mikil, *n* mikit, *acc m* mikinn; *comp* meiri, *superl* mestr) *adj* big, large, great; much; (of rivers) swollen, running high; **mikill fyrir sér** strong, powerful, mighty
mikit *adv* much (*see* **mikill**)
miklu *adv* [*w comp*] much (*n dat sg of* **mikill**)
milli *prep* [*w gen*] between; **standa milli** separate, set at odds
minn (*f* mín, *n* mitt; *acc m* minn, *f* mína, *dat m* mínum, *n* mínu, *gen m/n* míns; *pl m* mínir, *f* mínar, *n* mín, *acc m* mína, *dat* mínum; *see* 16.4) *poss adj* my, mine
minni *comp adj* littler, smaller, lesser (*see* **lítill**)
minnr *comp adv* less (*see* **lítt**)
minnst *superl adv* least (*see* **lítt**)
minnstr *superl adj* littlest, smallest, least (*see* **lítill**)
mín *pron, see* **ek** (*see also* 3.6)
mjólk *f* milk
mjólk-á *f* milk-stream, river of milk
mjǫk (*comp* meir(r), *superl* mest) *adv* much, greatly, very; almost
móðir (*acc/dat/gen* móður; *pl* mœðr, *dat* mœðr, *gen* mœðra; *see* 9.5, 14.8) *f* mother
móti *prep* [*w dat*] toward, against
muna (man, muna; mundi; munaðr) *vb* remember
munnr *m* mouth
munu (mun, munu; mundi; *pret inf* mundu) *vb* will, shall (*future*), be likely
mylja (muld-) *vb* crush to pieces
myndi *vb, see* **munu**
mæla (-t-) *vb* say, speak; **mæla við** say to, speak to
mær (*acc* mey, *dat* meyju, *gen* meyjar; *pl nom/acc* meyjar, *dat* meyjum, *gen* meyja) *f* girl, maiden

mǫgr (*dat* megi, *gen* magar; *pl* megir, *acc* mǫgu) *m* boy, youth

N

nafn (*pl* nǫfn) *n* name
nakkvat *var of* **nǫkkut** (*see* **nǫkkurr**)
nam *vb, see* **nema**
nauð *f* need
nauðgjald *n* forced payment
ná (-ð-) *vb* [*w dat*] reach, attain
nábúi *m* neighbor
nám *n* acquisition, occupation; **land-nám** land-taking, settlement
nár (*gen* -s; *pl* -ir, *dat* nám) *m* corpse, dead man
nátt *var of* **nótt**
náttstaðr *m* night-quarters, lodging for the night
nefna (-d-) *vb* name, call; mention by name
neinn (= **né einn**) (*n* neitt) *indef pron* no, not one; [*w neg*] (not ...) any
neitt *indef pron, see* **neinn**
nema *conj* but (that), except
nema (nemr; nam, námu; numinn) *vb* take; **nema á brott** abduct
nes (-j-) *n* headland, peninsula
neyta (-tt-) *vb* [*w gen*] use, make use of
né *conj* nor
niðr *adv* down; **setja niðr** settle (a dispute)
niðri *adv* down (in)
nítján *num* nineteen

níu *num* nine
Njáll *m* Njal (*personal name*)
norðanverðr *adj* northern
norðr *adv* north
norðrhálfa *f* northern region
Norðrlǫnd *n pl* Northern Lands (Northern Europe) (*place name*)
norn *f* Norn
Nóregr *m* Norway
nótt (*gen* nætr; *pl* nætr) *f* night
nú *adv* now
nær *prep* [*w dat*] near
nær *adv* near, nearly
nær *conj* when
næst *adv* next (following); **því næst** then, next, thereupon
nǫkkurr (*f* nǫkkur, *n* nǫkkut) *indef pron* some, someone; any, anyone; one, a certain; (*n*) something, anything
nǫkkut *n adj as adv* somewhat, in some degree (*see* **nǫkkurr**); **nǫkkut hafask at** undertake ('have at') something; **vera nǫkkut við** be somehow connected with
Nǫrvasund *n pl* the Straits of Gibraltar (*place name*)
Nǫrvi *m* Norvi (*personal name*)

O

oddr *m* point
of *adv* too
of *prep* [*w acc/dat*] over (*distance*); for, during (*time*)
ofan *adv* down, from above; **ofan frá** below
ok *conj* and (in addition); as
okkarr *poss adj* our (two); **okkrum mundi þykkja** it would seem to us
okkr *pron, see* **vit** (*see also* 16.3)
opt *adv* often
orð *n* word
orðinn *ppart, see* **verða**

ormr *m* snake, serpent
ormslíki *n* form of a snake
ormstunga *f* 'Serpent's Tongue' (*nickname*)
orrosta *f* battle
oss *pron, see* **vér** (*see also* 3.6)
otr (*gen* -rs; *pl* -rar) *m* otter
Otr *m* Otr (*mythological name*), Otter, son of Hreidmar
otrbelgr *m* otter skin
otrgjǫld *n pl* otter's ransom, wergild (blood money) for a dead otter
oxi (*pl* øxn) *m* ox

Ó

ó- (*also* **ú-**) *pref* un-, in-

Óðinn *m* Odin (*mythological name*), chief god of the Æsir

ójafnaðr (*gen* -ar) *m* injustice; unfairness

ójafnaðarmaðr *m* unjust man, quarrelsome and overbearing, difficult to deal with

Óláfr *m* Olaf (*personal name*)

ólíkligr *adj* unlikely

ólíkr *adj* unlike, different; **ólíkr sýnum** different in appearance;

ólíkari reyndum more different in reality

ór (*also* **úr**) *prep* [*w dat*] out of, from; **ór hendi þér** out of your hands

óráð *n* evil plan, ill-advised plan

óreyndr *adj* unproved

ósáttr *adj* unreconciled, at odds

ótiginn *adj* not noble (of family), of common descent

óttask (-að-) *refl vb* fear

óvinr (*gen* -ar; *pl* -ir) *m* enemy

óœðri *comp adj* lower

P

penningr *m* penny, coin

R

Ragnarr *m* Ragnar (*personal name*)

rak *vb, see* **reka**

Randalín *f* Randalin (*personal name*)

rangr (*f* rǫng) *adj* wrong; crooked

rani *m* snout

rann *vb, see* **renna**

rauðavíkingr *m* 'red' viking, a particularly fierce and violent viking

rauðr *adj* red

ráð *n* counsel, advice, plan; match, marriage; **synja ráðs** refuse a proposal of marriage; **taka til ráða** adopt a plan

ráða (ræðr; réð, réðu; ráðinn) *vb* [*w dat*] advise, counsel; decide, determine; control, rule, govern; prevail in; **ráða fyrir** rule over; **ráða um við [e-n]** consult with [sb]; **þá er eigi ráðit** then there is no help for

Refill *m* Refil (*mythological name*), name of a sword

Refr *m* Ref ('Fox') (*personal name*)

Reginn *m* Regin (*mythological name*), son of Hreidmar and foster-father of Sigurd

reið *vb, see* **ríða**

reiði *f* anger

reiðr (*n* reitt) *adj* angry, wrathful

reka (rekr; rak, ráku; rekinn) *vb* be carried along, drift; **reka fyrir strauminum** drift with the current

renna (rennr; rann, runnu; runninn) *vb* run, flow

Reykjanes *n* Reykjanes ('Smoky Headland'), peninsula in Southwest Iceland (*place name*)

reykr (*gen* -jar; *pl* -ir) *m* smoke, steam

reyna (-d-) *vb* try, prove; experience; **reyna með** put to the test

reynd *f* experience; **reyndum** in reality

réð *vb, see* **ráða**

rétt *adv* straight (*see* **réttr**)

réttlátr *adj* just

réttr *adj* straight; right, just

ríða (ríðr; reið, riðu; riðinn) *vb* ride, go on horseback; [*w dat of animal, acc of road or place*]; **ríða hesti** ride a horse; **ríða leið sína** ride on one's way

ríkr *adj* powerful, mighty

ríki (-j-) *n* realm, kingdom; power; **setja til ríkis** put in power

rísa (ríss, reis, risu, risinn) *vb* rise

róg *f* stife, discord

rógmálmr *m* metal of strife

runnu *vb, see* **renna**

rýrr *adj* thin

ræðr *vb, see* **ráða**

rǫdd (*gen* raddar; *pl* raddir) *f* voice

Rǫgnvaldr *m* Rognvald (*personal name*)

rǫnum *m, see* **rani**

S

saga *f* story

sagði, sagt *vb, see* **segja**

salr (*dat* sal, *gen* -ar; *pl* -ir) *m* room, hall

saltr *adj* salt(y)

saman *adv* together; **bera saman** collect, gather together

samr *adj* same

sá (*f* sú, *n* þat; *acc* þann, *dat* þeim, *gen* þess; *pl* þeir; *see* 12.1) *dem pron/adj* that (one)

sá *vb, see* **sjá**

sár *n* wound

sátu *vb, see* **sitja**

segi *m* slice, strip, shred

segja (sagð-) *vb* say, tell; **segja frá** relate, tell about; **segja til** tell, inform of

seinþreyttr *adj* slow to stir up; **seinþreyttr til vandræða** slow to be drawn into a quarrel

selagnúpr *m* 'Seal-Cliff' (*nickname*)

selja (-d-) *vb* deliver, hand over; **selja í hendr** turn over (to)

sem *rel pron* who, which, that; *conj* as; [*w subjunct*] as if; [*w superl*] as ... as possible; **sem mest** as much as possible; **sem skjótast** at once, as soon as possible; **þar sem** there where

senda (-nd-) *vb* send

serkr (*gen* -s/jar; *pl* -ir, *gen* -ja) *m* shirt

setja (-tt-) *vb* set, put, place; **setja [e-n] fyrir** order [sb] to keep watch; **setja niðr** settle (a dispute); **setja til ríkis** put in power; *refl* **setjask** settle oneself, sit down

sex *num* six; **sex tigir** *num* [*w gen*] sixty

sextán *num* sixteen

sé *vb, see* **vera** (*see also* 16.2)

sér *refl pron, see* **sik**

sér *vb, see* **sjá**

sigla (-d-) *vb* sail

sigling (*pl* -ar) *f* sailing; voyage by sail; **sjau dœgra sigling** a sail of seven days

sigra (-að-) *vb* conquer, vanquish, be victorious, overcome; *refl* **sigrask** gain victory

Sigríðr *f* Sigrid (*personal name*)

sigrsæll *adj* victorious

sigrumsk *vb, see* **sigra**

Sigmundr (*gen* -ar) *m* Sigmund (*personal name*); son of Volsung and father of Sigurd

Sigurðr (*gen* -ar) *m* Sigurd (*personal name*); legendary hero who slays Fafnir the dragon

sik (*dat* sér, *gen* sín) *refl pron* him-/her-/it-/oneself, themselves

silfr *n* silver

sinn *n* a time, instance, occasion; **mǫrgu sinni** many a time, on many occasions

sinn (*f* sín, *n* sitt; *acc m* sinn, *f* sína, *dat m* sínum, *n* sínu, *gen m/n* síns; *pl m* sínir, *f* sínar, *n* sín, *acc m* sína, *dat* sínum; *see* 14.3) *refl poss adj* his, her, its, their (own)

sitja (sitr; sat, sátu; setinn) *vb* sit

sitt *refl poss adj* (*n*), *see* **sinn** (*see also* 14.3)

síð *adv* late

síðan *adv* then, later, afterwards, after that

síðar *comp adv* later (*see* **síð**)

síðr *comp adv* less; **þótt ek ætla þat síðr mun vera** although I think that is less likely

sín, sína, síns, sínum *refl poss adj, see* **sinn** (*see also* 14.3)

sín *refl pron, see* **sik**

Síreksstaðir *m pl* Sireksstadir ('Sirek's Farmstead') (*place name*)

sjau *num* seven; **sjau tigir** *num* [*w gen*] seventy

sjautján *num* seventeen

sjá (= þessi) *dem pron/adj* this (one)

sjá (sér; sá, sá; sénn) *vb* see

sjálfr *adj* self, him-/her-/it-/oneself, themselves

sjóða (sýðr; sauð, suðu; soðinn) *vb* boil, 'seethe'

sjón *f* sight, eyesight

sjóni *m* 'The Seer' (*nickname*)

sjónlítill *adj* having poor eyesight

skal *vb*, *see* **skulu**

Skalla-Grímr *m* Skalla-Grim (*personal name*)

skammr (*f* skǫmm, *n* skam(m)t; *comp* skem(m)ri, *superl* skem(m)str) *adj* short, brief

skapa (-að-) *vb* shape, form

skarpr *adj* sharp

skaut *vb*, *see* **skjóta**

skáld *n* poet, 'skald'

Skáldskaparmál *n pl* 'Poetic Diction', the second section of *The Prose Edda*

skáldskapr (*gen* -ar; *pl* -ir) *m* poetry, 'skaldship'

skemmstr *superl adj*, *see* **skammr**

skemmtiliga *adv* entertainingly

skera (skerr; skar, skáru; skorinn) *v* cut, carve, 'shear'

skildi, skildir *m*, *see* **skjǫldr**

skilja (-d-) *vb* part, divide, separate; discern, understand; *refl* **skiljask** part

skilnaðr *m* parting

skip *n* ship

skipakostr *m* naval force

skipta (-pt-) *vb* [*w dat*] divide, share; **skipta í helminga** divide into two equal portions

skína (skínn; skein, skinu; skininn) *vb* shine

skírr *adj* pure

skírskota (-að-) *vb* refer to, appeal to; **skírskota ek undir þik** I call you to witness

skjóta (skýtr; skaut, skutu; skotinn) *vb* shoot; **skjóta af** shoot with

skjǫldr (*dat* skildi, *gen* skjaldar; *pl* skildir, *acc* skjǫldu, *gen* skjalda; *see* 11.5, 17.6) *m* shield

skotit *ppart*, *see* **skjóta**

skógr (*gen* -ar; *pl* -ar) *m* forest, woods

skór (*dat* skó, *gen* skós; *pl* skúar, *acc/gen* skúa, *dat* skóm) *m* shoe

skreið *vb*, *see* **skríða**

skríða (skríðr; skreið, skriðu; skriðinn) *vb* crawl, creep

Skuld *f* Skuld ('Debt'), one of the Norns

skulu (skal, skulu; skyldi; *pret inf* skyldu) *vb* shall (necessity); must

skúa *m*, *see* **skór**

skúta *f* small boat, skiff

skyldi, skyldu *vb*, *see* **skulu**

skǫmm *f* shame

sleikja (-t-) *vb* lick

slíkr *adj* such

smár *adj* small

smiðr *m* smith

smíða (-að-) *vb* work in wood or metals, make, build

smyrja (smurð-) *vb* anoint, 'smear'

smæri *comp adj* smaller (*see* **smár**)

snemma (*also* **snimma**) (*comp* snemr, *superl* snemst) *adv* early, soon

sneri, sneru *vb*, *see* **snúa**

Snorri *m* Snorri (*personal name*); Snorri Sturluson, author of *The Prose Edda*

snúa (snýr; snøri/sneri; snúinn) *vb* turn; *refl* **snúask** turn oneself

snær (*gen* snævar/snæfar) *m* snow

Snæfellsnes *n* Snæfellsnes ('Snow Mountain's Headland'), peninsula in Western Iceland (*place name*)

sofa (sefr; svaf, sváfu; sofinn) *vb* sleep

sogit *ppart*, *see* **súga**

Sogn *n* Sogn, area in Western Norway (*place name*)

Sólundir *pl* Solundir, islands off Sogn in Western Norway (*place name*)

sonargjǫld *n pl* ransom, wergild (blood money) for a son

sonr (*dat* syni, *gen* sonar; *pl* synir, *acc* syni/sonu; *see* 3.4, 14.4) *m* son

sól *f* sun

spakr *adj* wise

spekingr *m* wise man, sage

speni *m* teat

spilla (-t-) *vb* [*w dat*] spoil, destroy

spillir *m* spoiler; **spillir bauga** *poet* generous lord, spoiler (= distributor) of rings

spjót *n* spear

spurði, spurðr *ppart*, *see* **spyrja**

spyrja (spurð-) *vb* ask; **spyrja eptir** ask about

spýja (spýr; spjó, spjó; spúinn) *vb* spew

staddr *adj* present; placed, situated

staðr (*gen* -ar; *pl* -ir) *m* place; stead,

parcel of land

Staðr (*gen* -ar) *m* Stad, a peninsula in Western Norway (*place name*)

stakkr *m* haystack

standa (stendr; stóð, stóðu; staðinn) *vb* stand, be located; **standa milli** separate, set at odds; **standa við** withstand

stangarhǫgg *n* Staff-Struck (*nick-name*)

Starkaðr *m* Starkad (*personal name*)

steði (-ja) *m* anvil

steðr *f pl, see* **stoð**

steig *vb, see* **stíga**

steikja (-t/ð-) *vb* roast

Steinarr *m* Steinar (*personal name*)

Steinbjǫrn *m* Steinbjorn ('Stone-Bear') (*personal name*)

steinn *m* stone; stone dwelling, cave

sterkr *adj* strong; **sterkr at afli** strong

stilla (-lt-) *vb* restrain, calm, still

stilltr *adj* calm, composed

stíga (stígr; steig/sté, stigu; stiginn) *vb* step (up); **stíga á bak** mount on horseback

stoð (*pl* steðr) *f* pillar

stokkinn *ppart* spattered, stained (*esp* with blood) (*from* **støkkva**)

stokkr *m* stock of an anvil

stóð, stóðu *vb, see* **standa**

stóll *m* chair

stólpi *m* post

stórlyndr *adj* magnanimous

stórr *adj* big, great, important

stórráðr *adj* ambitious

stórskip *n* large ship

straumr *m* stream, current

stund (*dat* -u; *pl* -ir) *f* length of time, a while

stundum *adv* sometimes (*dat pl of* **stund**); **stundum... stundum...** sometimes... at other times...

Sturlubók *f* 'Sturla's Book', version of the **Landámabók** made by Sturla Thordarson

stýra (-ð-) *vb* [*w dat*] steer; rule, govern

støkkva (støkkr; stǫkk, stukku; stokkinn) *vb* spring, burst, leap; be sprinkled, spattered

stǫng (*gen* stangar; *pl* stangir/stengr) *f* pole, staff

suðr (*gen* suðrs) *n* the south; *adv* southwards; **í suðr** south(wards)

Suðrríki *n* Southern Realm (Southern Europe) (*place name*)

sumar (*dat* sumri) *n* summer

sumr *adj* some

sund *n* sound, strait, channel

sundr (*also* **í sundr**) *adv* apart, asunder

sunna *f* sun

sunnan *adv* from the south; on the south side; **fyrir sunnan** [*w acc*] to the south of

sunnanverðr *adj* southern; **á sunnanverðum enda** on the southern end

Sunnudalr (*dat* Sunnudal(i)) *m* Sunnudal ('Sun Dale') (*place name*)

sú (*acc* þá, *dat* þeiri, *gen* þeirar; *pl* þær; *see* 12.1) *dem pron/adj* (*f*), that (one) (*see* **sá**)

súga (sýgr; saug/só, sugum; soginn) *vb* suck

Súrr *m* Sur (*personal name*)

Svalbarði *m* Svalbard ('Cold Coast'), archipelago in the Arctic Ocean (*place name*)

svalr *adj* cool, fresh

svara (-að-) *vb* [*w dat*] answer, reply

svardagi *m* oath

Svartálfar *m pl* black elves

Svartálfheimr *m* world of the black elves

svartr (*f* svǫrt, *n* svart) *adj* black

svá *adv* so, thus, in this way; such; **svá ... at** so ... that; **ok svá** and also

sváfu *vb, see* **sofa**

sveigja (-ð-) *vb* bend; **sveigja at** deal with harshly

svelgja (svelgr; svalg, sulgu; sólginn) *vb* swallow

sveinn *m* boy, lad

sveiti *m* sweat; blood

sverð *n* sword

sverðsegg (-j-) *f* sword's edge

sverja (svarð-) *vb* swear

svipta (-pt-) *vb* [*w dat*] sweep, pull quickly

Svíakonungr *m* king of the Swedes

Svíar *m pl* Swedes
Svíþjóð *f* Sweden
svíkja (svíkr; sveik, sviku; svikinn) *vb* betray
svǫrt *adj, see* **svartr**
syngja (*older* **syngva**) (syngr; sǫng, sungu; sunginn) *vb* sing
syni, synir *m, see* **sonr**
synja (-að-) *vb* [*w gen*] refuse, deny
systir (*acc/dat/gen* systur; *pl* systr, *dat* systrum, *gen* systra; *see* 9.5, 14.8) *f* sister
sýn (*pl* -ir) *f* sign, vision, appearance; **ólíkr sýnum** different in appearance; **fegri sýnum** more beautiful (in appearance)
sýna (-d-) *vb* show; *refl* **sýnask** [*w dat*] appear, seem (*impers*); **sýnisk mér** it seems to me

sæti *n* seat
sætt *f* settlement, agreement, reconciliation; **vera/verða at sætt** constitute a settlement or agreement
sættask (-tt-) *refl vb* become reconciled
sœkja (sótt-) *vb* seek; **sœkja sǫkum** prosecute
sœnskr *adj* Swedish
sǫgðu *vb, see* **segja**
sǫðull *m* saddle
sǫgu *f, see* **saga**
sǫk (*gen* sakar; *pl* sakar/sakir) *f* reason, cause, sake; prosecution, lawsuit; **sǫk til [e-s]** reason for [sth], cause of [sth]; **fyrir … sakar** on account of, because of
sǫkkva (søkkr; sǫkk, sukku; sokkinn) *vb* sink

T

taka (tekr; tók, tóku; tekinn) *vb* take, catch, seize; reach, stretch forth, touch; receive (a person); begin; [w inf] begin to do; *refl* **takask** begin, happen; **taka af** take away, remove from; **taka á** touch; **taka hǫndum** take hold of, seize with the hands; **taka í sundr** cut in two; **taka til ráða** adopt a plan; **taka [e-m] vel** receive [sb] well; **taka við** receive; **taka undir sik** take charge of
tala (-að-) *vb* speak; **fegrst talaðr** most eloquent
Tálknafjǫrðr *m* name of a fjord in NW Iceland
tekit *ppart, see* **taka**
temja (tamd-) *vb* tame
tiginn *adj* noble (of family)
tigr (*gen* -ar; *pl nom* -ir, *acc* -u) *m* ten, group of ten; **sex tigir** *num* [*w gen*] sixty; **sjau tigir** *num* [*w gen*] seventy; **þrír tigir** *num* [*w gen*] thirty
til *prep* [*w gen*] to, until; for; with respect to, for the sake of; **til þess** the reason for this; **til þess at** to, in order to; **til þess er** until; **búask til** prepare for; **gera brúðlaup til** marry; **jafna til** compare with; **sem**

hon átti ætt til which was characteristic for her family
til *adv* **vera til** to exist, be at hand; **bœta til um** improve; **ganga til** approach, go up to a thing; **leggja til (orð)** say
tíðendi *n pl* news, tidings; **er þetta var tíðenda** when this happened
tími *m* time; **þenna tíma** at this time; **í þann tíma** at that time
tíu *num* ten
topt *n* toft, site of a house; foundation or bare walls, ruins of a house
Toptavǫllr *m* Toptavoll ('Field of Ruined Walls') (*place name*)
tók, tóksk, tóku *vb, see* **taka**
tólf *num* twelve
trúa (-ð-) *vb* [*w dat*] trust
Tryggvi *m* Tryggvi (*personal name*)
tunga *f* tongue
tuttugu *num* twenty
tveir (*f* tvær, *n* tvau; *acc m* tvá, *all dat* tveim(r), *all gen* tveggja; *see* 14.1) *num* two
tylft (*pl* -ir) *f* dozen, group of twelve; a half day's sail
tæla (-d-) *vb* betray; entice, entrap
tœki *vb, see* **taka**

U

ull (*dat* ullu) *f* wool
ullarlagðr *m* tuft of wool
um *prep* [*w acc*] around, about, in regard to; during, in (*time*); **um alla hluti** in all respects; **um fram** in addition; **um várit** in the spring; **bœta til um** improve
umhverfis *adv* around, round about
undan *adv* away; **biðjask undan** be evasive; **komask undan** escape
undir *prep* [*w acc/dat*] under
ungmenni *n* young people, children
ungr *adj* young; **á ungum aldri** young
unna (ann, unnu; unni; unn(a)t) *vb*

[*w dat of person, gen of thing*] grant, allow; [*w dat*] love
upp *adv* up (*motion*), upwards; **upp með** up along; **koma upp** come about, happen
Uppsalir *m pl* Uppsala ('Upper Halls'), a town in Sweden (*place name*)
Urðarbrunnr *m* 'Urd's Well' (*place name*)
urðarmaðr *m* outlaw; **gera at urðar-manni** to outlaw
Urðr *f* Urd ('Fate'), one of the Norns (*see* **verða**)
urðu *vb, see* **verða**

Ú

ú- *pref, see* **ó-**
úlfr *m* wolf
úr *prep, see* **ór**
út *adv* out (*motion*), outwards
útan *adv* from without, from outside;

fyrir útan [*w acc*] outside; out beyond
úti *adv* outside (*location*)
útlenzkr *adj* foreign
útsjár *m* ocean

V

Valaskjálf *f* 'Vali's Seat' (*place name*)
valda (veldr; olli, ollu; valdit) *vb* [*w dat*] wield, control, rule over; cause
valði *vb, see* **velja**
vandliga *adv* carefully
vandræði *n pl* trouble, difficulty
var *vb, see* **vera**
vara (-ð-; *ppart* varat) *vb* give (one) a foreboding of; **þat varir [e-n]** [sb] has a presentiment
varð *vb, see* **verða**
varr *adj* aware; **verðr [e-m] varr við [e-t]** [sb] becomes aware of [sth]
vaskligr *adj* brave, bold
vaskr *adj* brave, valiant
vatn (*pl* vǫtn) *n* water
vágr *m* bay
vágskorinn *adj* scored with bays
ván (*pl* -ir) *f* hope; expectation, prospect
vándr (*n* vánt) *adj* bad, wretched
vápn *n* weapon; **bera vápn á [e-n]** raise a weapon against [sb]

Vápnafjǫrðr *m* Vápnafjord ('Weapon's Fjord') (*place name*)
vár *n* spring; **um várit** in the spring
vár *pron, see* **vér** (*see also* 3.6)
várr *poss adj* our
váru *vb, see* **vera**
veggr (*gen* -jar/s; *pl* -ir) *m* wall
vegr *m* way, path, road
veiða (-dd-) *vb* catch; hunt
veiðr (*acc/dat* veiði, *gen* veiðar; *pl* veiðar) *f* catch
veikr *adj* weak
veit *vb, see* **vita**
veitt *ppart, see* **veiða**
veizla *f* feast, party
vekja (vakt-) *vb* wake
vel (*comp* betr, *superl* bezt) *adv* well, very, very much; **vel viti borinn** intelligent, endowed with good sense
veld *vb, see* **valda**
velja (valð-) *vb* choose, select
venja (vanð-/vand-) *vb* accustom, train

vera (er; var, váru; verit) *vb* be; **vera nǫkkut við** be somehow connected with; **vera til** exist, be at hand; **er/var [e-m] [e-t]** [sb] has/had [sth]; **[e-t] er/var at** it is/was [sth]

verða (verðr; varð, urðu; orðinn) *vb* become; happen, come to pass; **verða af** come about, appear; **verða at** [*w inf*] must, need to, be obliged to [do sth]; **verða [e-m] at meini** cause [sb] harm; **verða varr við [e-t]** become aware of [sth]; **eigi mun svá mikill brestr orðinn** such a great break is not likely to have occurred

Verðandi *f* Verdandi ('Becoming', *pres part of* **verða**), one of the Norns

verit *ppart, see* **vera**

verr *comp adv* worse (*see* **illa**)

verri *comp adj* worse (*see* **illr**)

verst *superl adv* worst (*see* **illa**)

verstr *superl adj* worst (*see* **illr**)

vestr *n* the west; *adv* west, westwards; **í vestr** west(wards)

vetr (*gen* vetrar; *pl* vetr) *m* winter; year (*in reckoning time*); **um vetrinn** during the winter

Vé *m* Ve, brother of Odin (*mythological name*)

vér (*acc/dat* oss, *gen* vár; *see* 3.6) *pron* we (*pl*)

Vésteinn *m* Vestein (*personal name*)

við *prep* [*w acc*] with, to; at, by, close to; according to, after; **lifa við** live on, feed on; **mæla við** say to, speak to; **taka við** receive; **vera nǫkkut við** be somehow connected with

viðr (*dat* við(i)) *m* tree

vilja (vill; vildi; viljat; *pret inf* vildu) *vb* want, wish, will

vinátta *f* friendship

vinna (vinnr; vann, unnu; unninn) *vb*

gain, overcome, conquer; win; work, perform, do; till, cultivate (land); **vinna at [e-m]** do away with, kill [sb]

vinr (*gen* -ar; *pl* -ir) *m* friend

vinsæll *adj* popular, blessed with friends

virðask (-rð-) *refl vb* [*w dat*] seem, think (*impers*); **mér virðisk** it seems to me

vissi, vissu *vb, see* **vita**

vist (*gen* -ar; *pl* -ir) *f* food, provisions

vit (*acc/dat* okkr, *gen* okkar; *see* 16.3) *pron* we (two)

vit *n* good sense, wit, intelligence; **vel viti borinn** intelligent, endowed with good sense

vita (veit, vitu; vissi; vitaðr) *vb* know

vitja (-að-) *vb* [*w gen*] visit

vitr (*gen* vitrs) *adj* wise

vígja (-ð-) *vb* ordain, consecrate

víking *f* sea-raiding; **vera í víking** be engaged in sea-raiding

víkingr *m* a viking, sea-raider

Vílir *m* Vili, brother of Odin (*mythological name*)

vísa *f* verse

víss *adj* certain, sure

vænn *adj* fine, handsome, beautiful

væri *vb, see* **vera** (*see also* 16.2)

vættr (*dat* vætti, *gen* vættar, *pl* vættir) *f* creature, being; **ekki vætta** nothing at all

vǫllr (*dat* velli, *gen* vallar; *pl* vellir, *acc* vǫllu, *gen* valla; *see* 11.5, 17.6) *m* field

Vǫlsungr *m* Volsung (*personal name*); father of Sigmund

vǫxtr (*dat* vexti, *gen* vaxtar; *pl* vextir, *acc* vǫxtu, *gen* vaxta; *see* 11.5, 17.6) *m* size, stature; **mikill vexti** big, great in stature

Y

yðar *pron, see* **þér** (*see also* 3.6)

yðarr *poss adj* your (*pl*)

yðr *pron, see* **þér** (*see also* 3.6)

yfir *prep* [*w acc/dat*] over, above; **konungr yfir** king of

yfirkonungr *m* supreme king

yfirlit *n* look, personal appearance

yfirmaðr *m* leader, chieftain

Yggdrasill *m* the tree of life

Ymir *m* Ymir, the first giant (*mythological name*)

Ynglingar *m pl* line of early Swedish kings

Yngvarr *m* Yngvar (*personal name*)

yrði *vb, see* **verða**

yztr *superl adj* outermost (*compare* **út**)

Þ

þaðan *adv* from there, thence

þak *n* roof

þagði *vb*, *see* þegja

þangat *adv* (to) there, thither; þangat til to there

þann *dem pron/adj*, *see* sá (*see also* 12.1)

þar *adv* there; þar eptir thereafter, accordingly; þar sem there where

þat (*dat* því, *gen* þess; *pl* þau; *see* 5.1) *pron* (*n*) it

þat (*dat* því, *gen* þess; *pl* þau; *see* 12.1) *dem pron/adj* (*n*) that (one) (*see* sá)

þau (*dat* þeim, *gen* þeira; *see* 5.1) *pron* they (*n and mixed*)

þau (*dat* þeim, *gen* þeira) *dem pron/ adj* those (*n*) (*see* þat *and* þeir; *see also* 12.1)

þá *pron*, *see* þeir (*see also* 5.1)

þá *dem pron/adj*, *see* sú *and* þeir (*see also* 12.1)

þá *adv* then; þá er *conj* when

þáttr (*dat* þætti) *m* short story, tale

þegar *adv* at once, immediately; *conj* as soon as

þegja (þagð-; *ppart* þagat) *vb* be silent; þegja við remain silent

þegnskapr (*gen* -ar) *m* generosity, open-handedness

þeim *pron*, *see* þeir (*see also* 5.1)

þeim *dem pron/adj*, *see* sá *and* þeir (*see also* 12.1)

þeir (*f* þær, *n* þau; *acc* þá, *dat* þeim, *gen* þeira; *see* 5.1) *pron* they (*m*)

þeir (*f* þær, *n* þau; *acc* þá, *dat* þeim, *gen* þeira) *dem pron/adj* those (*m*) (*see* sá; *see also* 12.1)

þeira *pron*, *see* þeir (*see also* 5.1)

þeira *poss pron* their, theirs

þeira *dem pron/adj*, *see* þeir (*see also* 12.1)

þeirar, þeiri *dem pron/adj*, *see* sú (*see also* 12.1)

þekja (þakð-) *vb* cover, thatch

þenna *dem pron/adj*, *see* þessi (*see also* 12.1)

þess *dem pron/adj*, *see* sá *and* þat (*see also* 12.1)

þessi (*f* þessi, *n* þetta; *see* 12.1) *dem*

pron/adj this (one); þenna tíma at this time

þetta *dem pron/adj*, *see* þessi (*see also* 12.1)

þér (*acc/dat* yðr, *gen* yð(v)ar; *see* 3.6) *pron* you (*pl*)

þér *pron*, *see* þú (*see also* 3.6)

þiggja (þiggr; þá, þágu; þeginn) *vb* accept

þik *pron*, *see* þú (*see also* 3.6)

þing *n* assembly

þingbrekka *f* slope on which assembly meetings were held

þingheimr *m* the attendance (those in attendance) at a þing

þinn (*f* þín, *n* þitt; *acc m* þinn, *f* þína, *dat m* þínum, *n* þínu, *gen m/n* þíns; *pl m* þínir, *f* þínar, *n* þín, *acc m* þína, *dat* þínum; *see* 16.4) *poss adj* your (*sg*)

þit (*acc/dat* ykkr, *gen* ykkar; *see* 16.3) *pron* we (two)

þín *pron*, *see* þú (*see also* 3.6)

Þjóð *f* Thjod ('People') (*place name*, modern province of Thy in Jutland, Denmark)

þola (-d-; *ppart* þol(a)t) *vb* suffer, endure

þora (-ð-) *vb* dare, have courage

Þorgeirr *m* Thorgeir (*personal name*)

Þorgerðr *f* Thorgerd (*personal name*)

Þorgils *m* Thorgils (*personal name*)

Þorgrímr *m* Thorgrim (*personal name*)

Þorkell *m* Thorkel (*personal name*)

Þormóðr *m* Thormod (*personal name*)

þorp *n* village, hamlet

Þorsteinn *m* Thorstein (*personal name*)

þó *adv* yet, though, nevertheless

Þóra *f* Thora (*personal name*)

Þórarinn *m* Thorarin (*personal name*)

Þórbjǫrn *m* Thorbjorn (*personal name*)

Þórdís *f* Thordis (*personal name*)

Þórðr *m* Thord (*personal name*)

Þórir *m* Thorir (*personal name*)

Þórólfr *m* Thorolf (*personal name*)

þótt (= þó at) *conj* [*w subjunct*] although, even though

þótti, þóttu *vb*, *see* þykkja

þrettán *num* thirteen
þriði *ord num* third
þrír (*f* þrjár, *n* þrjú; *acc m* þrjá, *all dat* þrim(r)/þrem(r), *all gen* þriggja; *see* 14.1) *num* three; **þrír tigir** *num* [*w gen*] thirty
þrǫngr *adj* narrow
þurfa (þarf, þurfu; þurfti; þurft) *vb* [*w gen*] need, have need of
þú (*acc* þik, *dat* þér, *gen* þín; *see* 3.6) *pron* you (*sg*); **ór hendi þér** out of your hands
því *pron*, *see* þat (*see also* 5.1)
því *dem pron/adj*, *see* þat (*see also* 12.1)
því *conj* because (*n dat of* þat); **(fyrir) því at** because

þykkja (þótt-) *vb* [*w dat*] seem (*impers*); **Ásum þótti ørvænt hans heim** the gods gave up hope of his returning home; **okkrum mundi þykkja** it would seem to us; *refl* **þykkjask** seem to one, consider oneself; **þykkjask vita** feel convinced
þyldi *vb*, *see* þola
þysja (þust-) *vb* rush
þær (*dat* þeim, *gen* þeira; *see* 5.1) *pron* they (*f*)
þær (*dat* þeim, *gen* þeira) *dem pron/ adj* those (*f*) (*see* sú *and* þeir; *see also* 12.1)
þœtti *vb*, *see* þykkja
þǫkðu *vb*, *see* þekja

Æ

Æsa *f* Æsa (*personal name*)
Æsir *pl of* Áss
æti *vb*, *see* eta
ætla (-að-) *vb* think, intend; agree
ætt (*pl* -ir) *f* family; **sem hon átti ætt til** which was characteristic for her family
ætti *vb*, *see* eiga
ævi *f* time, lifetime, age

Œ

œðri *comp adj* higher
œgir (*gen* -is) *m* one who frightens
œgishjálmr *m* helmet of dread
œrinn *adj* sufficient, enough
œska *f* youth, childhood
œxla (-t-) *vb* multiply, increase

Ǫ

ǫðru, ǫðrum *adj*, *see* annarr
ǫflugr *adj* strong, powerful
ǫld (*gen* aldar; *pl* aldir) *f* age
ǫll, ǫllu, ǫllum *adj*, *see* allr
Ǫlvir *m* Olvir (*personal name*)
ǫnnur *adj*, *see* annarr
Ǫnundr *m* Onund (*personal name*)
ǫr (-v-) *f* arrow
ǫrn (*dat* erni, *gen* arnar; *pl* ernir, *acc* ǫrnu, *gen* arna; *see* 11.5, 17.6) *m* eagle
ørvænt *adj* past hope; **Ásum þótti ørvænt hans heim** the gods gave up hope of his returning home
øxn *m*, *see* oxi
Øxna-Þórir *m* Thorir 'of the Oxen' (*personal name*)

FURTHER SUGGESTED READINGS
OLD NORSE - OLD ICELANDIC LANGUAGE, RUNES, SOCIETY, AND CULTURE...

THE VIKING LANGUAGE SERIES

A modern introduction to Old Norse language, runes, Icelandic sagas, Viking history and literature. Perfect for the modern classroom, online teaching, and the self-learner.

Viking Language 1: Learn Old Norse, Runes and Icelandic Sagas (2nd Edition) is a new introduction to Old Norse, Icelandic sagas, and runes. Everything from beginner to advanced in one book: graded lessons, vocabulary, grammar exercises, pronunciation, and extensive maps. Includes sections on Viking history, literature, and myth. Innovative word-frequency method greatly speeds learning and Modern Icelandic has changed little from Old Norse; students are well on the way to mastering Modern Icelandic. EBOOK AVAILABLE.

Viking Language 2: The Old Norse Reader is a treasure trove of Scandinavian lore, immersing the learner in a wide variety of Old Norse sources and runes. *The Reader* offers a large vocabulary, chapters on Eddic and skaldic poetry, and a full reference grammar: the latter can be invaluable while learning to read sagas. It includes complete sagas, runic inscriptions, myths, creation stories, legends, with Eddic poems about Scandinavian gods, monster-slayers, dwarves, giants, and warrior kings and Valkyries.

PRONUNCIATION ALBUMS
Audio Lessons 1-8, Audio Lessons 9-15

Two MP3 albums teach the pronunciation of saga passages and runes in *Viking Language 1*. The pronunciation is a slightly archaic Modern Icelandic as used in the saga and language courses at the University of Iceland. Both albums are available on Amazon and iTunes for download and purchase. Check out free sample lessons at oldnorse.org.

FURTHER OLD NORSE RESOURCES FROM JULES WILLIAM PRESS...

Old Norse–Old Icelandic: Concise Introduction to the Language of the Sagas answers the need for a modern method to learn the language of the sagas. This new primer requires no previous language knowledge, and the beginner quickly starts reading original passages from Icelandic sagas, mythological texts, and sources about the Viking Age. Designed for quick learning on one's own or in class, the lessons supply all necessary grammar, exercises, and vocabulary.

Supplementary Exercises for Old Norse - Old Icelandic complements *Old Norse-Old Icelandic: Concise Introduction to the Language of the Sagas* by providing additional exercises and vocabulary activties. Together, these two books make the sagas accessible for anyone learning Old Norse and the Viking Age.

AUCH IN DEUTSCH ERHÄLTLICH
(Also Available in German)

Altnordisch I: Die Sprache der Wikinger, Runen und isländischen Sagas gliedert sich in fünfzehn inhaltlich aufeinander aufbauende Lektionen bestehend aus altnordischen Textpassagen, Runen, Grammatikbaukästen, Übungen, Karten. Das Buch enthält ein vollständiges Wörterverzeichnis, eine Kurzgrammatik sowie Hinweise zur (rekonstruierten) Aussprache.

COMING SOON FROM JWP...

THE ICELANDIC SAGA SERIES

Our Icelandic Saga series includes new English translations together with the original Old Norse, as well as introductions, vocabulary, grammar, maps and notes.

The Tale of Thorstein Staff Struck (Þorsteins þáttr stangarhöggs) is a short saga set in Iceland's East Fjords during the 10th-century Viking Age. Thorstein, a peaceful young man, is forced to live with the humiliating nickname "staff struck." Even Thorstein's father, an old Viking, looks down on his son as a coward. But Thorstein is no coward. Waiting for the right moment to take revenge, Thorstein reclaims his good name in a way that brings honor both to him and his chieftain.

The Saga of the Families of Weapon's Fjord (Vápnfirðinga saga) is a classic Icelandic saga of feuding chieftains and their families struggling for power and survival. Set during the 10th-century Viking Age in Iceland's East Fjords, the saga recounts how a rich Norwegian merchant stirs the greed of the local inhabitants. Sons avenge fathers, while wives and mothers demand honor for their families. In this new edition, a world in the far North Atlantic opens for the modern reader.

Egil's Bones: Icelandic Sagas, Blood Feud, and Viking Archaeology (The Writings of Jesse Byock) explores Viking Age Iceland — its origins, sagas, heroes, society, and archaeology. The studies provide a comprehensive picture of this North Atlantic island founded more than 1,000 years ago. The pages explore the background of legendary heroes such as the Viking warrior poet, Egil Skalla-Grimsson and his archaeological bones as well as Sigurd the dragon slayer, whose saga influenced J.R.R. Tolkien and Richard Wagner's Ring Cycle.

OTHER WORKS BY JESSE BYOCK

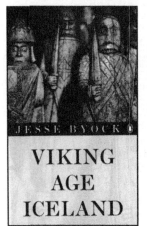

VIKING AGE ICELAND

Viking Age Iceland combines anthropology, archaeology, and history offering crucial insights into the Icelandic sagas and the inner workings of a feuding society with intriguing proto-democratic tendencies. Unusual for Western Europe, Iceland had no king, no foreign policy, no defence forces, and no great lords. It should have been a utopia, yet its sagas are dominated by blood feud and killings. Reasons for this, argues Jesse Byock, lie in the cultural codes and processes of conflict within the island's social order and the Viking world.

Feud in the Icelandic Saga explores conflicts at the core of the Old Icelandic sagas. Jesse Byock shows how the dominant concern of medieval Icelandic society was the channeling of violence into accepted patterns of feud and the regulation of conflict, processes that are reflected in the family and the *Sturlunga* sagas. This comprehensive study of narrative structure and the control of violence explores the sagas as revealing expressions of medieval social thought.

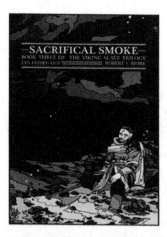

Printed in Great Britain
by Amazon

26696591R00119